The Elizabethan
Dumb Show

DIETER MEHL

The Elizabethan Dumb Show

THE HISTORY OF A
DRAMATIC CONVENTION

1966
HARVARD UNIVERSITY PRESS
CAMBRIDGE   MASSACHUSETTS

Contents

Preface

This book has gone through several stages. Its subject was first suggested to me in a seminar on *Hamlet* held by Professor Wolfgang Clemen. Under his supervision I wrote a doctoral dissertation on dumb shows which was accepted by the Faculty of Arts in the University of Munich in 1960. It was then thoroughly revised and expanded, and published by the German Shakespeare Society. The present version is a rather free translation, and I am very grateful to the President of the Deutsche Shakespeare Gesellschaft-West and his committee for permission to reprint my material in this new form. I have again made a considerable number of changes and additions; my chief aim has been to provide a useful work of reference rather than an exercise in academic criticism.

I have been fortunate in having had Professor W. Clemen as teacher and adviser for many years, and it gives me great pleasure to record my gratitude for all the encouragement and help I have had from him. To his outstanding scholarship and his stimulating criticism this book owes more than can be acknowledged here. I have also benefited greatly from the expert advice and criticism of several scholars, to all of whom I am deeply grateful, especially to Professor Helmut Bonheim, Dr Werner Habicht, Professor Hermann Heuer, Professor Hugo Kuhn, Professor Clifford Leech, Dr Ernest Schanzer, and the late Professor Levin L. Schücking. I hope their friendly interest in my work has not been entirely wasted. Professor Lloyd G. Gibbs (South Carolina), who was writing a dissertation on dumb shows at the same time as I, very generously placed a copy of his unpublished thesis at my disposal. My debt to him and to all previous investigators in the same field is acknowledged in the footnotes.

My greatest thanks are due to my wife, who has borne the lion's share in the arduous work of translation and adaptation

vii

and who has saved me from many blunders. Those that still remain are entirely my own.

München   D. M.

Abbreviations

Archiv	*Archiv für das Studium der neueren Sprachen und Literaturen*
EETS (ES)	*Early English Text Society (Extra Series)*
ELH	*Journal of English Literary History*
ESts	*English Studies*
JEGP	*Journal of English and Germanic Philology*
Malone Soc.	*The Malone Society Reprints* (General Editor, W. W. Greg)
MLR	*Modern Language Review*
PMLA	*Publications of the Modern Language Association of America*
PQ	*Philological Quarterly*
RES	*Review of English Studies*
ShJ	*Shakespeare-Jahrbuch*
ShQ	*Shakespeare Quarterly*
ShS	*Shakespeare Survey*
TFT	*Tudor Facsimile Texts*, ed. John S. Farmer

Introduction

This study of the dumb show and its function in a number of Elizabethan plays is intended as a contribution to the history of sixteenth- and seventeenth-century drama as a whole. In the past dumb shows have been mainly treated from a purely historical point of view: that is to say, critics inquired into the origins of this convention and looked for models in the English drama of the Middle Ages and in Italian Renaissance drama.[1] However justified this line of approach may be, it does not reveal so very much about the real nature of Elizabethan drama which is better understood not by studying the sources drawn upon by individual dramatists, but by seeing how they made use of them and incorporated them in their plays. Playwrights vary considerably in this respect, and so any attempt to point out general lines of development can only be based on a more exact analysis of individual plays. Such an examination should automatically contribute to an understanding of the whole and not merely treat some aspects out of their context. It should also, by showing the varied use of the pantomime, throw light upon the individual peculiarities of dramatists and their personal technique, as I shall demonstrate with a series of selected examples. It is particularly interesting to see how the pantomime is fitted into the drama in question and what contribution

[1] See especially: John W. Cunliffe, 'Italian Prototypes of the Masque and Dumb Show', *PMLA*, XXII (1907), pp. 140–56, and George R. Kernodle, *From Art to Theatre* (Chicago, 1947). For the purely historical matters I have been able to make use of some valuable studies: Frances A. Foster, 'Dumb Show in Elizabethan Drama before 1620', *Englische Studien*, 44 (1911–12), pp. 8–17, and B. R. Pearn, 'Dumb-show in Elizabethan Drama', *RES*, XI (1935), pp. 385–405. The dissertation by Lloyd Graham Gibbs, *A History of the Development of the Dumb Show as a Dramatic Convention* (University of South Carolina, 1959), is also more historical and descriptive in method. See also the brief account by Robert Y. Turner, 'The Causal Induction in Some Elizabethan Plays', *Studies in Philology*, LX (1963), pp. 183–90.

it makes to the whole. For, while in some cases it appears to be only a primitive technical device, in others it fulfils some important dramatic function and underlines the theme of the play. The part played by the dumb show also varies according to the type of drama in which it occurs. It does not usually have the same function in tragedy as it has in chronicle plays. It is also worth noting that the dumb shows in England, unlike the *intermedii* in Italy, are to be found almost exclusively in serious plays. Where they occur in comedies they are mainly in the form of parodies, imitating the manner of great tragedy. The best known example of this is the performance of the craftsmen in *A Midsummer Night's Dream* with its preceding dumb show.[1]

Defining the exact meaning and limits of the term 'dumb show' presents some difficulty. Pearn's definition[2] is certainly rather narrow and does not cover all existing examples. Any piece of silent action where one would normally expect dialogue may be called a dumb show, as for example the pantomime in Shakespeare's *Hamlet*. However, one can usually apply the term dumb show to all cases where one or more characters advance and retire without having spoken. The brief appearance of De Flores before the third act of Middleton's *The Changeling* is an example.[3] Conversely, extensive masque-like performances, when they are accompanied by speeches or introduce dialogue, are not normally termed dumb shows. Thus the beginning of Dekker's *The Honest Whore* with the appearance of the funeral procession is not a dumb show in the exact sense of the word; while the beginning of the second act of Marston's *Antonio's Revenge*, where Piero enters with the funeral procession and remains alone on the stage, is. I shall pay little attention to the detailed stage directions, suggestive of pantomimes, which are frequently to be found in the moralities and interludes. These have little to do with the tradition of the dumb show and can only in some few cases be considered as early forms of it.[4] The same is true of dances, songs and brawls in dramas. There are, however, many different transitional forms which can tell us a

[1] See Chapter 7.

[2] 'A part of a play which presents by means of action without speech an element of plot which would more naturally be accompanied by speech.' (Op. cit., p. 385.)

[3] '*In the act time* (i.e. between the two acts) *De Flores hides a naked rapier behind a door.*' (III, 1.) [4] See below, Chapter 6.

lot about the development of the dumb show, but make a precise classification difficult. The list of dramas containing dumb shows, which appears at the end of this book, includes a number of such doubtful cases where it is often difficult to decide whether they really assumed the character of dumb shows in performance. The absence of dialogue distinguishes the dumb show from the device of the play within a play so popular in Elizabethan drama.[1] Here also we find something like a second stage set up on the real stage, where scenes are enacted which are often quite different in character and style from the rest of the play. In the case of the dumb show, however, we rarely come across that interplay between the two planes of dramatic action which constitutes the particular appeal of the play within a play. This intentional confusion of the two levels of the real and the make-believe the majority of dumb shows lack, but we shall see that dumb shows are most effective where their use resembles most nearly the technique of the play within a play. *Hamlet* is of course the most famous example of a simultaneous use of both devices, but there are also some other plays where a clear distinction is hardly possible.

In the first section of this book I shall try to outline the various sources and models of the earliest dumb shows, and then continue with a brief account of their different forms in Elizabethan drama. In the second part I shall show, by examining a series of selected examples, how the individual dramatists used dumb shows in their plays and what a variety of functions those dumb shows could perform.

I have thought it necessary to give a fair number of quotations, as many of the plays discussed are not of the kind every reader will be thoroughly familiar with, and some are not easily accessible. I have on the whole preferred old-spelling editions, but I have corrected obvious errors, modernized the titles of plays, and, for the sake of consistency, used italics throughout for all stage directions and dumb shows. Speech headings are given in full.

[1] See Joachim Voigt, *Das Spiel im Spiel* (Diss., Göttingen, 1954); Arthur Brown, 'The Play within a Play: An Elizabethan Dramatic Device', *Essays and Studies* (1960), pp. 36–48, and my article 'Zur Entwicklung des "Play within a Play" im elisabethanischen Drama', *ShJ*, 97 (1961), pp. 134–52.

PART I

1

Origin and Beginnings

Speech and action have been the two basic elements of drama in every age; their mutual interplay is one of the most complex and interesting problems in the history of drama. Thus in tracing the development of early Elizabethan drama we shall see how various attempts were made to strike a balance between the two extremes, action without speech and speech without action, until with the emergence of Shakespeare's major plays a perfect, if temporary, fusion of the two seems to have been achieved.[1] In this process the dumb show which was deliberately employed even in the first English classical tragedies undoubtedly played an important part.

Very early in the history of the English stage one finds examples of attempts to illustrate the spoken word by simultaneous silent action, or, conversely, of a pantomime explained to the audience by a commentary. Some poems by John Lydgate are among the oldest examples of such attempts and, as Wickham has shown,[2] are to be understood as a commentary on a mime performed simultaneously or subsequently. These are the so called 'mummings' or 'disguisings', festive parades, usually in allegorical guise, which were frequently presented on special occasions, such as after a solemn banquet. Some of these poems expressly announce a mime, others give a running commentary on it and call to mind the later figure of the 'presenter'.[3] In his

[1] Cf. Ingeborg Glier, *Struktur und Gestaltungsprinzipien in den Dramen John Websters* (Diss., München, 1957), p. 61.

[2] See Glynne Wickham, *Early English Stages* 1300–1660, Vol. I (London, 1959), pp. 191 ff., and *The Minor Poems of John Lydgate*, Part II, ed. Henry MacCracken, *EETS*, 192 (1934), pp. 668 ff. *Mumming at Windsor* (pp. 691 ff.), for instance, contains an account of how the fleur-de-lis became the emblem of the French Kings. At the end the speaker announces a visual presentation of what he has described, presumably a kind of dumb show.

[3] Thus we find in *Mumming at London* (pp. 682 ff.) an explicit introduction of allegorical characters while the poet gives his account: 'Loo, first

Troy Book Lydgate himself describes more exactly how such a performance is to be imagined, even though the scene is set in a Trojan theatre and not in Lydgate's London:

> Al þis was tolde and rad of þe poete.
> And whil þat he in þe pulpit stood,
> With dedly face al devoide of blood,
> Singinge his dites, with muses al to-rent,
> Amydde þe theatre schrowdid in a tent,
> þer cam out men gastful of her cheris,
> Disfigurid her facis with viseris,
> Pleying by signes in þe peples siȝt,
> þat þe poete songon hath on hiȝt;[1]

This is not so different from the way in which some pantomimes are commented on by a figure appearing as a presenter in Elizabethan drama more than a century later. In Lydgate's 'mummings', which for the most part were intended for the court of the king himself or for presentation before the Lord Mayor of London, a deliberate attempt was made to exploit different artistic means for the same purpose to bring home the meaning as clearly and forcefully as possible. Such experiments are of great importance in the history of English drama. They provide the background not only for the dramatic efforts of the guilds, universities and Inns of Court, but also for the numerous semi-dramatic spectacles, the 'mummings' and Lord Mayor's Shows which are so typical of the period and whose importance in the history of English drama has been increasingly recognized of late. This common habit of employing various artistic means simultaneously also explains why rhetorical tragedies in the Senecan tradition were never really at home in England as they

---

komeþe in Dame Fortune.' He then goes on to describe Fortuna's appearance, mentioning a few examples of her power. In another *Mumming* we read that it was 'brought and presented vn to þe Mayre by an heraude, cleped Fortune', i.e. Fortuna is here acting as a 'presenter'. It is worth noting in this connection that Fortuna appears several times in later drama as well as in dumb shows (e.g. *The Rare Triumphs of Love and Fortune*, and *Jocasta*, V).

[1] *EETS ES*, 97 (1906), II, ll. 896–904. Wickham and Gibbs also quote this passage. In the Middle English Poem *Sir Degrevant*, we find a brief description of a 'disguising' in which the douzepers of France perform a dance. See *EETS*, 221 (1949), ll. 1869–72.

were in Italy and France. Neither the classical tragedies of the Inns of Court nor the similar experiments of Ben Jonson achieved striking successes, while a crude, patchwork, romantic fairytale-drama like *Mucedorus* went through seventeen editions. It is therefore not surprising that the authors of even the first classical tragedies, such as *Gorboduc* and *Jocasta*, tried to relieve the monotony of the formal structure by inserting scenes of a pantomimic nature which present the moral of the play in the form of a pageant appealing vividly to the eye. These are the so-called dumb shows, whose origin has been the subject of much scholarly argument.

Surprisingly enough, foreign models were looked for first. John Cunliffe, one of the first to concern himself with this question, refers continually to the Italian *intermedii*, which he considered to be the immediate predecessors of the dumb show.[1] However, as he himself noticed, there was a very important difference between the two forms: the English dumb shows always had a connection with the drama in which they occurred and formed a part of it, while the *intermedii* were originally only an inserted extra to entertain the audience during the intervals between the acts. A further difference is that the *intermedii* in Italy were at first mainly used in comedy, and only much later in tragedy. They were originally intended as lively interludes and consisted chiefly of songs and dances, comparable to the 'Bergomask dance' in the last scene of Shakespeare's *A Midsummer Night's Dream*. Later on the *intermedii* were used in the rhetorical tragedies. Since the chorus usually remained on the stage during the pauses between the acts in these plays such interludes had not at first been considered necessary. Dolce's *Troiane*, which is the first known example of the use of *intermedii* in tragedy, was written several years after the first performance of *Gorboduc*.

Luigi Alamanni's comedy *La Flora* provides a typical example of how the *intermedii* were used in Italian drama.[2] In this play Cupido, together with various allegorical characters, appears between the acts to sing madrigals, but there is never

---

[1] See particularly 'Italian Prototypes of the Masque and Dumb Show', and *Early English Classical Tragedies* (Oxford, 1912), pp. xl ff.

[2] *La Flora, Comedia di* Lvigi Alamanni, *con gl'intermedii di* Andrea Lori, In Fiorenza, MDLVI.

any pantomime in the real sense and no clear link with the rest of the drama except, perhaps, in the choice of the allegorical figures. It is also worth noting that the *intermedii* were added by some other author and not by Alamanni himself, a procedure which can occasionally be found in Elizabethan drama.[1] The *intermedii* were not, therefore, an indispensable part of the play in which they occurred, but an independent addition to divert the audience during the intervals. They could be exchanged and used in several different plays. Furthermore they were often omitted from the printed edition.

Cunliffe's theory went undisputed for a long time and has often been accepted tacitly in more recent criticism.[2] Nevertheless the differences between the *intermedii* and the English dumb shows are too obvious and the similarities he points out not convincing enough to prove the point.[3] George R. Kernodle has therefore every reason for opposing this theory about the origin of the dumb shows in his influential work *From Art to Theatre*, where he indicates particularly the numerous English entertainments which, in his opinion, explain their appearance and form much better than the Italian *intermedii*.[4] Much new

---

[1] Cf. Thomas Hughes, *The Misfortunes of Arthur*, where several authors of the dumb shows are mentioned by name.

[2] Cf. A. P. Rossiter, *English Drama from Early Times to the Elizabethans* (London, 1950), pp. 134–5, where the dumb shows are explained as an 'Italian innovation'. A similar view is expressed by Karl Brunner in his review of Ernst Th. Sehrt, *Der dramatische Auftakt in der Elisabethanischen Tragödie* (Göttingen, 1960), *ShQ*, XIII (1962), pp. 353–4. Professor Brunner seems to me to overestimate the gulf between 'University drama' and popular pageantry.

[3] Cunliffe himself, to be sure, was prepared to admit that other influences may have been at work (op. cit., p. xl).

There is also a certain resemblance between the *intermedii* and the *entremeses* in Spanish drama of the same period, gay interludes with song and dialogue, inserted between the acts of serious plays. There seems to have been no apparent connection between those *entremeses* and the plays in which they occurred. The *entremeses*, like those of Cervantes, are often rather farcical comedies. They have hardly a single feature in common with the English dumb shows except, perhaps, that both meet an apparent need for relief from the rigid formality of the main play. See Cervantes, *Comedias y entremeses*, Vol. IV (Madrid, 1918), and H. Heidenreich, *Figuren und Komik in den spanischen 'Entremeses' des Goldenen Zeitalters* (Diss., München, 1962).

[4] Op. cit., especially Chapter IV.

material concerning the partly static, partly dramatic performances and festive processions of the late Middle Ages and the
Renaissance has been uncovered in recent years and it is today
much easier for us than it was for Cunliffe to imagine these
spectacular forms of entertainment with their appeal to popular
as well as sophisticated and courtly audiences.[1] Whatever part
the *intermedii* may have played, the origin and the various forms
of dumb show cannot be explained without reference to the
Royal Entries, City Pageants and Lord Mayor's Shows. All
these forms of entertainment, which were so typical of the
period, contain important characteristics which we find in later
dumb shows, indeed, one could probably find a parallel in these
Civic Entertainments for every figure and convention used in
the dumb shows.

These various forms should of course be seen against the
general background of late medieval life and art, in which the
'show' element played a very prominent part. It made its appearance in every sphere, the secular as well as the spiritual, the
popular and the aristocratic, influencing at the same time
fashion on the one hand and the church service on the other,
which of course contained, as has often been noticed, germs of
later drama. For instance, the Corpus Christi processions in the
larger towns were often magnificent pageants, interspersed with
pantomimes and *tableaux vivants*. On special holidays and at the
reception of English or foreign rulers there were also 'ridings',[2]
sword dances, tournaments, allegorical processions, and in-

---

[1] See Rudolf Brotanek, *Die englischen Maskenspiele* (Wien-Leipzig,
1902); E. K. Chambers, *The Mediaeval Stage* (Oxford, 1903); Robert
Withington, *English Pageantry*, 2 vols. (Cambridge, 1918–20); Enid
Welsford, *The Court Masque* (Cambridge, 1927); G. Wickham, op. cit.;
G. K. Hunter, *John Lyly: The Humanist as Courtier* (London, 1962),
pp. 89 ff. For the Lord Mayor's Shows see the volume *Collections III*, ed.
J. Robertson and D. J. Gordon, *Malone Soc.* (1954). For the influence of
pageantry on Elizabethan drama see the excellent book by Alice S.
Venezky, *Pageantry on the Shakespearean Stage* (New York, 1951).

[2] See the often quoted passage from Chaucer's *Cook's Tale;*
> For whan ther any ridyng was in Chepe,
> Out of the shoppe thider wolde he lepe—
> Til that he hadde al the sighte yseyn,
> And daunced wel, he wolde nat come ayeyn—

(*The Works of Geoffrey Chaucer*, ed. F. N. Robinson, 2nd ed. (London,
1957), I, ll. 4377–80.)

numerable spectacles of this kind, combining outward pomp and significant gesture. The idea of the pageant found its way into world literature at an early date. In Dante's *Purgatorio* there is an extensive and elaborate allegorical procession, representing the history of the Church. It can be partly explained as a kind of supranatural Corpus Christi procession, in which Beatrice occupies the position of the Sacrament, and it becomes quite impossible to make a clear distinction between allegory and reality.[1]

From this wealth of material I shall only draw upon those examples which throw most light on the development of the dumb shows or which can be brought into direct connection with them. The wide field of Civic Entertainments is particularly important in this respect, for it was in these that the active community spirit of the burgher classes and their positive relationship with the higher nobility and the court, so typical in Elizabethan England, found vivid expression.

Not only the Royal Entries but also the Lord Mayor's Shows, which became increasingly popular from the sixteenth century onwards, made use principally of allegorical, mythological and historical characters. Allegories such as Time, Truth, Ambition, or Charity, mythological figures such as Cupid, Neptune, and Venus, and historical or legendary characters like King Arthur or Alphonsus occur again and again in these performances, and most of them reappear in the pantomimes of Elizabethan dramatists. The means of presentation, too, were often very similar. The pageants and Lord Mayor's Shows consisted of either silent *tableaux* or brief scenes, characteristic episodes with some reference to contemporary affairs, especially the political situation. However, pantomimes, like the early dumb shows, often had a double meaning and had to be interpreted in the light of current events by the audience themselves. To make this easier,

---

[1] See Dante Alighieri, *The Divine Comedy: Purgatory*, translated by Dorothy L. Sayers (Harmondsworth, 1955), pp. 298 ff. For the general background see the works mentioned in note 1, p. 7, and J. Huizinga, *The Waning of the Middle Ages* (Harmondsworth, 1955); Karl Young, *The Drama of the Medieval Church* (Oxford, 1933), and the collection of articles: *Les Fêtes de la Renaissance, Études réunies et présentées par* Jean Jacquot (Paris, 1956). The dissertation by L. G. Gibbs also contains a great number of relevant examples and devotes far more space to antecedents of the dumb show than I have done.

the pageants were often accompanied by speeches which explained them fully, but allowance had to be made for the fact that the majority of the spectators would not be able to understand them in the general noise and turmoil. Consequently these performances had to appeal above all to the eye and try to attract attention by magnificent costumes, properties, and special visual effects. On reading accounts of such performances one is surprised many a time at the lavish use of money, ingenuity, and artistic skill. Some few examples from Elizabethan times may suffice to illustrate this and to show at the same time how striking the relationship is between the pageants and the later dumb shows.[1]

As Elizabeth I rode through London in the year 1558, immediately before her coronation, extremely elaborate pageants were presented at various spots on the route. One of them is described as follows:

> Over the two syde portes was placed a noyes of instrumentes. And all voyde places in the pageant were furnished with prety sayinges, commending and touching the meaning of the said pageant, which was the promises and blessinges of Almightie God made to his people.[2]

As the Queen proceeded she was met by Time, *'apparaylled as an olde man, with a sythe in his hande, havynge wynges artificiallye made'*.[3] A little later Truth appeared, carrying an English Bible, which was ceremoniously presented to the Queen. She kissed the book before the assembled people and held it to her breast.[4]

In 1575 the Queen visited Kenilworth Castle where she was received and entertained with much pomp. The entertainments began as soon as she arrived at the gateway; at the approach of the illustrious guest a group of trumpeters appeared who were

---

[1] These examples are taken from John Nichols, *The Progresses, and Public Processions of Queen Elizabeth* (London, 1788–1821), 4 vols., still the most comprehensive collection of pageants and royal entertainments of the Tudor period.

[2] J. Nichols, op. cit., Vol. I, 1558, p. 12.

[3] Ibid., 1558, p. 16.

[4] It is worth noting that a very similar episode occurs in Thomas Heywood's play *If You Know Not Me, You Know Nobody*, Part I. In a dream, staged as dumb show, an English Bible is presented to the Queen. See Chapter 6.

taller than all the other people present. The descriptive text explains the meaning of the scene:

> And by this dum shew it was ment, that in the daies and reigne of King Arthure, men were of that stature; so that the Castle of Kenilworth should seeme still to be kept by Arthur's heires and their seruants.[1]

It is worth noting that here even the term 'dum shew' is used, but in other respects also the style of these 'stage directions' has great similarities with the early dumb shows. There are also similarities in the characters employed and in some of the dramatic effects. Thus in 1578 on the occasion of the Queen's visit to Suffolk and Norfolk Venus and Cupid appeared '*out of Heaven*', as happens also in R. Wilmot's *Tancred and Gismund* and in R. Greene's *King Alphonsus*.[2] All these pageants were, like the dumb shows, accompanied by music, suited to the type of scene it was used for. The total effect must, therefore, have been very similar.

Although it is perhaps not possible to find an exact model in these pageants for every single Elizabethan dumb show, the numerous obvious parallels are sufficient to show that the one influenced the other. The pantomime before the first act of *Gorboduc*, the first dumb show ever used in Elizabethan drama, may serve as an example. It begins with the appearance of '*sixe wilde men clothed in leaues*' on the stage. The inclusion of such figures in a classical tragedy seems strange at first. A more careful examination, however, reveals that they were very popular and commonly used characters in the pageants.[3] 'Wilde

---

[1] J. Nichols, op. cit., Vol. I, 1575, p. 59.

[2] Ibid., Vol. II, pp. 64 ff. 'At Kenilworth, and every other place where the Queen was entertained, the whole Heathen Mythology was pressed into her service' (ibid., Vol. IV, i, p. 70).

[3] Cf. R. Withington, op. cit., Vol. I, pp. 72 ff., and G. Wickham, op. cit., pp. 391–2 and Plate I. Nichols tells about a pageant in which the Queen is addressed by a '*wilde man . . . cladde in ivie*' (op. cit., Vol. II, 1591, pp. 3–4). Later dumb shows do not make use of this character. It is, however, a particularly interesting link between the pageants and early drama. See E.Th.Sehrt, op. cit., pp. 11 ff.

In George Whetstone's play *Promos and Cassandra* we witness the preparations for a pageant on the stage in the course of which '*Two men, apparelled, lyke greene men at the Mayor's feast*' appear to clear a passage for the King.

men' or 'wode men' frequently appeared in them, usually as advance performers who headed the procession and made the way clear for the actual performance. At the sight of those figures entering the stage the audience must have been immediately reminded of the pageants and noticed the connection between the two forms of entertainment.

Another feature often found in Elizabethan drama is the appearance of a 'presenter' and again this seems to have been suggested by the pageants. Most of the *tableaux* and processions described by Nichols included such a figure who explained to the spectators the meaning of the 'show'.[1] In the earliest dumb shows there was no such presenter, and the meaning of the pantomime was explained by a chorus or – at least in the printed versions – in the 'argument'. In *Gorboduc* the chorus appears only at the end of each act to comment on the dumb shows. It is possible that the written 'argument' was handed to the more important people in the audience at the beginning of the performance, as in Middleton's *Women Beware Women*, so that at least they were able to follow the action closely and understand its deeper significance. Similarly, at the pageants only the Queen and her immediate followers were informed about the meaning of the show, while the rest of the audience had to be content with the outward spectacle and splendour.[2]

In later, more popular plays, the meaning of the dumb show was usually explained and commented on by some character

[1] Children were often employed to do this, as in the pageant of 1558 (see Nichols, op. cit., Vol. I). For the origin of the 'presenter' see also F. A. Foster, op. cit., p. 11 n. Foster mentions the chorus of classical drama and the 'expositor' of the moralities as possible models.

A striking parallel is found in the German *Fastnachtsspiele* of the later Middle Ages, where at the beginning a *praecursor* or *Einschreier* appeared, whose task it was to introduce the actors and to explain the initial situation of the play to be performed. Like the 'presenter' he served as a link between the play and the audience. See Eckehard Catholy, *Das Fastnachtsspiel des Spätmittelalters. Gestalt und Funktion* (Tübingen, 1961), p. 47 and *passim*.

[2] In this connection it is particularly interesting to note what Thomas Heywood says in describing one of his Lord Mayor's Shows (*Londini Speculum*, 1637): '*The third Pageant or Show meerly consisteth of Anticke gesticulations, dances, and other Mimicke postures, devised onely for the vulgar, who are better delighted with that which pleaseth the eye, than contenteth the eare.*' (*The Dramatic Works of Thomas Heywood*. London, 1874, Vol. IV.)

acting as chorus. This tradition, however, originated only partly in the pageants and the expression 'presenter' is used only in a few plays.[1] Very often mythological or legendary figures serve as chorus, as they also do in some of Seneca's tragedies. The Furies and other characters embodying the spirit of revenge seem to have been particular favourites,[2] but a glance through the numerous plays containing dumb shows reveals that a wide variety of characters could be used as chorus and that many different influences must have been at work.[3] The figure of the presenter reflects the tendency, so typical of the popular Elizabethan drama, to make everything as clear and impressive as possible. Everything had to be said more than once, using different artistic means, in order to impress it on every single member of the audience.

The strong relationship between the various semi-dramatic forms of entertainment, the pageants, masques, and Lord Mayor's Shows on the one hand, and actual drama on the other, is also illustrated by the fact that very often the same men were active in both fields. The best known example from the time of James I is of course Ben Jonson who gained a reputation for himself as a dramatist and as the author of numerous masques. But many other dramatists also tried to supplement their sometimes rather meagre income by devising such Civic Entertainments. The Lord Mayor's Shows in particular were often written by successful dramatists such as Anthony Munday, Thomas Dekker, Thomas Heywood and Thomas Middleton, although this practice was usual mainly in the reign of James I. It is only natural that such a personal connection should result in one form influencing the other, and we can be sure that the

---

[1] E.g. in Peele's *The Battle of Alcazar*, Heywood's *The Four Prentices of London*, and Middleton's *Your Five Gallants*.

[2] Cf. Megaera in Wilmot's *Tancred and Gismund* and Gager's *Meleager*, Nemesis in Gwinne's *Nero*, Ate in *Locrine*, and others.

[3] Cf. Mercury in *The Rare Triumphs of Love and Fortune*, 'Tragedy' in *A Warning for Fair Women*, 'Fame' in Day's *The Travails of the Three English Brothers*. Frequently characters are used who have some vague connection with the plot of the play, like Josephus in *Herod and Antipater* by Markham and Sampson, Homer in Heywood's *Ages*, Guicciardine in Barnes' *The Devil's Charter*, and others. Quite often only the word 'chorus' is used, as in *Captain Thomas Stukeley*, *The Bloody Banquet*, and Daborne's *A Christian turned Turk*.

dramatists liked to make use in their own plays of certain effects and new technical developments employed successfully in the popular shows. In particular at the Inns of Court, where the first classical tragedies were produced, festivals and so-called 'revels' seem to have been very popular. Certain festivals, especially Christmas, were celebrated by 'revels' and 'mummings',[1] so that here again both formal drama and pageantry appeared side by side and benefited each other.

In considering the English pageants and other semi-dramatic forms, however, it has to be admitted that there were certain equivalents in Italy. The so-called *trionfi*,[2] which contained many elements found in pageants and dumb shows, should be mentioned here. Very often allegorical and mythological characters appeared in these festive processions. Scenes from the Bible or classical mythology were presented as silent *tableaux* and moved through the streets mounted on large carts. The stationary pageant seems to have been less common. On the whole these Italian festive processions give a rather aristocratic impression whereas the English shows include a more popular and homely element, but again it is difficult to make any definite statement about the possible influence of these *trionfi* on English drama. Undoubtedly English Renaissance drama received strong impulses from the Italian theatre and shows clear marks of its influence. On the other hand, it developed a characteristic style of its own which differed considerably from the Italian one. One must also bear in mind that classical mythology and thinking in terms of allegory were so general and so much a part of the common store of knowledge in Europe during the Renaissance that one or two similarities and parallels do not count for much.

In a discussion of the various influences which affected the development of the dumb show mention must also be made of the emblems, whose technique is remarkably similar to that of the early dumb shows and reveals the same liking for puzzles and allegories as do the pantomimes and pageants. They were used to illustrate an abstract idea or moral lesson in the form of a

---

[1] For these Revels see Brotanek, op. cit. Texts in *Gesta Grayorum, Account of the Christmas revels at Gray's Inn in 1594–5, Malone Soc.* (1914), and *Certaine Deuises and shewes presented to her Maiestie by the Gentlemen of Grayes-Inne at her Highnesse Court in Greenewich* (London, 1587).

[2] See Werner Weisbach, *Trionfi* (Berlin, 1919).

mythological or allegorical scene accompanied by a short motto.[1] Such emblems had been employed in many pageants. The figures taking part often carried emblematic crests indicating their character. An example can be found in the *Gesta Grayorum*, where several such *impresses* are described.[2] A different use of the emblem within a pageant is made when certain virtues and vices are personified by historical and legendary figures. At the marriage celebrations of James IV of Scotland the four virtues, Justice, Fortitude, Temperance, Prudence, appeared represented by Nero, Holofernes, Epicurus, and Sardanapalus.[3] By frequent use many of these characters were so closely identified with certain moral qualities that they could then almost be considered emblems. Here the close relationship between emblem and allegorical representation becomes especially obvious.

It is interesting to note that the expression dumb show is occasionally used by contemporaries for these emblems, and Rosemary Freeman has shown that these two forms are in many cases nearly identical.[4] They have in common the fact that they both, because of their abstract representation and stylization,

---

[1] See especially Rosemary Freeman, *English Emblem Books* (London, 1948). 'There are very few poets of the period in whose work the matter, if not the manner, of the emblem books cannot somewhere be traced.' (p. 99). The use of emblems is of course not confined to poetry. We frequently find it, for instance, in Elizabethan embroidery. The famous 'Cavendish Tapestry', probably the joint work of Mary Queen of Scots and the Countess of Shrewsbury (Bess of Hardwick), and now in the possession of the Victoria and Albert Museum, contains a large number of simple emblematic designs. In the centre there is a more elaborate emblem with a Latin motto. See also C. Tourneur's *The Atheist's Tragedy*, IV, 1.

[2] E.g. 'A Flag of Fire wavering upwards.—*Tremet & ardet* . . . A Tortois, with his Head out of the Shell.—*Obnoxia*.' (*Malone Soc.*, p. 67.) Very similar emblems are used in the opening dumb show of Robert Wilson's *The Three Lords and Three Ladies of London*: 'Pollicie' enters with a shield, 'the ympreze, a *Tortoys*, the word *Prouidens securus*'. Cf. also the emblematic dumb show before the last act of Hughes' *The Misfortunes of Arthur*.

[3] This pageant described in R. Withington, op. cit., Vol. I, pp. 168–9. Animals were also frequently used in these pageants; cf. ibid, pp. 64 ff.

[4] 'Indeed the *dumb show* of the stage is in both form and function only a more elaborate version of the pictures in an emblem book', op. cit., p. 15. The term 'dumb showes' used by G. Wither in his *Collection of Emblems* (1635).

For emblems in drama see C. W. Hodges, *The Globe Restored* (London, 1953), pp. 77 ff.; and G. Wickham, op. cit., Vol. II, Part I, pp. 206 ff.

are somewhat removed from reality and that the visible scene is only a vehicle for some deeper meaning. This is the exact opposite of the realism often found in Elizabethan drama, in fact, it is just this contrast which often produces the special effect of the dumb show.

Emblematic scenes can be found even in the first dumb shows, particularly in *Gorboduc* and *Jocasta*, where historical figures also appear as the embodiments of particular virtues and sins. Thus the pantomime before the first act of *Jocasta* is: '*Representing vnto vs Ambition, by the hystorie of Sesostres king of Egypt.*' Similarly in R. Greene's *James IV*, Semiramis, Kyrus, and Sesostris are shown as representatives of the vanity of the world. The consistent use of the emblem in the tragedy *Locrine* is especially striking. In this play the animal representations, common in the emblem books, and the Latin mottoes, which were also an important part of every collection of emblems, can both be found, as well as the historical and mythological figures. Here the close connection between emblem and dumb show is particularly clear, but it reveals itself – often in very small details – in the work of many dramatists, as for instance in Middleton's comedy *Your Five Gallants*, where such emblems and their Latin mottoes are employed to achieve a very funny effect.[1] Here too, it is hardly possible to prove direct influence in every individual case. Yet it should suffice to show how closely the various artistic forms of Elizabethan times are interrelated and that none of them can be explained and understood on its own.

It should also be noted that there had been definite pantomimic elements in early English drama long before the first appearance of the dumb show, indeed some of them could almost be considered predecessors of the dumb shows, although a direct connection is very unlikely. Examples can be found in several of the surviving moralities. A short scene in the morality *Wisdom* (*c.* 1460) reminds one particularly of the later pantomimes. In it 'Wisdom' reveals to 'Mind' his own corrupt soul. *Anima* appears as a hideous figure and 'Wisdom' explains the incident:

> As many dedly synnys as ye haue vsyde,
> So many deullys in yowur soule be.

[1] See Chapter 10.

Be-holde wat ys þer-in reclusyde!
Alas, man! of þi soule haue pyte!
(*Here rennyt owt from wndyr þe horrybyll mantyll of þe Soull vı
small boys in þe lyknes of Dewyllys, & so retorne a-geyn.*)[1]

Here, as in some of the later dumb shows, the allegorical meaning is made clear and emphasized by direct and visual means,
Wisdom acting as presenter and explaining the meaning of the
pantomime. Although this short passage has little in common
with the type of dumb show performed between the acts of the
classical tragedies, it is not unlike some later forms of dumb
show found in popular drama.

A similar form of pantomime is also included in Skelton's
Magnificence, where an allegorical incident is again made more
dramatic by a little piece of silent action, but here there is no
presenter.[2]

All these earlier forms appear at least to show that the introduction of pantomimes into sixteenth-century drama was no
completely new idea, but rather the continuation of an older
custom. Of course this does not explain the sudden appearance
of extensive dumb shows between the acts of *Gorboduc*. Here
undoubtedly the influence of the pageants played a more important part. The available material suggests that we need
hardly turn to the Italian *intermedii* to explain satisfactorily the
origin of the English dumb shows. I do not of course wish to
dispute the fact that Italian literature, especially drama, exer-
cised a decisive influence on developments in England. It is
impossible to imagine the classical tragedies of the Inns of Court
without the models of Giraldi, Dolce, and others. Probably the
idea of filling the pauses between the acts with some more
spectacular entertainment was also taken over from the Italian
dramatists. Such an idea was just what the English writers
needed because all the earlier popular plays had more than satisfied the liking of the spectators for movement and action, and

[1] *The Macro Plays*, ed. F. J. Furnivall and Alfred W. Pollard,
EETS ES, 91 (1904), p. 65.

[2] Ed. R. L. Ramsay, *EETS ES*, 98 (1908), following l. 324:
'Magnyfycence' is silently reading a letter. 'Interim superueniat cantando
Counterfet Countenaunce suspenso gradu, qui uiso *Magnyfycence* sensim
retrocedat; at tempus post pusillum rursum accedat *Counterfet Countenaunce* prospectando et uocitando a longe; et *Fansy* animat silentium
cum manu.'

the purely rhetorical tragedies must have appeared as something completely strange at first. For the actual content of the dumb shows the English dramatists could draw on the inexhaustible store of native pageantry and it is completely unnecessary to look for Italian models to explain the details of the pantomimes. At the same time the English dramatists could count upon spectators even more used to such performances than the Italians and to whom allegorical allusions were familiar. Citizens who prepared such splendid and costly pageants for their Queen certainly found the inclusion of similar elements in serious drama natural and suitable.

Here we have what seems to be the most likely explanation for the origin of the dumb show.[1] The close connection between the theatre and the various other forms of public entertainment, particularly the pageants, suggests that the dumb shows developed chiefly out of these popular spectacles. In no other country did they become such a widespread tradition and such an integral part of drama as in England. They are an outcome of a characteristic trend of the time, the desire to make abstract spiritual experiences and conflicts visible as concrete scenes and to impress a moral idea on the spectators by appealing directly to the senses. The drama as well as the prose literature of the Elizabethan period expresses a strong desire for explicitness and repetition. To be considered effective, everything had to be said more than once, if possible in continually new and hitherto untried ways. All these shows and emblems must also be understood as the products of an allegorical habit of mind which found its most magnificent expression in Spenser's *Fairy Queen*, but has also left innumerable less conspicuous traces. A nice illustration is the little scene described by Nichols, where Elizabeth during one of her processions sees a pageant in which an allegory of Time appears, whereupon she adds a general comment on the subject.[2]

---

[1] I find that L. G. Gibbs, after a far more detailed analysis than mine, arrives at the same conclusion (op. cit., pp. 52 ff.).

[2] 'Sone after that her Grace passed the Crosse, she had espyed the pageant erected at the Little Conduit in Cheape, and incontinent required to know what it might signifye. And it was tolde her Grace, that there was placed Tyme. Tyme? quoth she, and Tyme hath brought me hether. And so furth the hole matter was opened to her Grace' (op. cit., Vol. I, 1558, p. 13).

The Elizabethan Dumb Show

The tradition of the dumb show appears as the expression of a particular way of thinking in art and life and it is necessary to keep this in mind when discussing Elizabethan pantomimes. A more detailed consideration of the various forms of the dumb shows and the characters appearing in them will demonstrate that they should not be seen out of their context and that numerous links exist between them and the semi-dramatic performances discussed in this chapter.

2

Forms of the Dumb Show

Mention has already been made of the fact that the same figures appear over and over again in the early dumb shows, but a glance at the work of J. Nichols and similar collections reveals that in the pageants too the characters were usually of the same type and the same allegorical or mythological figures appear very often. In many cases it is impossible to make a clear-cut distinction between allegory and mythology because, as in the emblem books, moral qualities are often represented by classical heroes or deities. The example encountered most frequently is the personification of love by the figure of Venus or Cupid.[1] Such figures are as common in the dumb shows as they were in the pageants. To this universally familiar store, drawn upon by nearly every artist of the period, belong personifications, such as Time, Truth, Ambition, Chastity and numerous others.[2] On the other hand, figures, such as Megaera, Nemesis, and Ate, which appear in several dumb shows, hardly ever occur in the pageants; they probably date back to the Senecan tragedies. Conversely, the personification of certain localities, such as 'London' or 'Thamesis', which were a distinctive feature of many pageants and the later masques, were not taken over by the authors of the dumb shows.[3]

By this frequent inclusion of the allegorical and the mythological the range of characters in Elizabethan drama was considerably extended. In many of the early dumb shows figures appear which had not previously been employed in English

[1] Cf. R. Withington, op. cit., Vol. I, pp. 210 ff. Examples are Greene's *Alphonsus*, R. Wilmot's *Tancred and Gismund* and Hymen in Kyd's *Spanish Tragedy*.

[2] See also Chapter 1 on the emblems. I shall in the course of this chapter only give a few characteristic examples for each type. Further details are given in the list of plays containing dumb shows (Appendix I).

[3] See, however, the prologue to R. Wilson's *The Three Lords and Three Ladies of London* which is spoken by '*a Lady very richly attyred, representing London*'.

drama, like the '*six wilde men*' in *Gorboduc*. Others had, it is true, already been used earlier in popular drama, but now found their way for the first time into classical tragedy as, for instance, the various representations of particular virtues and vices, or the figure of Fortune in *Jocasta* (V).

Another group of characters, which were introduced into drama chiefly via the dumb shows, is that of the famous heroes of history and legend. They are particularly prominent in *Gorboduc* (IV) and *Jocasta* (I, III), but also occur in later pantomimes.[1] Usually they too serve to emphasize some moral, just as we frequently find in these plays references to history and legend with the same end in view. However, an important development in the history of the dumb show is the gradual replacing of the allegorical and mythological figures by the characters from the actual play. The style and technique of Elizabethan drama developed on such different lines from the pageants that the figures which had appeared in the early dumb shows were then no longer acceptable. The pantomimes became more and more like any other scenes in the plays and eventually included exactly the same characters. There are, however, some rather curious transitional forms.

While in the early dumb shows only allegorical or mythological characters appeared, and in the later ones only characters from the drama itself, we find some pantomimes in which characters from the play and allegorical figures appear simultaneously. Although a marked difference between the actual play and the dumb show still persists, it is nothing like as obvious and clear-cut as it was in the classical tragedies. This mixed form is still related to the pageants, in which there was also a strong connection between the sphere of the play and that of real life: personifications and real characters often met on the same stage. This same juxtaposition of allegory and reality could be found too in the popular interludes, such as *Appius and Virginia*, Pickering's *Horestes*, and Garter's *Susanna*, in which figures such as Vice, Fame, Conscience, and other personifications are common, and inner arguments and conflicts are frequently ex-

---

[1] Cf. Greene's *James IV*, Kyd's *Spanish Tragedy* (I, 5) and *Herod and Antipater* by Markham and Sampson, where the example of some historical and legendary heroes greatly influences Antipater's own decisions.

pressed in allegorical dialogue. Here the allegorical and the real are merged at various points while in those plays in which allegory was confined to the pantomimes they are kept separate.

The most interesting example of this use of the 'mixed' dumb show occurs in the tragedy *A Warning for Fair Women*. Here the sphere of real life is abandoned at certain important points and an allegorical pantomime is employed to portray mental processes and moral decisions.[1] Similarly in Dekker's *The Whore of Babylon* and Middleton's *The Mayor of Queenborough* the pantomimes are used to give the drama an extra dimension by adding to the scenes of ordinary dialogue something in the nature of a morality play. One suspects that often the writer's inability to cope with these matters in straightforward dialogue made him resort to the dumb show as an easy way out.

As has been shown, the range of characters in the dumb shows alone is nearly as wide and varied as that in Elizabethan drama as a whole, although a certain narrowing of the range can be detected in the course of development. The same applies to drama where allegorical characters played a much less important part after 1600 than before. In the early dumb shows we therefore find mainly allegorical and mythological figures, whereas one can say that the characters in the later pantomimes are practically identical with those of the play itself.

Leaving the characters aside, it is far more difficult to find in the dumb shows features of style which can be said to be common to them all. We find the same diversity in the elements of plot used in the dumb shows as we did in the case of the characters. At first sight it seems as if there is hardly any dramatic situation which has not been used in one of the dumb shows. Of course the capacity for expression in the pantomimes is severely limited by the absence of dialogue and not every scene which is effective in real drama can be easily converted into a dumb show. As one would expect, scenes which involve the weighing of decisions, persuasive argument, and elaborate planning are not suitable for presentation in pantomimic form. Where such dumb shows do occur in plays they are usually not very satisfactory and have to be explained by the chorus in lengthy

[1] See the more detailed analysis of this play in Chapter 6.

speeches.[1] On the other hand, any striking and obvious gesture, any of the spectacular encounters in which Elizabethan drama is so rich, lends itself to this form, indeed sometimes such a silent scene is even more effective than it would be if accompanied by dialogue.[2] Generally the style of the dumb shows is governed by the necessity of replacing by powerful and even exaggerated movement and action that which is inevitably lost by the absence of spoken words.

The simplest form of the pantomime is the formal procession where a group of people, usually distinguished by their magnificent attire and ceremonial mien, appears and crosses the stage in silence. If dialogue follows immediately, without any transition, we can only speak of a particularly impressive opening for a scene and the expression dumb show is not justified.[3] It is another matter when the group passes round the stage several times and withdraws before the actual scene begins. This form of dumb show was used above all in the classical tragedies.[4] Its usual function was only to create a certain atmosphere, as of sombre foreboding or of victorious triumph. External splendour and costumes play an important part, whether a train of courtiers, an army, or a group of mourners is represented. The similarity to the Royal Entries and pageants is particularly obvious here and it is significant that this form of pantomime is hardly ever to be found in later plays,[5] just as dumb shows whose function is to create an atmosphere appropriate to the following act occur only in earlier drama.

Another form of pantomime, which involves more than merely

---

[1] Cf. *Captain Thomas Stukeley*, Marston's *Antonio's Revenge* (III), Heywood's *The Golden Age* (V), *The Silver Age* (IV), *The Brazen Age* (III) and, in a different way, *A Warning for Fair Women*.

[2] See particularly Marston's use of the pantomime (Cf. Chapter 8.).

[3] See the beginning of Dekker's *The Honest Whore*, Part I, and Tourneur's *The Revenger's Tragedy*. There are some splendid processions in the anonymous plays *The Stately Tragedy of Claudius Tiberius Nero* and *Look About You*. Marston's *Sophonisba* is perhaps a border-line case (see Chapter 8).

[4] Cf. *Gorboduc* (III, IV), *Jocasta* (I), and *The Misfortunes of Arthur* (I, V).

[5] See the use of this type in Middleton's *Your Five Gallants*, where it has a distinctly archaic flavour and makes some scenes of the play rather like some popular morality which, I think, was precisely the author's intention.

a ceremonial procession round the stage, but which does not contain the details of a complete scene, goes a step further. Very often only a short significant gesture or a brief meeting, important for the development of the plot, is shown. This form can also be found as early as the classical tragedies, where the gesture is mostly symbolic or allegorical.[1] In later plays it is usually a means of presenting small episodes which have some direct bearing on the plot, thus dealing with them as quickly as possible.[2] In this way a prearranged meeting between two persons or parties from the play can be acted.

A third and perhaps the most frequent type of dumb show is the presentation of a whole scene, complete in itself, without dialogue. This type, too, is as old as the dumb show itself and makes its appearance in *Gorboduc* (I, II) and *Jocasta* (III, IV). In both plays the pantomime tells a moral or instructive tale which summarizes the content of the following act in a didactic manner. In the majority of later dumb shows important scenes of the play are presented and thus take up much less time in performance than normal scenes with dialogue. Often the only reason for the use of this technique seems to be that the playwright despaired of managing his material in any other way, as can be seen in Heywood's drama of adventure *The Four Prentices of London* where this is openly admitted:

> Now to auoide all dilatory newes,
> Which might with-hold you from the Stories pith,
> And substance of the matter wee entend:
> I must entreate your patience to forbeare,
> Whilst we do feast your eye, and starue your eare.
> For in dumbe shews, which were they writ at large
> Would aske a long and tedious circumstance:
> Their infant fortunes I will soone expresse,
> And from the truth in no one point digresse.

[1] Cf. the discharging of guns in *Gorboduc* (V). Further examples are in *Jocasta* (V) and *The Misfortunes of Arthur*. War-like fights are frequently presented in dumb show, as in Pickering's *Horestes*, Wilson's *The Three Lords and Three Ladies of London*, and Legge's *Richardus Tertius*.

[2] Cf. Middleton's *The Changeling* (III) and *A Game at Chess*, Marston's *The Insatiate Countess* (III) and Heywood's *The Fair Maid of the West*. In all these plays only a rather brief scene is acted in pantomime which is, however, important for the further development of the plot and was probably introduced to save time in performance.

It is obvious that Heywood wanted more action on the stage than could be fitted into a play of normal length and so he resorted to the dumb show as an easy way out of his difficulty. We shall find, however, that more skilful playwrights often make a less clumsy use of the pantomime.

Although the individual pantomimes differ considerably from each other in content, certain motives recur frequently, suggesting that some dramatic situations enjoyed particular popularity. The representation of a murder, especially when executed in some ingenious and novel way, was often the subject of a dumb show. One of the earliest examples occurs in Peele's *The Battle of Alcazar*. Shakespeare employs this motive in a particularly original way in *Hamlet*, and Webster in *The White Devil* even uses it twice in succession, the second murder exceeding the first, if possible, in sadistic cruelty.

Another favourite motive was the big state-occasion, frequently staged as a dumb show, because this device emphasized the ceremonial and solemn character of the scene. Thus Hieronimo's installation as marshal in *The First Part of Ieronimo*, the coronation of Alexander Borgia as Pope in Barnaby Barnes' *The Devil's Charter*, and Ward's conversion to Islam in Daborne's *A Christian turned Turk* are all presented as dumb shows.[1] Very often the dumb shows consist of scenes in which a king appears, followed by his courtiers, to receive an ambassador, to hear a petition or to pass judgment.[2] In connection with such state-scenes, but also in other contexts, magic and supernatural apparitions are often included to create spectacular stage-effects.[3] Admittedly one cannot talk of dumb shows in the strict sense of the term in all these cases. Often such apparitions are little more than stage-effects, lacking the characteristics of pantomimes, and in other examples the ghosts which have been conjured up begin to speak, as in Chapman's *Bussy D'Ambois*.

[1] See also Webster's *The Duchess of Malfi*.

[2] Cf. *Captain Thomas Stukeley*, Dekker's *Match Me in London*, Heywood's *If You Know Not Me, You Know Nobody*, Part I, Daborne's *A Christian turned Turk*, Brome's *The Queen and Concubine*, and others.

[3] Only a few particularly typical examples may be mentioned: Greene, *Friar Bacon and Friar Bungay; John of Bordeaux;* Marlowe, *The Tragical History of Doctor Faustus*, particularly the edition of 1616; William Rowley, *The Birth of Merlin*; Heywood, *The Silver Age* (V); Barnes, *The Devil's Charter*; Fletcher, *The Prophetess*.

The dumb shows were, on the other hand, a favourite means of bringing such supernatural elements on to the stage, at the same time separating them clearly from the rest of the play. This applies even to the early play *The Rare Triumphs of Love and Fortune*, but similar dumb shows are still to be found in Shakespeare's *Macbeth* and *The Tempest*. Dreams also are often acted as pantomimes, as in Lyly's *Endimion*, where again the absence of dialogue makes the incident seem more unreal and striking.

The large number of stage properties used in many dumb shows also deserves brief mention.[1] Most common among them are probably the torches. These had been an indispensable feature of most pageants,[2] but played an even more important part in drama, because the stage was usually unlit at the beginning of a performance and many dramatists incorporated the bringing on of torches into the initial scene of the play, thus providing a natural beginning, as in Marston's *What You Will*, quoted in a later chapter. Torchbearers appear frequently in dumb shows, especially when the dumb show comes at the beginning of a new scene and we often find them lighting a bridal chamber or accompanying a wedding procession.[3]

To sum up, the dramatic style of the dumb shows does not differ materially from that of the plays themselves, although certain motives and situations are employed more frequently in the dumb shows and there is a more marked reliance on the sensational and spectacular. While the early dumb shows deal mainly with allegorical and mythological subjects and are clearly related to the street pageants, the later ones usually contain a telescoped version of a scene from the play itself, preferably one of a strikingly unusual or ceremonial character. In these plays the dumb shows develop further and further away from their original models, the pageants, and become increasingly more like the other scenes of the play, often dis-

---

[1] Cf. banquet and tree in Peele's *The Battle of Alcazar* and in *A Warning for Fair Women*, chariot in *Jocasta* (I); see also J. Nichols, op. cit., Vol. II, 1581, p. 139, for the description of a chariot in which there was room for a full orchestra.

[2] Cf. G. Wickham, op. cit., Vol. I, p. 224.

[3] Cf. Kyd's *The Spanish Tragedy*, Marston's *The Malcontent* and *Sophonisba*, Webster's *The White Devil*, Middleton's *A Game at Chess*, Heywood's *If You Know Not Me, You Know Nobody*, Part I, and *A Maidenhead Well Lost*.

tinguished only by the absence of dialogue. Their dramatic function also brings them closer to the actual play, of which, in many cases, they become an integral part.

This leads us directly to the main subject of this book, which is the structural relationship between the dumb shows and the plays in which they occur. This question is discussed in the following section. It has of course been necessary to limit the analysis to some selected and particularly characteristic examples; all the extant dumb shows could not have been treated with equal thoroughness, but it would be easy enough to fit those not dealt with at length into the general pattern of development which emerges.[1]

[1] For this the appended list of plays containing dumb shows provides further material.

PART II

3

The Classical Tragedies

Although the pantomimic element played in general a much more important part in popular drama, in the moralities, 'interludes' and chronicle plays, than in the classical tragedies, the characteristic form of the dumb show appears for the first time in the plays written under the influence of Seneca and the Italian tragedians and is at first confined to them. It is therefore with those plays that an account of the history of the dumb show must begin.

The dumb show as a dramatic convention in its own right did not gradually develop out of small beginnings, but appears in *Gorboduc* as a finished product; it became less and less distinctive in the course of its history, until at last it merged completely into the drama. Even in *Gorboduc,* and in *Jocasta,* which was strongly influenced by the earlier play, the individual dumb shows are amazingly varied and it is not easy to find a formula which could be applied to each of them. Most of the descriptions usually given are too narrow and do not fit every example.[1]

All dumb shows at this first stage have in common that they are inserted between the acts – indeed they are, like the Italian *intermedii,* only possible in plays which are strictly divided into acts – that they have a marked didactic or moralizing tendency, and that they stand out in relief against the stiff and formal rhetoric of the plays themselves. In sharp contrast to the popular comedies and history plays with their lively pantomimic scenes,[2] the dumb shows here are anything but 'realistic', if by realistic we mean close to real life. On the contrary, they are even further removed from reality than the action of the play. They emphasize the festive and ceremonial character of the performance, and its general meaning.

In spite of these common features, we find even in the early

---

[1] See the description of these first dumb shows by F. A. Foster (op. cit.) and B. R. Pearn (op. cit.).

[2] See, for instance, the brawls in Preston's *Cambises.*

tragedies noticeable differences in the treatment of the dumb shows. For instance, the characters appearing in them may be purely allegorical or mythological figures, or personifications of various kinds. The pantomimes can be either processions round the stage, *tableaux* with brief characteristic gestures, or proper scenes containing complete episodes. It is important to note that the two spheres, dialogue without action and action without dialogue, are kept entirely separate at first.[1] Only in the course of further development is an organic relationship between dumb show and drama established, most clearly in Wilmot's *Tancred and Gismund*, where the dumb shows lead directly into the dialogue.

THOMAS NORTON AND THOMAS SACKVILLE: 'GORBODUC'

Any systematic study of the dumb show has to begin with *Gorboduc*.[2] Here for the first time we come across that curious custom of introducing each act with a pantomimic prologue. That is to say, the play begins, not with a chorus or a dialogue, but with a silent scene. There is a musical prelude, or rather background music,[3] followed by the appearance of '*sixe wilde men clothed in leaues*' on the stage.[4] Whereas most scenes in classical tragedies include only very few characters, we see here a larger group entering together. In other respects, too, the pantomime is strikingly different from the rest of the tragedy. It introduces lively and theatrical movement. As in some popular plays the actors appear to have been given something of a free

[1] Cf. Wolfgang Clemen, *English Tragedy Before Shakespeare* (London, 1961), pp. 56 ff. (for *Gorboduc*).

[2] Ed. John W. Cunliffe in *Early English Classical Tragedies* (Oxford, 1912). On *Gorboduc* cf. also Agostino Lombardo, *Il Dramma Pre-Shakespeariano* (Venezia, 1957), pp. 171 ff., where the dumb shows are briefly touched on and the old theory that they derive from the *intermedii* is repeated (p. 189).

[3] On the music accompanying the dumb shows see Cunliffe's note (op. cit., p. 299) and the interesting article by F. W. Sternfeld, 'La Musique dans les tragédies élisabéthaines inspirées de Sénèque', in *Les Tragédies de Sénèque et le Théatre de la Renaissance*, ed. Jean Jacquot (Paris, 1964), pp. 139–51.

[4] For these figures see Chapter 1. For the opening dumb show of *Gorboduc* see E. Th. Sehrt, op. cit., pp. 10 ff., where the pantomime as an introduction to the play is very well treated.

hand; thus the scene could easily degenerate into a riot although of course no comedy of any kind was intended:

> *The order of the domme shew before the first act, and the signifi-cation therof.*
>
> *First the Musicke of Violenze began to play, during which came in vpon the stage sixe wilde men clothed in leaues. Of whom the first bare in his necke a fagot of small stickes, which they all both seuerally and together assayed with all their strengthes to breake, but it could not be broken by them. At the length one of them plucked out one of the stickes and brake it: And the rest plucking out all the other stickes one after an other did easely breake them, the same being seuered: which being conioyned they had before attempted in vaine. After they had this done, they departed the stage, and the Musicke ceased. Hereby was signified, that a state knit in vnitie doth continue strong against all force. But being diuided, is easely destroyed. As befell vpon Duke Gorboduc diuiding his land to his two sonnes which he before held in Monarchie. And vpon the discention of the brethren to whom it was diuided.*[1]

In contrast to other pantomimic episodes, as we find them in many popular plays of the period, here a complete, rounded-off scene is presented, and its allegorical significance for the play that is to follow is explicitly stated and commented on. In other words, even before the beginning of the actual play the audience was entertained by a lively, engrossing spectacle, a moral tale which could be understood even without commentary. The scene addresses itself to the audience only and has at first sight no direct connection with the play itself. No character from the play appears in it, nor are the events depicted an exact parallel to the plot of the tragedy. That there is some relationship, how-ever, becomes clear as early as in the first scene of the following act where Videna informs her son of the impending division of the kingdom and foresees the final catastrophe. Even before

---

[1] On the origin of the motives see E. Th. Sehrt, ibid. Professor Sehrt doubts if the audience would understand the significance of the scene. It is, of course, difficult to prove the contrary, but I am inclined to think that the more educated spectators, who at the Inns of Court must have been in the majority, were so much accustomed to such allegorical presentations that their meaning and application presented no difficulty to them. This is also the reason, I am sure, why the dumb shows in *Gorboduc* are not explained straightaway, as in most popular plays, but only at the end of the act.

Gorboduc himself announces his decision in the second scene, the evil that will come of this weakening of the realm is strongly suggested. The fatal outcome is, however, hinted at only in the form of a general moral, not by means of an appropriate atmosphere, as in later dumb shows. The function of the scene is therefore not so much a dramatic as a didactic one. The whole pantomime, in spite of its liveliness, is abstract and there is no indication of place and time. It is not so much a preview of what is to come as a moral that applies to the whole play. This function is stressed by the explanation included in the printed text of the play and quoted above, as well as by the commentary of the chorus at the end of the act where the didactic intention is finally driven home:

> And this great king, that doth deuide his land . . . (19)
> A myrrour shall become to Princes all,
> To learne to shunne the cause of suche a fall.

This use of tragedy as a means of political instruction, which makes *Gorboduc* a kind of dramatized *Mirror for Magistrates*, is clearly emphasized by the opening dumb show, so that the latter on the one hand obviously strengthens the play's didactic and theoretical character while at the same time counter-balancing its static and formal rhetoric. The two dramatists seem to have been struck by the idea of employing two entirely different dramatic means to point their moral, i.e. sententious dialogue and colourful pageantry. If any proof were needed that they considered the didactic content of their play more important than its dramatic qualities, this opening pantomime would furnish it.

The second dumb show is of a slightly different kind. Here a scene is presented which even in its atmosphere bears a direct relation to the following act. Again great pains seem to have been taken to give plenty of colour and movement to the incident. Although in the text of the play itself we find no indication of any stage properties or supernumeraries being employed, the king here is surrounded by '*a nombre of his nobilitie and gentlemen*' and '*a chaire of estate*' is brought in for him. The following episode consists of two movements which stand in sharp contrast to each other, just as in the first panto-mime we had the two attempts to break the bundle of sticks.

Again the visual element predominates and the significance of every gesture is immediately obvious:

> *The order and signification of the domme shew before the second acte.*
>
> *First the Musicke of Cornettes began to playe, during which came in vpon the stage a King accompanied with a nombre of his nobilitie and gentlemen. And after he had placed him self in a chaire of estate prepared for him: there came and kneled before him a graue and aged gentelman and offred vp a cuppe vnto him of wyne in a glasse, which the King refused. After him commes a braue and lustie yong gentleman and presentes the King with a cup of golde filled with poyson, which the King accepted, and drinking the same, immediatly fell downe dead vpon the stage, and so was carried thence away by his Lordes and gentlemen, and then the Musicke ceased. Hereby was signified, that as glasse by nature holdeth no poyson, but is clere and may easely be seen through, ne boweth by any arte: So a faythfull counsellour holdeth no treason, but is playne and open, ne yeldeth to any vndiscrete affection, but geueth holsome counsell, which the yll aduised Prince refuseth. The delightfull golde filled with poyson betokeneth flattery, which vnder faire seeming of pleasaunt wordes beareth deadly poyson, which destroyed the Prince that receyueth it. As befell in the two brethren Ferrex and Porrex, who refusing the holsome aduise of graue counsellours, credited these yong Paracites, and brought to them selues death and destruction therby.*

This pantomime, even more than the first one, has developed into a complete dramatic scene, a kind of play within a play. This development is important because nowhere in the play itself do we find anything as striking in its appeal to the eyes of the spectators. Of course there is still that rigid division between mime and dialogue which is so typical of *Gorboduc*. The dumb show was a convenient means of providing true theatre without actually enlivening the stiff and inflexible dialogue, and of conveying to the audience something which the authors were apparently unable or unwilling to express through the medium of speech.

The introduction of such pantomimes before the acts must have strongly influenced the audience's response to the rest of the play. Having watched the impressive spectacle of a king at the height of his power dropping dead from his throne, the spectators must have been far more impressed by the following dialogue, and the sententious warning uttered in it could not so easily have been forgotten. Even the most rhetorical chorus-speech could not have made the meaning and importance of the tragedy more clear than such a vivid scene. The Fall of Princes, probably the most popular tragic subject of the Middle Ages and the Renaissance, was presented in a novel way: a pageant, followed by a classical tragedy which explained and illustrated it. Whereas the moralities tried to combine allegory and dialogue, the two are here kept entirely separate, allegory being confined to the pantomimes, while dialogue is only used for the actual story.

Like the first pantomime, this second one is only intended for the spectators, and the characters of the play have nothing to do with it. There are, however, some more obvious parallels to the events described in the play. In both cases the action takes place at the court of a king. The two scenes of the following act show us the same incident, a prince listening to two advisers, twice. As indicated in the printed text of the dumb show, there is in each case an old and well-meaning counsellor and a young flatterer. Thus the same basic situation is in fact repeated three times, a primitive but very effective means of dramatic intensification.

Another important function of this second pantomime is to foreshadow coming events; for both scenes of the following act stop at the point where the prince seems to accept the advice of the young flatterer, while the spectators, remembering the dumb show, can draw their own conclusions and foresee the inevitable ruin of the princes. The gloomy prophecies of the chorus contribute to the effect.

Thus the second dumb show is not only an abstract moral as is the first, but gives in very thin allegorical disguise an outline of what is to happen in the following act and at the same time foreshadows the tragic end of the play. It drives home the meaning of the performance even to the less intelligent spectator and thus again emphasizes the didactic character of the play. It has been noticed that the two council-scenes of the second act are not so much debates as a series of mostly unrelated speeches in which each character affirms his particular standpoint without either listening to the opponent's arguments or even trying to persuade him.[1] The same tendency is found in the dumb show

[1] See W. Clemen, op. cit., pp. 68 ff.

where again the characters are personifications of certain principles and attitudes rather than living people. The role of the pantomime is therefore very similar to that of the chorus: to make an authoritative statement of the play's moral intention.

The third dumb show is quite different in character and function. Its main purpose is to create an appropriate atmosphere for the following act and to convey a vague foreboding of coming disaster. Even a cursory reading reveals that prophecy and anticipation play a very important part in *Gorboduc*. Thus both scenes of the second act end on a note of sinister warning and premonition (II, 1, ll. 194ff.; II, 2, ll. 67ff.). The second of the two speeches is addressed directly to the audience and paints a gloomy picture of the future:

Lo here the end of these two youthful kings . . . (67)

The dialogue suddenly turns into a string of *sententiae*. The chorus continues in this vein and adds an explanation of the preceding dumb show:

Loe, thus it is, poyson in golde to take,
And holsome drinke in homely cuppe forsake. (25–26)

This is immediately followed by the next pantomime:

> *The order and signification of the domme shewe before the thirde act.*
> *Firste the musicke of flutes began to playe, during which came in vpon the stage a company of mourners all clad in blacke betokening death and sorowe to ensue vpon the ill aduised misgouernement and discention of bretherne, as befell vpon the murder of Ferrex by his yonger brother. After the mourners had passed thryse about the stage, they departed, and than the musicke ceased.*

The scene presents no special difficulty to the spectator. It derives its effect mainly from the black robes and the solemn movement. There is no particular grouping of characters and no actual plot as there was in the earlier dumb shows. There is also much less pantomimic action. A procession of mourners would be quite possible in any other play and does not necessarily have to be a dumb show,[1] but here the scene is again kept

---

[1] Funeral processions occur frequently in plays of the period. Cf. Munday's *The Death of Robert, Earl of Huntingdon*, the beginning of Dekker's *The Honest Whore*, Part I, Middleton's *A Chaste Maid in Cheapside*, and others.

completely separate from the rest of the play and explicitly described as a dumb show. It may also have been more elaborate in performance than the printed text suggests. In the play itself we find nothing like that ceremonial marching round the stage and the *'company of mourners'*. The contrast is heightened by Gorboduc's rhetorical and declamatory lament at the beginning of the next scene, which is a good specimen of the play's undramatic style.[1] This speech is of course prepared for by the dumb show and is the more effective for it. We see here two completely different and unrelated attempts to find an adequate dramatic expression for grief and suffering. This juxtaposition of mime and lament is a typical example of the way in which various dramatic devices are used side by side in pre-Shakespearean drama without being integrated. The dramatists obviously did not know how to make gesture subservient to dramatic speech and to fuse pantomime and dialogue.

There is in this third pantomime no apparent connection with the characters of the play as we have noticed it in the second act. One might perhaps point out a superficial similarity between the group of mourners and the chorus in this tragedy, but of course the function of the chorus is purely rhetorical and didactic whereas there is nothing didactic about this pantomime. Its function, as has been noted, is mainly to create an atmosphere of tragic expectation.[2] This connection is borne out by the events of the following act, in which news arrives of the sons preparing for war and the sinister prophecies begin to come true.

Something similar is to be found in the fourth act where the dumb show is far more colourful and lively, as can be seen from the printed description:

> *The order and signification of the domme shew before the fourth act.*
>
> *First the musick of Howboies began to plaie, during which there came*

---

[1] Cf. the interpretation of this speech by W. Clemen, op. cit., pp. 253 ff.

[2] This in some cases was also the purpose of the *intermedii* (cf. J. W. Cunliffe, op. cit., p. xl). Thus De Sommi recommended the appearance of the Fates or the Furies whenever tragic deaths or horrible crimes were the subject of the following act. On the *intermedii* see also Heinz Kindermann, *Geschichte des europäischen Theaters*, Vol. II: *Die Renaissance* (Salzburg, 1959), pp. 70 ff.

from vnder the stage, as though out of hell three furies. Alecto, Megera, and Ctesiphone, clad in black garmentes sprinkled with bloud and flames, their bodies girt with snakes, their heds spred with serpentes in stead of heare, the one bearing in her hand a Snake, the other a Whip, and the third a burning Firebrand: ech driuing before them a king and a queene, which moued by furies vnnaturally had slaine their owne children. The names of the kings and queenes were these. Tantalus, Medea, Athamas, Ino, Cambises, Althea, after that the furies and these had passed about the stage thrise, they departed and than the musicke ceased: hereby was signified the vnnaturall murders to follow, that is to say. Porrex slaine by his owne mother. And of king Gorboduc and queene Viden, killed by their owne subiectes.

The entrance of the figures '*from vnder the stage, as though out of hell*' is peculiar to this scene and is to be found nowhere else in the play. The use of mythological characters, too, is unique because up to now there were only personifications of a more general kind ('*a King*', '*a graue and aged gentleman*', etc.). The appearance of the Furies, however, makes the division between the sphere of the pantomimes and that of the play even more marked, and the impression is deepened that we are watching a performance on two entirely different levels. The use of classical mythology is strongly reminiscent of the Italian *intermedii*, but also of many of the native pageants which often introduced similar allegorical and mythological processions.[1] After *Gorboduc* the Furies became a favourite tradition with English playwrights whenever tragic events involving crime and punishment were staged.[2]

The description of the Furies again emphasizes the visual aspects of this dumb show. The love of the sensational, which was perhaps the most powerful stimulus behind popular Elizabethan drama, is very much apparent here and makes the contrast with the following act even more glaring. The appearance of the Furies alone, as for instance in *Tancred and Gismund*, would give the pantomime a striking atmosphere, but the dramatists went even one step further by including characters from the Greek myths, driven round the stage by the Furies. One can probably take it for granted that the audience was quite clearly

[1] See Chapter 1.
[2] Cf. Hughes' *The Misfortunes of Arthur* (I) and Wilmot's *Tancred and Gismund* (IV, 1).

informed – either by written notices, typical costumes or recognizable emblematic designs – as to the identity of the figures whose names the reader finds in the printed edition. We can also be sure that their symbolic significance and their relation to the action of the play did not escape the audience. For the spectator familiar with classical mythology this pantomime must have been an even more explicit indication of what was to follow than the previous ones because here the events in the tragedy are quite closely paralleled and some specific incidents anticipated. The parallel is not suggested by pantomimic presentation but by drawing the spectator's attention to some similar classical examples; the general effect, however, is not very different. This technique is akin to the numerous classical allusions in the dramatic laments and other set speeches of pre-Shakespearean drama, which also serve to add weight and general significance to the particular situation.[1]

Here again there is no pantomimic scene, but a procession three times round the stage; the dumb show depends for its effect on the unusual garb and manner rather than on dramatic movement. The didactic element is less obtrusive than in the first two dumb shows; in its function the pantomime resembles the third one: it creates a suitable atmosphere for what follows. At the same time the spectator is most forcefully made to realise the unnatural hideousness of the crimes described in the following scenes by being confronted with famous murderers from classical myth, like Medea and Tantalus. A similar effect is sometimes achieved by such references in dramatic speech.

The last dumb show relies on noisy spectacle even more than do the earlier ones. The introductory music with its drums and flutes, if conclusions can be drawn from the scanty stage direction, strikes a more lively note, and is obviously intended to suggest a military band:

> *The order and signification of the domme shew before the fifth act.*
>
> *First the drommes & fluites, began to sound, during which there came forth vpon the stage a company of Hargabusiers and of Armed men all in order of battaile. These after their peeces discharged, and that the armed men had three times marched about the stage, departed, and then*

[1] On the use of 'mythological parallels' in dramatic lament see W. Clemen, op. cit., pp. 230–2. See also Gorboduc's lament in III, 1.

the drommes and fluits did cease. Hereby was signified tumults, rebellions, armes and ciuill warres to follow, as fell in the realme of great Brittayne, which by the space of fiftie yeares & more continued in ciuill warre betwene the nobilitie after the death of king Gorboduc, and of his issues, for want of certayne limitacion in succession of the crowne, till the time of Dunwallo Molmutius, who reduced the land to monarchie.

It is a short piece of realistically portrayed action, involving probably more actors than any of the other dumb shows, and in its total effect rather like some scenes in popular plays. There could be no greater contrast to the purely rhetorical effects of the play itself. Mythology plays no part here and the scene is dramatically on quite a different level from the third dumb show to which it bears some superficial resemblance. The one is a symbolic expression of the sorrow that is to come over the land, a very abstract and general kind of foreboding. This one, however, is to a certain extent a concrete anticipation of the plot, a realistic presentation of some event which could not be staged within the tragedy itself because of its formal character, but could only be reported by messengers.

Here we touch on a problem which is of the greatest importance for the further development of Elizabethan drama, that is, the relationship between dramatic speech, and action presented on the stage. While the producers of popular comedies, chronicles, and biblical plays did not scruple to perform any kind of action on the stage, *Gorboduc* follows the example of Seneca and Renaissance tragedy on the Continent in that all action is excluded from the stage and only described in the course of speeches and messenger-reports. The dumb shows can be explained as an attempt to bring some life and movement on to the stage at least between the acts of the play, and to give a visual representation of some important events, if only in a symbolical and abstract form. The second act was an example of how this procedure could lead to the same incident being shown more than once, first as a mime and then by means of static and rhetorical declamation. In the fifth act, however, the connection between dumb show and play is even closer. The dumb show does not just prepare for a certain scene, but in it events are enacted which could obviously not be included in a play of this kind, but are nevertheless part of the plot.

The original intention of the playwrights was, I believe, to give only some general foreshadowing of the wars described in the following act. For the spectator, however, the scene is almost a part of the play, especially as he is told at the beginning of the next act that civil war has broken out. He feels that he has already seen some war-like action in the pantomime. In later plays, as we shall see, dumb shows are often employed to fill in some gaps in the plot and to cut long scenes short by omitting dialogue.[1] This use of the dumb show is at least vaguely suggested here, although the main function of the pantomime is still of a more general kind.[2] The didactic element, so conspicuous in the first two dumb shows, is lacking and the pantomime refers only to the actual plot, not so much to its symbolic and moral significance. This of course brings the dumb show much closer to the play itself and made it easier for later dramatists to incorporate such scenes into their plays.

To sum up, all five dumb shows in *Gorboduc* have in common that they are strictly separated from the play, although, as I have tried to point out, the play's total appeal is strongly influenced and heightened by them. This clear division is of course underlined by the formal five-act structure of the play. The audience is, so to speak, addressed from two different levels. The visual and dramatic spectacle elucidates the sententious speeches and makes it easier for the spectator to grasp the meaning of the tragedy. Thus the dumb shows are anything but an entertainment to fill in the pauses between the acts and to amuse the audience as most of the *intermedii* were; they are a very important part of the performance.

The various forms and functions of the dumb shows in *Gorboduc* suggest that several influences were at work, although it would be hard and perhaps not very rewarding to trace them exactly.[3] The second dumb show, for instance, seems to owe a great deal to the moralities, while the fourth appears to be particularly close to some pageants, at the same time including elements from Senecan tragedy.

---

[1] See, for instance, *Captain Thomas Stukeley* (1596). This is but one of many examples.

[2] See the explanation in the printed text: '*Hereby was signified tumults, rebellions, armes and ciuill warres to follow,*'

[3] Cf. Chapter 1.

At any rate, this first example of the use of dumb shows in England seems to prove that the Elizabethan playwrights were not content to divert the audience with spectacular pageants, but tried to link these pageants with their play in a fairly clear and effective manner. The pantomimes also make it appear quite certain that *Gorboduc*, for all its literary qualities and somewhat lifeless dialogue, was intended not so much for the study as for the stage.[1]

GEORGE GASCOIGNE AND FRANCIS KINWELMERSH: 'JOCASTA'

Jocasta is after *Gorboduc* the second English play containing dumb shows.[2] It is a translation of *Giocasta* by Lodovico Dolce, and is consequently of particular interest for the history of the dumb show because here the pantomimes were added to a play already in existence.

At first sight the tragedy has much in common with *Gorboduc*: the five-act structure, the strong emphasis on rhetorical speech, and the static nature of the scenes. At the same time it reveals a much higher degree of technical skill. Although no vivid action is presented on the stage, there are occasional dramatic outbursts and passionate verbal exchanges which have no parallel in *Gorboduc*. It is also noticeable that the dialogue is accompanied by more detailed stage directions giving precise information about entrances and exits, the number and type of accompanying persons, as well as the stage set (see, for instance, the placing of the gates of Thebes). The dialogue does not consist merely of instructive speeches, but is more directly related to what is happening on the stage than in *Gorboduc*.[3] This fact alone would facilitate a closer connection between the dumb shows and the drama.

Cunliffe believes, I think rightly, that it was the example of *Gorboduc* which led to the introduction of dumb shows in this

[1] This is also suggested by the fact that *Gorboduc* did not appear in print until nine years after its first performance. The reference on the title page '*set forth without addition or alteration but altogether as the same was shewed on stage before the Queenes Maiestie, about nine yeares past*' also points in this direction.

[2] Ed. J. W. Cunliffe in *Early English Classical Tragedies*.

[3] Cf. the sudden appearance of Eteocles in II, 1, and the following dialogue. See also the skilful use of stichomythia in II, 2, and III, 1.

play.[1] This influence is not surprising as both plays originated at the Inns of Court and *Gorboduc* seems to have enjoyed a certain popularity there. For this reason it is well worth enquiring which were the characteristics that most impressed the imitators and what contribution was made by *Jocasta* to the further development of the dumb shows.

The first dumb show at once reveals that it was the magnificent and sensational more than anything else which invited emulation. This justifies the conclusion that the audience must have strongly felt the lack of movement and splendour in the strictly classical tragedies and demanded something to compensate for it. A glance at the contemporary pageants and some other types of drama, such as the miracle plays and interludes, makes this demand easy enough to understand. The beginning of *Jocasta* seems therefore almost like an attempt to incorporate something of the style of the interludes into the classical rhetoric drama, as can be seen from the description of the opening pantomime:

> *The order of the dumme shewes and Musickes before euery Acte. Firste, before the beginning of the first Acte, did sounde a dolefull & straunge noyse of violles, Cythren, Bandurion, and such like, during the whiche, there came in vppon the Stage a king with an Imperial crown vppon his head, very richely apparelled: a Scepter in his righte hande, a Mounde with a Crosse in his lefte hande, sitting in a Chariote very richely furnished, drawne in by foure Kinges in their Dublettes and Hosen, with Crownes also vpon their heades. Representing vnto vs Ambition, by the hystorie of Sesostres king of Egypt, who beeing in his time and reigne a mightie Conquerour, yet not content to haue subdued many princes, and taken from them their kingdomes and dominions, did in like maner cause those Kinges whom he had so ouercome, to draw in his Chariote like Beastes and Oxen, thereby to content his vnbrideled ambitious desire. After he had beene drawne twyce about the Stage, and retyred, the Musicke ceased, and Iocasta the Queene issued out of hir house, beginning the firste Acte as followeth. Iocasta the Queene issueth out of hir Pallace, before hir twelue Gentlemen, following after hir eight Gentlewomen, whereof foure be the Chorus that remayne on the Stage after hir departure. At hir entrance the Trumpettes sounded, and after she had gone once about the Stage, she turneth to one of hir most trustie and esteemed seruaunts, and vnto him she discloseth hir griefe, as foloweth.*

[1] Op. cit., p. lxxxv.

The scene certainly appears to have outshone *Gorboduc* in sheer magnificence, lavishness and splendour. A king in his rich chariot, drawn by four conquered princes – that was a spectacle which up to then had only been possible in some costly pageant. Marlowe was the first to include similar scenes in his plays.[1] Here, however, it is still an independent 'show' before the beginning of the actual play. The pantomime has no plot of its own, but is a kind of *tableau*, comparable to the Italian *trionfi*. An example from history is used to give a vivid representation of the vice Ambition. As in *Gorboduc* the theme of the play is indicated, but no details of plot are revealed to the audience. Again the dumb show does not just refer to the first act, but introduces the whole play, like an overture. The king in his chariot of triumph is not merely an historical figure, but embodies Ambition itself and may thus more or less be regarded as a personification. He cannot be identified with any particular character of the play, but rather he represents the vice that is the driving force behind several of its characters and incidents.[2] The dumb show is only related to Jocasta herself in so far as it is she who is directly affected by the ambition of her sons, which causes them to destroy each other.

Here also the emphasis is on the moral content of the play, not on its dramatic plot. The pantomime is a kind of visual warning prefacing the whole tragedy. It does not contribute to the exposition, nor does it hint at the events of the following act. In this respect it is hardly different from the *intermedii* and dramatically less effective than the dumb shows in *Gorboduc*.

The dumb show before the second act, however, is quite different:

The order of the second dumbe shewe.
Before the beginning of this seconde Acte dyd sound a very dolefull noise of flutes: during the which there came in vpon the stage two coffines couered with hearclothes, & brought in by viij. in mourning weed: & accompanied with viij. other mourners: & after they had caried the coffins about the stage, there opened & appeared a Graue, wherin they buried ye coffins & put fire to them: but the flames did seuer & parte in twaine, signifying discord by the history of two brethren, whose discord in their life was not onely to be wondred at, but being buried both in one Tombe (as some writers affirme) the

---

[1] Cf. the triumphal processions of Tamburlaine.
[2] Cf. the speeches of the servant and the chorus in the first act.

flames of their funeralls did yet parte the one from the other in like
maner, and would in no wise ioyne into one flame. After the Funerals
were ended & the fire consumed, the graue was closed vp again, the
mourners withdrew them off the stage, & immediately by ye gates
Homoloydes entred Pollinyces accompanied with vj. gentlemen and a
page that carried his helmet and Target: . . .

The idea of the funeral procession is probably taken over from
Gorboduc (III), but is connected far more skilfully with the plot
of the play. The scene – two coffins burning in an open grave –
is certainly a strikingly unusual sight. In the well-known tale
of the two flames that refused to unite, the disunity of the
brothers is more effectively expressed than in an abstract fable
like *Gorboduc* (I). Although the scene may not necessarily refer
to the characters in the tragedy, the parallel is obvious and
significant. In both cases the theme is the enmity of the two
brothers and their mutual hatred which survived even death.
The spectator is not only reminded of the disastrous results of
dissension in a most impressive way, but the denouement
(which unites both brothers in death) is also clearly revealed to
him. The didactic element has here retired into the background.
The playwrights have endeavoured to achieve a greater
dramatic effect, although it is again by means of a *tableau* rather
than by an actual scene. Outward spectacle is still more important
than real action even though the pantomime is more than just a
procession round the stage. The preparations for the funeral and
the cremation itself give rise to a certain stir and the whole
scene probably took longer in performance than the first dumb
show in the play.

Although this scene stands out in relief against the rest of
the play, the writers' attempt to blend the two spheres and to
increase the dramatic effect of the tragedy by adding these pantomimes is apparent. The use of the dumb show as a kind of
forecast becomes particularly clear when Polinices enters and
speaks of his enmity with Eteocles, at the same time expressing
the hope that it will be possible to bring about a reconciliation
with him. The audience, however, knows from the dumb show
as well as from the myth that all attempts to mediate will
eventually fail. The dumb show thus emphasizes the tragic irony
of the scene by partly revealing its eventual outcome. In the
violent dialogue which immediately follows, the implacability of

their hatred comes to the fore, and the events of the play follow more or less the path indicated by the dumb show, although there is no marked correspondence of plot. The dumb show, then, goes a step further than those in *Gorboduc*, because it is employed to augment the total dramatic effect of the play and give a clear hint of coming events.

This purpose is fulfilled in an even more convincing manner before the third act. Unlike the preceding pantomimes this one has a highly dramatic plot. For the first time not all characters enter together; there seems to be some coming and going during the scene. The desperate attempts of the men and women to fill in the cleft in the earth bring more movement into the action, which culminates in the appearance of Curtius and his sacrificial death. As in *Gorboduc* a kind of play within a play is performed. This use of the Curtius-myth may have been suggested by Italian examples;[1] yet mythological figures as illustrations and models of certain moral qualities were frequent in the English pageants as well.

As in the earlier acts, the chief function of the dumb show is to forecast the development of the plot. The hero Curtius, an embodiment of patriotism ready to die for its ideal, corresponds of course to Meneceus, who is required to make the same sacrifice. The mythological reference gives the events more import than they would otherwise have and emphasizes the timelessness of the situation. The spectator is made aware that it is not here a question of the fate of one person, but of an ever-present tragic conflict. At first, however, there is something like tragic irony in the events of the following act, because they deviate from those of the pantomime. Instead of sacrificing his life for his country without hesitation, Meneceus appears to allow himself to be persuaded by his father to flee, but the audience knows more than the characters concerned, because against the background of the Curtius-myth the preparations for escape seem merely a vain attempt of man to rebel against his destiny.[2] The

[1] This is suggested by J. W. Cunliffe, op. cit., p. xl. The text of this and the following two dumb shows is quoted in Appendix II at the end of the book.

[2] Cf. the commentary of the chorus at the end of Act III:
But euery man is loth for to fulfill
The heauenly hest that pleaseth not his will. (50–51)

sacrifice of Meneceus' life is not reported until the fourth act, so that this pantomime stages an event, if only indirectly, which in the play itself is merely narrated. We shall often meet with this use of the dumb show in later drama.[1] The events of the following act are not only foreshadowed here, but they are also presented in such a way that an indirect comment is implied, which marks a definite advance in dramatic technique and the skilful employment of pantomime.

The fourth dumb show is even more full of tension and movement. The gun salute announcing the entrance of twenty men at arms is impressive enough, but the dramatic quality of the whole scene is even more striking. For the first time in the history of English tragedy a bitter struggle is represented on the stage. We have here a quite unprecedented attempt to include thrilling events in the performance of a serious play which before had only been possible in popular drama.

After a general skirmish three single combats are shown, so that the whole scene probably took considerably longer than the other dumb shows. Uncertainty as to the outcome of each fight adds to the tension and prevents the pantomime from appearing merely as a demonstration of some abstract moral. Although the didactic intention is obvious it does not here detract from the dramatic effect of the scene.

Its connection with the following act is also clear. Not only is the spectator prepared for the single combat between the brothers which is agreed on in the fourth act, but the result of it is revealed as well, if only in a general manner and not in the form of a direct parallel as in the third act. The audience is meant to see what follows in a new light after having watched and understood the dumb show. This becomes quite clear when Creon, even while the two brothers are arming themselves for the fight, announces his intention of seizing power in Thebes, thus taking advantage of their disunity. The two brothers are confronted by an enemy whom they could only overcome by ending their strife. The dumb show before the fourth act, however, indicates that this will not happen, thus supporting the admonition of the chorus, which concludes the act with a hymn to 'Blisful concord'. Here again one can see clearly, in comparison with

[1] See below, *The Misfortunes of Arthur* and *Tancred and Gismund*. Most of the later dumb shows have a similar function.

Gorboduc, how the didactic element is pushed into the background in order to enliven the pantomime and with it the whole performance. This also made it easier for the dumb shows to be merged with the actual play later on.

The last dumb show, however, is rather more similar in type to the first one, in that it does not stage a lively scene but illustrates a general moral idea. It is an allegorical *tableau* which achieves its effect more by magnificent display and choice costuming than by any particular action. The brief scene contains no dramatic plot as do the previous dumb shows, but only a symbolic gesture which strongly reminds one of the street pageants and civic entertainments. The didactic element predominates this time and the dumb show is less skilfully linked to the following act than are the preceding ones; in fact, it could just as well be tacked on to any other tragedy of this kind. It does not contribute much to our understanding of the final act, but merely underlines the warning (familiar to every reader of medieval or renaissance literature) spoken by the chorus, not to put one's trust in the constancy of Fortune. Fortunately it was not this kind of dumb show which achieved popularity in the next decades.

The treatment of the dumb show in *Jocasta* has, as we have seen, much in common with that in *Gorboduc*. For instance in both plays background music is employed to create the right atmosphere.[1] The two components of drama, speech and action, are still kept strictly separate. The dramatic quality of the dumb shows has as yet no influence on the play itself and the characters of the play are not in any way affected by the pantomimes, because these are only addressed to the audience and provide a commentary on the play. The characters appearing in them, too, are fundamentally different from those of the tragedy. They are allegorical or mythological figures who have nothing to do with the world of the play.

On the other hand, in comparison with *Gorboduc* some definite development can be pointed out. Not only does *Jocasta* surpass *Gorboduc* in magnificence and splendour, in the number of actors, properties and stage-technique, but at the same time an attempt is made to increase the dramatic tension of the individual scenes

---

[1] Cf. '*a very dolefull noise of flutes*' before the funeral (Act II) and '*the Trumpets, drummes and fifes sounded*' before the fight (Act IV).

presented in the dumb shows. Thus before the third and fourth acts there are small plays within the play, and the stage has for the first time become a show-place for real movement and conflict. Above all, the playwrights have tried to strengthen the connection between the dumb shows and the tragedy itself. This is the more remarkable as the play had been on the stage in Italy before, and the dumb shows were only added afterwards by the translators. An outward sign of the writers' efforts in this direction is that the scenes of the play, as the stage directions indicate, followed the pantomimes immediately so that there was no break between the dumb shows and the beginning of the dialogue. Similarly the subject-matter of the dumb shows is more directly related to the events in the play without exactly paralleling them. Often there is a clear correspondence between the characters in the dumb shows and those in the play. The third dumb show is an excellent example of this, but also in the other pantomimes the intention to make these interludes more than just independent extras can be clearly seen. They are all meant to point to the tragedy itself and throw light upon its meaning, although they are not actually an integral part of it and the play would be quite complete without them. Soon after *Jocasta* we find plays in which lively events and dramatic movement form a necessary part of the action. Within the tradition of classical tragedy, however, these pantomimes were for the time being the only concession to that general trend.

THOMAS HUGHES: 'THE MISFORTUNES OF ARTHUR'

It is a remarkable fact that – if we exclude the Latin university drama – no play seems to have been written between 1567 and 1587 which continued the tradition of classical tragedy in England. The influence of that school on contemporary drama must therefore have been much less important than is often assumed. Similarly, the peculiar form of the dumb show as found in *Gorboduc* and *Jocasta* was not at first imitated, although some of its elements found their way into the plays of Kyd and the 'University Wits'.

In Thomas Hughes' tragedy *The Misfortunes of Arthur* the tradition of classical drama in the style of Seneca is, however, once more revived,[1] and with it the idea of introducing each act by a formal pantomime. The dumb shows in this tragedy are even more lively and original than those in the two earlier plays, with which on the whole they have much in common. It will be seen, however, that they are much more closely linked to the actual drama. There is, to be sure, still that clear-cut division between dialogue and action, but there are in several places intermediate stages which suggest the later forms of the dumb show.

In the first dumb show we do not find much of this development. It is a formal procession like *Gorboduc* (III) and *Jocasta* (I), and the characters appearing in it, too, are on the whole conventional:

The Argument and manner of the first dumbe shewe.
Sounding the musicke, there rose three furies from vnder the stage apparelled accordingly with snakes and flames about their blacke haires and garments. The first with a Snake in the right hande and a cup of wine with a Snake athwart the cup in the left hand. The second with a firebrand in the right hande, and a Cupid in the left: The thirde with a whippe in the right hande and a Pægasus in the left. Whiles they went masking about the stage, there came from another place three Nuns which walked by them selues. Then after a full sight giuen to the beholders, they all parted, the furies to Mordreds house, the Nuns to the Cloister. By the first furie with the Snake and Cup was signified the Banquet of Vther Pendragon, and afterward his death which insued by poysoned cup. The second furie with her firebrande & Cupid represented Vthers vnlawfull heate and loue conceyued at the banquet, which neuer ceased in his posteritie. By the third with her whip and Pægasus was prefigured the crueltie and ambition which thence insued and continued to th'effecting of this tragidie. By the Nuns was signified the remorse and dispaire of Gueneuora, that wanting other hope tooke a Nunrie for her refuge. After their departure, the fowre which represented the Chorus tooke their places.

It is easy to see that this dumb show differs from those described so far in one or two important points. Of course there had been Furies in Italian tragedy as well as in *Gorboduc*. More

[1] Ed. J. W. Cunliffe in *Early English Classical Tragedies*. The play is part of the *Certaine Deuises and shewes presented to her Maiestie by the Gentlemen of Grayes-Inne at her Highnesse Court in Greenewich* (London, 1587). The dumb shows were contributed by several authors whose names are given at the end of the play, one of them being Francis Bacon.

interesting, however, is the simultaneous use of mythological figures and distinctly Christian elements like the group of nuns, which is likely to arouse the interest of the spectators by its novelty and at the same time makes a more specific contribution to the play. The explanation of the scene in the printed text introduces a new element in that it explicitly refers to events which are supposed to have taken place before the beginning of the actual tragedy. The audience is given some idea of what the play is about and what has gone before. This is particularly important in the case of the Arthur-legend because some knowledge of the earlier part of the story is essential to an understanding of the play. More than half the 'argument' provided for the readers of the printed version is concerned with events not presented in the play, but which lead up to the final catastrophe. Only this last phase, the tragic result of Pendragon's guilt, is the subject of the tragedy. The earlier part of the story had therefore to be reported in some form and the dumb shows were a convenient means to that end.

Of course this first dumb show only alludes to events which must have been familiar to most of the audience anyway and the symbolic hints were probably understood by nearly all the spectators who came to see such an academic play. For the others the ghost of Gorlois, appearing at the beginning of the first act, provided a more straightforward explanation. Here we have an early form of the presenter, who in later plays was often employed to interpret complicated dumb shows for the audience and make clear their relationship to the plot.[1] This innovation of course helps to make the transition from mime to dialogue much easier and to link the two planes of action. Though the dumb show here does not actually replace the exposition of the play as in some later examples, it makes a significant contribution to it and helps the spectator to understand the plot by conveying its antecedents and deeper causes.

The pantomime is thus very much more than an allegorical representation of the play's moral. The characters appearing in it also seem to correspond closely to those in the play. This is particularly true of the nuns, who are supposed to suggest the queen's retreat from the world. They are not just abstract personifications, but appear to be on the same dramatic level as the

[1] On the origin of this figure see Chapter 1.

queen herself. Nevertheless, the pantomime remains separated from the play and is not really indispensable; indeed this can be said of all five dumb shows in *The Misfortunes of Arthur*. The tragedy would be perfectly intelligible without them. In this respect they do not differ materially from those in *Gorboduc* or *Jocasta*.

The second dumb show again proves that its author was anxious to make its relationship to the following act as clear as possible.[1] This is made easier by the fact that a certain part of the stage, presumably a door like the gates of Thebes in *Jocasta*, was marked as '*Mordred's House*'. The king entering the stage from that side was thus for the audience clearly associated with Mordred although he is, as the text of the dumb show indicates,[2] not to be identified with him. Probably both characters were played by the same actor and the costumes served to underline the similarity. It was only a very little step from this kind of dumb show to the later type in which characters from the play appeared.

However, while the king is plainly an indirect representation of Mordred, the other characters of the dumb show are more like the older kind and are purely allegorical. The gifts offered by the nymphs are a symbolic expression of Arthur's desire to arrive at a peaceful settlement, while Revenge and Fury are traditional personifications. The king, though contemptuously refusing any kind of reconciliation, already appears as one haunted rather than triumphant, which strongly suggests his later downfall. Thus the pantomime presents a close parallel to the events in the play, if only in a slightly veiled and symbolic form. While the dumb shows in *Gorboduc* were chiefly concerned with the moral underlying the play, they here refer only to the action.

It is also worth noting that in this tragedy lively movement is no longer strictly confined to the pantomimes; there are effective scenes within the play itself, at least when compared with the two earlier classical tragedies.[3] The dumb shows are no longer justified as a relief from the static monotony of the

[1] The text of this dumb show is given in Appendix II, where the fourth and fifth dumb shows are also quoted.
[2] *The King represented Mordred.*
[3] Cf. W. Clemen, op. cit., pp. 85 ff.

dialogue, and the dramatists therefore tried to put them to other purposes as well. All dumb shows in this play go a step further than the earlier ones in that they contain figures which in an obvious manner stand for certain characters from the play. They can thus foreshadow the events of the following act much more directly, as can best be seen in the third pantomime, where Arthur and Cador appear and receive the message of defiance from Mordred. The scene is closely linked with the preceding act, in which we have watched Mordred and his followers gaining in strength and confidence. Now the spectators' attention is by means of the dumb show directed to the opposite camp:

> *The Argument and manner of the third dumbe shewe.*
> *Dvring the Musicke after the second Act. There came vppon the stage two gentlemen attyred in peaceable manner, which brought with them a Table, Carpet, and Cloth: and then hauing couered the Table they furnisht it with incense on the one ende, and banqueting dishes on the other ende: Next there came two gentlemen apparelled like Souldiers with two naked Swordes in their handes, the which they laide a crosse vpon the Table. Then there came two sumptuously attyred and warre-like, who, spying this preparation smelled the incense and tasted the banquet. During the which there came a Messenger and deliuered certaine letters to those two that fedde on the daineties: who, after they had well viewed and perused the letters, furiously flung the banquet vnder feete: and violently snatching the Swordes vnto them, they hastily went their way. By the first two that brought in the banquet was meant the seruaunts of Peace, by the second two were meant the seruaunts of Warre: By the two last were meant Arthur and Cador. By the Messenger and his Letters was meant the defiance from Mordred.*

Here, it is clear, we have on the one hand allegorical figures like the 'seruaunts of Peace' and a more symbolical treatment of the play's action; on the other hand, there are two characters representing Arthur and Cador, and the delivery of the letters to them as well as their anger about their contents are just what one would expect to see in the play itself. The dumb show can therefore be called only partly allegorical and not in any way didactic. An event which is supposed to take place between the acts of the tragedy is summarized by a pantomime and makes it much easier for the audience to grasp the situation in the following act.

The last two dumb shows perform a similar function. The brief scene introducing the fourth act (which is to show the misery of civil war) is not just a general *tableau* to create the appropriate atmosphere, but also gives a very dramatic picture of Mordred's end and the loss of his usurped crown. Here again we have that rather primitive technique of first showing events in mime and then reporting them by a *Nuntius*, which is done in quite a lively manner (IV, 2) although there is no actual movement on the stage.

The fifth dumb show is a curious mixture of more traditional and quite original ideas. Its function is to give a symbolic description of Arthur's victory, paid for so dearly. There are plenty of emblems, Latin mottoes and coats of arms, which suggests that the majority of the spectators must have been fairly well educated and quick to understand the heraldic and emblematic references, or else this sophisticated method of foreshadowing events would have been lost on them. The whole scene is very much like some of the older masques and pageants described in the first chapter.[1] At the same time it is so closely connected with the plot of the tragedy that it could not be lifted out of its context or added to any other play.

The dumb shows in *The Misfortunes of Arthur* thus mark a significant development in the history of this device. They are an attempt to add weight and dramatic force to the action and underline its most important episodes. For the first time they introduce characters from the play, although in superficial allegorical disguise. Still, there is a noticeable barrier between the two spheres of action; the pantomimes are outside the acts of the play and are intended only for the audience. None of the dumb shows is a really indispensable part of the play. Though the tragedy is much less static and rhetorical than *Gorboduc*, it must still have been rather weak and unexciting on the stage. In some measure, at least, it was still the purpose of the dumb shows to counterbalance the undramatic dullness of the spoken scenes and to provide some lively spectacle on the stage. They were the first, and for a long time only, attempt to bridge the wide gap between the academic tragedies and the more popular types of drama which were emerging at the same time.

[1] See for instance the *Plot for Masks at Nottingham* (1562) in *Collections*, II (*Malone Soc.*, 1908).

The Elizabethan Dumb Show

A later and particularly interesting example of the continued use of dumb shows in classical tragedy is Wilmot's new adaptation of *Gismond of Salerne*, which had first appeared some twenty-three years earlier. It has several times been noted that Wilmot tried above all to heighten the dramatic effect of the earlier version by livening up the dialogue and by bringing some more real movement on to the stage.[1] These alterations throw some light on the changes of literary taste in the last quarter of the sixteenth century. What is particularly interesting for the purpose of our enquiry, however, is that a kind of appendix with an *introductio* for each act (except the first) is added to the play. These 'introductions' are in fact brief dumb shows, though of a new kind. The original play contained, so far as we can see from the manuscripts (there is no print earlier than Wilmot's edition of 1591), no such pantomimes, although it is still an open question whether or not they had perhaps been performed without being included in the written text.[2] It seems more likely, however, that these pantomimes were added by Wilmot, because dumb shows had by then acquired some popularity and he may have felt the need to relieve the monotony of the classical play more acutely than the authors of the first play did twenty-three years before. The introductions are obviously attempts to make the play accord with the dramatic habits of the time and thus to increase its popularity.

The form of these dumb shows, too, seems to me to suggest a later date. While the appearance of Cupido *'out of the heauens in a cradle of flowers'* is still in the traditional manner, the

---

[1] *Gismond of Salerne*, ed. J. W. Cunliffe in *Early English Classical Tragedies; Tancred and Gismund*, ed. W. W. Greg (*Malone Soc.*, 1914).

On the relationship between the two plays see David Klein, 'According to the decorum of these daies', *PMLA*, XXXIII (1918), pp. 244–68; John Murray, '*Tancred and Gismund*', *RES*, XIV (1938), pp. 385–95; W. Clemen, op. cit., pp. 84–5.

[2] Cunliffe thought that the 'introductions' were already part of the older play (op. cit., p. lxxxvi). L. G. Gibbs arrives at the same conclusion (op. cit., pp. 84 ff.). For the opposite opinion see D. Klein, op. cit., pp. 257 ff. Thus before the fourth act the pantomime is followed by a dance of the Furies before Megaera addresses the audience. This double introduction seems to me to suggest a later redaction, but the text allows no conclusive proof.

appended introductions are quite different from any of the dumb shows discussed so far. For the first time characters from the play itself appear in the pantomimes, not only in an allegorical context, as in *The Misfortunes of Arthur*, but without any symbolic connotation. This means that the dumb shows are only distinguished from the drama proper by the absence of dialogue.

The introduction to the second act, for instance, is not much more than a lengthy and elaborate stage direction:

> *Introductio in Actum secundum.*
> *Before the second Act there was heard a sweete noice of stil pipes, which sounding, Lucrece entred, attended by a mayden of honor with a couered goddard of gold, and drawing the curtens, shee offreth vnto Gismunda to tast thereof: which when shee had done, the maid returned, and Lucrece rayseth vp Gismund from her bed, and then it followeth vt in Act. 2. Scen. 1.*

It was obviously the writer's intention to set the scene for the conversation which follows. A short typical gesture is meant to suggest the part played by the aunt. Thus a brief episode is shown which could have been represented just as well in a scene with dialogue, but which in this way took up less time in performance and remained more in the background. It is neither a procession round the stage nor a brief episode as in earlier plays, but a normal scene involving three characters from the play, one of whom withdraws after a few moments before the dialogue begins. Even in *The Misfortunes of Arthur* all figures leave the stage at the end of the dumb shows and a completely new scene starts. Here, however, two characters from the dumb show remain on stage and the act follows without a break. The silent scene does not contribute to the plot of the play, it only introduces Lucrece and prepares the way for the following dialogue. The reviser apparently wanted to stress the personal, individual characteristics of this tragedy. This can also be seen from seemingly insignificant changes like the extended address:

> Deare Aunt, my sole companion in distresse,
> And true copartner of my thoughtfull cares:[1]

The reviser's intention becomes even more clear in the *introductio* to the third act. In the older version Cupido appears at

[1] The older play only has:
> Dere aunt, when in my secret thought I weye
> my present state, . . .

the beginning of the act, assuming the role of a presenter and revealing his plans for Gismond and Guiskard:

> Now shall they know what mighty Loue can do,
> that proudely practise to deface his name.

In the manner of Senecan tragedy all events take place off stage. Cupido tells how Gismond has come to an arrangement with her lover (16) and in the third scene of this act we see Guiskard already in possession of her letter. Wilmot has, however, endeavoured to make the scene more vivid by presenting it visibly to the audience:

> *Introductio in Actum tertium.*
> *Before this Acte the Hobaies sounded a lofty Almain, and Cupid Vshereth after him, Guizard and Gismund hand in hand. Iulio and Lucrece, Renuchio and another maiden of honor. The measures trod, Gismunda geues a cane into Guiszards hand, and they are all ledde forrth again by Cupid, Et sequitur.*

Only here Cupido is presenter in the more precise meaning of the term because he introduces a *tableau* and, as was often the case in later plays, the characters of the drama are brought on stage by a mythological figure.[1] The brief scene between the lovers is explained by Cupid after their exit.

Here for the first time the dumb show presents an event which is important for the plot of the play. Consequently a closer connection between the pantomime and the rest of the play is established on the one hand, and on the other the formal scheme of classical tragedy is broken in an important respect. *Gismond of Salerne* is in its whole structure a rhetorical play on the lines of Italian Renaissance tragedy. By bringing action, which before had only been reported, on to the stage, the reviser speeds up the tempo of the play and makes it more dramatic. The same motive applies to the fourth act.[2] Scenes in which

---

[1] Thus in the popular *A Warning for Fair Women* 'Tragedy' calls in the Furies who bring in the dumb show:

> Dispatch, I say, and be their Ushers in.

[2] *Introductio in Actum 4.*

Before this Act there was heard a consort of sweet musick, which playing, Tancred commeth forth, & draweth Gismunds curtens, and lies down vpon her bed, then from vnder the stage ascendeth Guisz. & he helpeth vp Gismund, they amorously embrace, & depart. The king ariseth enraged, then was heard & seen a storm of thunder & lightning, in which the furies rise vp, Et sequitur.

something important is overheard by a third character were to become particular highlights in some of Shakespeare's plays. Wilmot evidently realized that the effect of such a scene would be far greater if it was acted out on the stage instead of being merely reported. Although the event is still reported afterwards, as in the original version, of course this narration has now a different function (IV, 2). The spectator knows as soon as Tancred enters the reason for his rage. He hears the incident he has just seen mimed repeated in the words of the angry father himself. The act is much easier to understand and dramatically more effective, because it is no longer alone responsible for informing the audience. Similarly Megaera's sudden entrance and the dance of the furies at the beginning of the act is motivated by the preceding action and is now more than a mere allegorical introduction, because the mythological figures are brought into close connection with the characters of the play.

While in Senecan drama each character had to introduce himself and, in a way, justify his appearance, Wilmot has tried to present the spectator with a more coherent and continuous action in which each scene develops naturally out of the preceding one. By this method, of course, a piece of dramatic narrative can sometimes lose part of its effect and events are occasionally presented twice over because Wilmot just added the pantomimes without making any corresponding cuts or alterations in the text. Thus Renuchio's report in act five loses much of its dramatic tension because it is preceded by a dumb show in which the same event is depicted.[1] This scene is particularly interesting because here again we find two different modes of dramatic expression juxtaposed without being in any way related to each other. The effect is only achieved incrementally, not by such a skilful blending of various elements as we shall find it in the work of some later dramatists. The introduction to the fifth act is also a sign of Wilmot's liking for crude scenic effects which do not necessarily contribute anything to the play

[1] See *Introductio in Actum quintum.*
Before this Act was a dead march plaid, during which entred on the stage Renuchio capten of the Guard, attended vpon by the guard, they tooke vp Guisz. from vnder the stage, then after Guiszard had kindly taken leaue of them all, a strangling cord was fastened about his neck, & he haled foorth by them. Renuchio bewayleth it, & then entring in, bringeth foorth a standing cup of gold, with a bloudy hart reeking whot init, and then saith ut sequitur.

or improve its dramatic quality. The visual representation of hideous cruelty and macabre detail is typical of that Elizabethan sensationalism which has often been described.[1]

In spite of their important dramatic function, however, Wilmot's 'introductions' are still additions in the sense that they appear as afterthoughts and do not form an organic part of the play. The dramatist does not rely on them completely when he wants to convey some particular information to the audience; he still retains, as we have seen, the messenger-speeches which sometimes repeat the content of the dumb shows. The introductions are not incorporated in the dialogue, but stand between the acts like the older kind of dumb show. On the other hand they are, of course, much more closely linked with the play. With the exception of Cupido and the Furies, who serve as a kind of chorus and comment on the action, only characters from the play itself appear in the pantomimes. They are thus neither of the didactic kind like those in *Gorboduc*, nor allegorical and symbolic like those in *The Misfortunes of Arthur*. On the contrary, they stress the more personal tone of the tragedy and show details of its plot which lend themselves less to rhetorical treatment, but come off best in such a visual representation. The pantomimes are thus quite different in kind from any of the earlier ones.

It remains to ask how this complete change was brought about. We must bear in mind that Wilmot does not use the actual term 'dumb show' for his introductions, and therefore it seems likely that he was not so much influenced by the earlier dumb shows as by other dramatic motives and ideas. His introductions have not much in common with the masques and pageants. Rather they seem an attempt to modify the strict form of the classical tragedy by introducing lively action and by providing some pantomimic 'background' for the rhetorical dialogue. In this Wilmot was probably influenced by the plays of the 'University Wits' and popular chronicle plays: in these we find that the liveliest action and the most sadistic detail is presented on the stage without any restraint. The introductions in *Tancred and Gismund* indicate that the tradition of the classical Senecan tragedy was coming to an end in England and that authors in

[1] See Levin L. Schücking, *Shakespeare und der Tragödienstil seiner Zeit* (Bern, 1947), pp. 14 ff.

that genre were beginning to submit to the influence of the more popular plays. A new kind of dumb show begins to evolve which is very unlike any Italian model and can perhaps be best described as an original combination of elements from the older pageant-like dumb shows and highly dramatic stage directions from popular drama. It was this type of dumb show which came to be so widely used in the following years, while the older, more allegorical kind survived only in a few later plays and was soon little more than an archaic curiosity which only very undiscriminating playwrights dared to use seriously.[1]

THOMAS LEGGE: 'RICHARDUS TERTIUS'

Legge's Latin play on the history of Richard III occupies a rather unique place in the history of English drama.[2] I have therefore referred it to the end of this chapter, although mere chronology would put it between *Jocasta* and *The Misfortunes of Arthur*. This play, which in its style and technique clearly belongs to the Senecan tradition, can yet justly claim to be the first English history play,[3] though it is at the same time remarkable how very little it has in common with the later dramatic chronicles in English. Static declamation and rhetorical dialogue take up far more room than dramatic action. The latter is, with a few exceptions, confined to pantomimic scenes inserted in various places. It is evident that Legge felt the strict classical tragedy to be a rather unsatisfactory medium for the staging of

[1] In this connection it is interesting to note that the ¦Latin ¦University drama, too, which usually followed the classical pattern particularly closely, was influenced by the pantomimes. Two of these plays at least contain dumb shows of a similar kind to those in *Tancred and Gismund*. In William Gager's *Meleager* there is a short scene before the second act in which the hunters pass over the stage. In Matthew Gwinne's *Nero* the three Furies and 'Nemesis' act as presenters. The dumb show gives a brief account of some events which took place before the beginning of the actual play. In both plays the characters appearing in the pantomimes are the same as those in the play proper. On Gager's *Meleager* see particularly F. S. Boas, *University Drama in the Tudor Age* (Oxford, 1914), pp. 165 ff.

[2] Ed. Barron Field (London, 1844) for the Shakespeare Society.

[3] Cf. George B. Churchill, *Richard the Third up to Shakespeare, Palaestra*, X (Berlin, 1900), pp. 265 ff.; F. S. Boas, op. cit., pp. 112 ff. and Walter F. Schirmer, 'Uber das Historiendrama in der englischen Renaissance', *Kleine Schriften* (Tübingen, 1950), pp. 112-13.

national history, but was unable to achieve a real fusion of dialogue and action. We have, therefore, especially in the last part, some very curious scenes in which stiff and formal dialogue is accompanied by a lively pantomime, performed simultaneously. The last scene, for example, in which the battle of Bosworth is presented, consists mainly of long speeches, but at the same time the following action takes place on the stage:

> *Heare let divers mutes, run over ye stage from divers places for feare.*
>
> *Let heare allso divers mutes, armed souldiers, run over the stage one after another to ye Earle of Richmond.*
>
> *After the like noise againe, let souldiers run from ye feild, over the stage one after another, flinginge of their harnesse, and att length let some come haltinge and wounded. After this let Henerye, Earle of Richmond come tryumphing, haveinge ye body of K. Richard dead on a horse: Catesby and Ratcliffe and others bound.*

After that a *Nuntius* appears and gives an account of the battle which is a straightforward and not very exciting translation from a chronicle.

What is particularly striking about these stage directions is that they are, unlike the play itself, written in English. They have so little in common with the rest of the tragedy that one is almost led to suppose they were, like the dumb shows in *The Misfortunes of Arthur*, the work of some other author or perhaps added for one particular performance. This observation does not, however, apply to the three elaborate processions at the end of each *Actio* which are, as far as outward splendour and ceremony is concerned, the highlights of the play. They are proper pageants, completely separate from the dialogue, and therefore more akin to the earlier dumb shows, but they are obviously part of the original play and were not inserted afterwards.

These processions and especially the English stage directions are closely related to the plot of the play and do not introduce allegorical figures. They try to suggest vivid events and political upheavals and partly succeed in making the play less static than most other classical tragedies, although the speeches and dialogue are not affected by this. It is also worth noting that the popular 'interludes', like Pickering's *Horestes* or Preston's *Cambises*, contain very similar stage directions. This is evidence that the formal University drama and the more popular types of comedy and chronicle influenced each other in several respects. Some dramatic devices and techniques seem to have been common to all of them. The history of the dumb show illustrates this mutual exchange of ideas and motives very well because we shall find dumb shows in nearly every kind of drama, the very sophisticated as well as the primitive.

In spite of many differences in detail, the dumb shows in all the classical tragedies can be said to have at least one thing in common: they are convincing proof of the fact that the Elizabethans did not find the formal rhetoric tragedy very congenial. Even the very first English plays of that type were 'improved' by the introduction of dumb shows, which in effect break the classical unities. The tragedies are thus made to express more than could normally be included in a play of this kind. This is why such different forms are piled on to each other and quite incompatible dramatic techniques are juxtaposed. The Elizabethan dramatists evidently did not believe in the classical principle of dramatic economy and sparing use of certain techniques. Consequently we find in the majority of Elizabethan plays such exuberance and astonishing diversity of dramatic modes of which the dumb shows are only one example.

The use of dumb shows can also throw some light on the much discussed relationship between audience and play. In the earlier classical tragedies the pantomimes help to remove the play even further from reality than it would be without them. By the symbolic interpretation of the action through the pantomimes before each act the spectator is continually reminded of the unreal character of the performance. The play is, so to speak, interrupted after every act and a direct address to the audience is delivered. Thus the spectator cannot see the play as anything but a rather abstract presentation of moral ideas, and no coherent world of illusion is created. It has been said that in this respect Elizabethan drama is more like the modern theatre of Brecht and his followers than like nineteenth- or early twentieth-century drama.[1] This is only partly true, because hand

[1] On these questions see M. Braun, 'Das Drama vor Shakespeare und seine Beziehungen zum Publikum', *ShJ*, 94 (1958), pp. 191–9, and *Symbolismus und Illusionismus im englischen Drama vor 1620* (Diss., München, 1962); E. Th. Sehrt, op. cit., pp. 199 ff., and particularly Anne Righter, *Shakespeare and the Idea of the Play* (London, 1962).

in hand with this 'anti-illusionary' element, as it may be called, there goes very often a powerful appeal to the spectator's imagination to supply the deficiencies of the stage and to create some higher kind of illusion. Many of the popular plays also try to present a more direct imitation of reality on the stage, though such attempts should not, of course, be confused with any modern conception of naturalism. The dumb shows in *Tancred and Gismund* and *Richardus Tertius* may be seen as an example of this. The lively movement on the stage and the realistic gestures bring the drama closer to reality, although the very idea of a silent scene is contrary to any 'realism' in the modern sense of the word. It is interesting to see that dumb shows could thus be employed either to destroy illusion on the part of the spectators or to encourage it. We shall find that in this particular respect later dramatists made very different use of dumb shows and departed a long way from the classical tragedies and their formal pantomimes.

4

Thomas Kyd

Whereas in the last two plays we considered, *The Misfortunes of Arthur* and *Tancred and Gismund*, the tradition of the classical University play was still predominant in spite of some more 'modern' traits, and the influence of the popular plays was not very marked, in Kyd's *Spanish Tragedy* many diverse influences contribute to the creation of a new kind of drama.[1] The rhetoric of the plays from the Inns of Court is used and modified by Kyd to achieve a more immediate dramatic effect, the dialogue has become a pointed verbal exchange and the plot works up to its climaxes in an unprecedented manner. Above all, the events represented on the stage are far more lively and vivid than in the earlier tragedies.[2] There are still, of course, some static scenes containing only long declamations,[3] but in contrast to them we find others in which the stage becomes an arena for breathtaking events, and the audience's love of spectacle and gruesome detail is well satisfied. The messenger's speech has almost completely disappeared[4] and the lively and unusual episodes in particular are brought on to the stage. The fourth and fifth scenes of the second act are excellent examples; they must have had a very startling effect on contemporaries. The sudden bursting in of the murderers on the lovers, the shocking bloody deed and Hieronimo's discovery of the dead bodies are completely new effects.

[1] This synthesis achieved by Kyd has often been commented on. See especially F. L. Lucas, *Seneca and Elizabethan Tragedy* (Cambridge, 1922), pp. 103 ff.; F. S. Boas, *An Introduction to Tudor Drama* (Oxford, 1933), pp. 94 ff.; P. W. Biesterfeldt, *Die dramatische Technik Thomas Kyds* (Halle, 1936); W. Clemen, op. cit., pp. 100 ff. Cf. also the editions by F. S. Boas (Oxford, 1901) and P. Edwards in the *Revels Plays* series (London, 1959). On the authorship see L. L. Schücking, 'Zur Verfasserschaft der "Spanish Tragedy"', *Bayerische Akademie der Wissenschaften, Phil.-Hist. Klasse, Sitzungsberichte* (1963, 4).

[2] Cf. T. M. Parrott and R. H. Ball, *A Short View of Elizabethan Drama* (New York, 1943), p. 77.

[3] On the new function of these scenes see W. Clemen, op. cit., pp. 100 ff.

[4] The report of the general in I, 2 is an exception to this.

Thus Hieronimo's rhetorical soliloquy has a new impact and purpose because of the dramatic situation in which it is placed.[1] This profound change in dramatic style is also reflected in the stage directions. The eloquent clarity of some of the gestures demanded there reminds one of the pantomimes in which gesture alone had to convey the meaning.[2] Thus Kyd satisfies, as far as possible, the audience's desire for lively action, and his work is the first attempt to combine rhetorical and popular drama, if at first only superficially, and by good craftsmanship rather than real poetic genius.

It might seem that such a play really needed no dumb shows. The pantomimes in the early tragedies were, as we saw, above all effective in that they relieved the static nature of the actual play. Consequently they were always separate and constituted a foreign element in the play. The dumb show can no longer fulfil this function when the dialogue scenes also include lively action and spectacle. The fact that Kyd nevertheless used the dumb shows as a dramatic device shows again his desire to profit from every technique that promised success and to make his play as many-sided and effective as possible. His actual treatment of the dumb show, however, is quite unlike that of previous dramatists and is important for its further development.

The Spanish Tragedy contains two pantomimes which are quite different from each other in type, content and function in the play. The first one comes at an important point in the tragedy; the war between Spain and Portugal is at an end and the reconciliation is being celebrated by a splendid banquet at the Spanish court in the presence of the Portuguese ambassador. All this is in sharp contrast to the events which are to follow in the play, and this contrast is also noted disapprovingly by the ghost of Andrea. The feast thus provides some effective dramatic suspense and the tragic turn of events seems the more fatal and sinister in contrast to that gay and courtly entertainment.

During the banquet Hieronimo, at the suggestion of the king, presents a short mime to amuse the guests at the feast. He him-

---

[1] Cf. W. Clemen, op. cit., pp. 108 ff.

[2] E.g. '*He flings away the dagger and halter*', '*He diggeth with his dagger*' (III, 12), '*He draweth out a bloody napkin*' (III, 13), '*She cuts down the arbour*' (IV, 2), and others. See also the murder of Serberine and the last scene.

self brings in some masked figures and explains their significance when asked by the king, who seems at first somewhat puzzled by their appearance. The subject of this dumb show, three English heroes who at different times defeated the Spanish, is rather like some of the earlier pantomimes: a legendary or historical figure is led across the stage, and no particular plot is evident. The static character of the performance is emphasized by its being repeated three times. It is only a short symbolic gesture, a historical *tableau* without any obvious relevance for the plot of the whole tragedy. The characters in this very conventional pantomime are quite different from those in the play. The only connection is that, by alluding to previous victories over Spain, the dumb show offers some consolation to the Portuguese ambassador for the defeat of his own people, flattering at the same time the Elizabethan audience which undoubtedly liked to be reminded of its national heroes.[1]

Hieronimo himself serves as a chorus to explain the meaning of the show. The explanation follows immediately after the pantomime and is provoked by an enquiry from one of the spectators. This procedure again suggests that the dramatists of the Inns of Court depended on the spectators' grasping the significance of the dumb shows and that therefore some short hint was sufficient to make clear their relevance for the play; an example of this is Act III of *Gorboduc*. Here, however, the audience must have been very much more heterogeneous and must have included many less educated playgoers. Consequently the dramatist had to be more explicit about the meaning of the dumb show and the king's admission, 'I sound not well the misterie', probably expressed the feelings of most of the spectators very accurately. Hieronimo's explanations and the king's comments are skilfully blended into the scene. Thus we have in *The Spanish Tragedy* that repetition which was typical of later dumb shows: the pantomime is immediately followed by explanatory narrative and the same events are presented twice in succession, the pantomime containing a typical gesture, while the narrative stresses the more individual part of the story and gives its general meaning.

In the role of Hieronimo in this scene Kyd has for the first time introduced the figure of the presenter into the drama

[1] Cf. P. W. Biesterfeldt, op. cit., pp. 66–7.

proper.[1] This innovation was of great importance for the further development of the dumb show, because by the introduction of a presenter the pantomime became much more a part of the play itself and a far more direct relationship with the audience was established. At the same time the use of the presenter made it possible to present more complicated incidents in pantomime and to explain them fully afterwards. There was no need for the audience to understand the dumb show immediately; in fact in later plays it often merely served as an illustration of a circumstantial narrative by the presenter or chorus.

Apart from this innovation Kyd's use of the dumb show differs from that of his predecessors in other important respects also. The dumb show is no longer, as in the classical tragedies, a rather inessential extra, but is an organic part of the play and occurs within one of the scenes. It is not, however, the content of the dumb show, but its actual presentation by one of the characters from the play, that is part of the plot. Here, probably for the first time in Elizabethan tragedy, the device of the play within a play is used. Within the main play a second 'play' is performed for the characters taking part. For such performances the dumb show was particularly suitable: the highly stylized plot and the silent and therefore particularly intensive acting made this scene stand out in relief against the actual play, and put it on a plane further removed from the audience in the theatre. Precisely this contrast, which hindered the achievement of an organic unity in the classical tragedies, has in this play become a special artistic device and adds quite a novel effect to it. Events on the stage gain in interest for the spectators because they see the characters in the play also in the role of spectators and for a time enjoy a performance together with them. They watch the pantomime and its audience at the same time. The dumb show, as well as Hieronimo's commentary, is not chiefly directed at the audience in the theatre, but at the Spanish court being entertained by this performance. In this respect Kyd's use of the dumb show differs considerably from the earlier pantomimes which were only directed at the audience proper.

The incident which is staged reminds one strongly of the tradition of the revels and masques. Weddings and visits of

[1] On the origin of this figure see Chapter 1.

foreign envoys were often the occasion for such performances.[1]
While the dramatists at the Inns of Court only took over the
form and content of such entertainments, Kyd included the
whole situation in which they occurred in his play, thus achieving
a vivid theatrical effect as well as a very close relationship
between pantomime and dialogue. This made the part played by
the dumb show in the whole tragedy far more important than it
had been in the classical tragedies. The different parts of the
play are more closely knit than before. For instance, the reconciliation scene, which appears to remove all tensions between the
various characters, stands in sharp contrast to the great festive
banquet at the end of the play where peace is about to be crowned
with a marriage and the catastrophe breaks upon the revelling
court. The contrast between the two festive scenes is emphasized
because on both occasions it is Hieronimo who is asked to
entertain the court with a dramatic interlude. In the first of the
two scenes, Hieronimo is introduced as a kind of official Master
of the Revels, and it seems therefore only natural that he should
fulfil the same office at the great marriage celebrations in the
last act. The idea of carrying out his revenge in such an unusual
way is therefore to some extent made plausible.[2] The harmless
pantomime prepares for the bloody ending, also a form of play
within a play, in which the court entertainment suddenly turns
into a scene of gruesome horror. This effective contrast between
the two state scenes is a particularly good example of Kyd's
masterly handling of various artistic means to create a vivid
impression.

The dumb show in *The Spanish Tragedy* fulfils an important
dramatic function. Hieronimo's personal tragedy is set against
the background of the court celebrating its triumphant success.
In this first scene he appears to be part of that court, but
immediately afterwards the tragic complications begin. At the
end of the play Hieronimo appears again, apparently in the same
role as at the beginning, but in fact completely cut off from the
rest and with an entirely different aim in view. The contrast is
heightened by the adroit use of dramatic means: the silent

[1] Cf. R. Brotanek, op. cit., pp. 90 ff.

[2] This has been noticed by F. S. Boas (*The Works of Thomas Kyd*): 'We
only realize later that this is an anticipation of the part he is to play at the
tragic crisis of the piece' (p. xxxiii).

tableau in the first act, and the pompous rhetoric of the play performed at the end. The dumb show is thus no longer apart from the main play, announcing its content and meaning, but is an important element in its structure, worked into a scene of normal dialogue, and therefore increasing its dramatic effect.

Something similar can also be said about the second pantomime, which is no less important for the total effect of the play although it is incorporated in a completely different way. It is added to the 'frame' of the play and is primarily meant to forecast the fatal events to come. Like the older dumb shows it is placed between two acts; typically, it comes immediately before the catastrophe.[1] Thus on the surface it occupies a position outside the play, similar to that of a chorus. In *The Spanish Tragedy* the chorus is linked with the play in a new and original way.[2] The chorus does not actually take part in the play, but watches it from the perspective of a passionately interested spectator. Thus the events on the stage are seen and commented on from outside. It was a particularly effective idea to give the function of the chorus to two distinct characters of which one (Revenge), like an omniscient spirit, occupies a position above the whole performance, while the other follows every movement in the play with rapt attention, eagerly awaiting the bloody end.[3] The inevitability of Fate is continually stressed by Revenge, while the Ghost of Andrea, on the other hand, grows increasingly impatient with every act, until after the third act he attempts to rouse his partner into action by a passionate speech. The dramatic tension is now at its highest and the last 'breathing-space'[4] before the final catastrophe is very effectively marked.

The spirit of Revenge answers to the accusations with a very superior gesture and allows Andrea a brief glance into the future by showing him the end of the tragedy in a symbolic pantomime. The performance is not a rehearsed play as it was in the

---

[1] Cf. P. W. Biesterfeldt, op. cit., pp. 67 and 93–4.

[2] Cf. ibid., p. 90, where the chorus is described as a kind of 'ideal pectator'.

[3] On the function of the ghost see H. Baker, *Induction to Tragedy* (London, 1958), pp. 215–35; P. Edwards, op. cit., pp. 1 ff.; A. Righter, *English Critical Essays, Twentieth Century, 2nd Series*, ed. D. Hudson (London, 1958), pp. 215–35; P. Edwards, op. cit., pp. 1 ff.; A. Righter, op. cit., pp. 78 ff.

[4] Cf. P. W. Biesterfeldt, op. cit., pp. 57–8.

first act, but is suddenly conjured up by Revenge. The scene is worth quoting because it is a good example of Kyd's ability to take over and adapt to his own purposes older conventions from different sources:

REUENGE: Beholde, Andrea, for an instance, how
                Reuenge hath slept, and then imagine thou
                What tis to be subiect to destinie.

                Enter a dumme shew.

GHOAST: Awake, Reuenge; reueale this misterie.

REUENGE: The two first the nuptiall torches boare
                As brightly burning as the mid-daies sunne:
                But after them doth Himen hie as fast,
                Clothed in Sable and a Saffron robe,
                And blowes them out, and quencheth them with
                    blood,
                As discontent that things continue so.

GHOAST: Sufficeth me; thy meanings vnderstood,
                And thanks to thee and those infernall powers
                That will not tollerate a Louers woe.
                Rest thee, for I will sit to see the rest.

It is easy to see what a curious mixture of Senecan and popular elements is here achieved. The inclusion of magic and visions was particularly frequent in popular Elizabethan drama and the dumb show proved to be a very effective means of presenting such apparitions on the stage. Here again it was precisely the strange and really undramatic features of the dumb show which were used to artistic ends, and the scope of the drama was thus widened considerably.[1]

It is important that this second pantomime too is introduced and explained by a kind of presenter who is asked to 'reueale this misterie'. By means of this symbolic scene the Spirit of Revenge wants to convey certain information and so the pantomime takes the place of a direct reply in dialogue. In this respect it is different from the previous one, which is primarily intended to entertain and whose content is not really relevant to the play itself. The second dumb show has a very definite connection with the play in that it foreshadows the denouement

[1] Cf. the lavish use of magic in Greene's *Friar Bacon and Friar Bungay*, W. Rowley's *The Birth of Merlin*, and Marlowe's *Doctor Faustus*, especially the 1616 version.

in an allegorical manner. As far as its form is concerned this pantomime could just as well occur in a play like *Gorboduc*. No characters from the play itself take part and the dumb show is limited to the abstract representation of events which are afterwards concretely enacted in the play. The sharp contrast between the marriage celebrations and the bloody ending is emphasized, thus drawing attention to one particular aspect of the tragedy and preparing the audience for the special effect of the final scene. The spectator receives a clear hint that the climax of the play, the tragic catastrophe, is now not far off, after being kept up to that point, like the Ghost of Andrea, in tense uncertainty about the outcome. This kind of foreboding is typical of pre-Shakespearean drama, where such gloomy forecasts of coming calamity are very frequent and are worked into the plot in various ways. Very often they take the form of hints and prophecies by the chorus. The entrance of the Furies in Senecan tragedy often has a similar function: to create an atmosphere of impending doom. In the case of *The Spanish Tragedy* this effect is heightened by the dialogue between the two spirits. Here again, therefore, the pantomime is skilfully built into a scene and could not be detached from the play.

As is often the case with Kyd, the dumb shows concentrate on broad theatrical effects; but these were nevertheless very important for the evolution of a more polished and subtle dramatic technique to which he made no small contribution. He very deliberately drew on the classical tragedies, adapting some of their artistic devices to his own ends. Thus he took over the pantomimes, which were rather an inessential part of classical drama, and provided some dramatic context for them by incorporating them in the play. I have tried to show how much was gained by this in the way of genuine dramatic effect.

It is largely owing to Kyd, then, that the convention of the dumb show was brought into a closer relationship with the play itself. In his tragedy the silent scenes have a specific function and cannot be taken out of their context. This can be seen from the fact that the dumb shows no longer stand in isolation between the individual acts, but within dialogue scenes, that characters from the play introduce them, watch them and comment on them. Thus the sphere of dialogue and that of silent action have come into much closer contact and the dramatist has devised a new dramatic form afterwards to be continually changed and improved on.[1] The plays of the 'University Wits', contemporaries of Kyd, show what new possibilities could now be exploited and what a popular device the dumb show had become.[2]

[1] There are some other scenes in which dialogue and pantomimic action are used side by side. Thus in I, 2 the victorious soldiers march Balthazar as prisoner. This provides an opportunity for the king to discuss the various characters and these are thus introduced to the audience. A similar technique is found in Shakespeare's *Troilus and Cressida*, I, 2, and in many other Elizabethan plays. Again it is obvious that the dramatist wanted to have as much action and spectacle on the stage as possible. Cf. A. Venezky, op. cit., pp. 87 ff.

[2] It is not necessary to discuss at length *The First Part of Ieronimo*, which is almost certainly not by Kyd. It is more like the popular history plays discussed in Chapter 6. In it Hieronimo's installation as marshal is presented as a silent but obviously splendid ceremony. See Appendix II for the text of this dumb show.

5

The 'University Wits'

Of the plays by the so-called University Wits *Locrine* is closest in style and structure to the tradition of classical tragedy. Although it was probably written a few years after *The Spanish Tragedy* the play is nevertheless on the whole less 'modern' and its attempt to fuse classical tragedy and low popular drama is not as convincing and successful as Kyd's achievement.[1] Its author did little more than juxtapose various styles, without arriving at a real unity through the mutual interplay of the individual elements. In spite of this failure it is interesting to examine what the anonymous dramatist took over from the large variety of models he had at his disposal, and which of their artistic means he considered most effective. As far as the dumb show is concerned, he retained it as an introduction to the individual acts in a way seldom found in later plays. Although he took over this framework from his predecessors almost as it stood, he did transform it for his own purposes and gave it a slightly different emphasis. One must take into account that the play, like Kyd's *Spanish Tragedy*, was directed at a far less educated audience than were the stricter forms of tragedy from the Inns of Court, an assumption which is confirmed by the form and use of the dumb shows.

While in *Gorboduc* and *Jocasta* the pantomimes were at first performed for the audience without any commentary, their connection with the actual play being hinted at only after the act by the chorus, there is in *Locrine* a kind of interpreter between the play and the audience in the form of Ate, goddess of Revenge. She fulfils a similar function to Revenge in Kyd's play, but, unlike her counterpart in *The Spanish Tragedy*, Ate remains

[1] Ed. T. Brooke in *The Shakespeare Apocrypha* (Oxford, 1908) and *Malone Soc.* (1908). Cf. also Baldwin Maxwell, *Studies in the Shakespeare Apocrypha* (New York, 1956), pp. 22 ff., and W. Clemen, op. cit., pp. 92 ff.

apart from the play and does not betray any personal interest in its events. She only points out their timeless significance and concludes the play with a general moral. Her most important function is to explain the pantomime to the audience. The whole plot of the dumb show is re-told in full and its connection with the play plainly and emphatically shown. In the figure of Ate, therefore, completely different traditions are combined. While her name and her appearance between the acts quite clearly betray her origin in classical drama of the Senecan type,[1] her function in this play is different from those models. In explaining the meaning of the dumb show to the audience Ate takes over the role of presenter from the pageants. Prologue, chorus and presenter are here united in one allegorical figure; the dumb shows help the chorus give a moral interpretation of the events in the play.

Thus, while in *Gorboduc* dumb show and chorus were kept strictly separate, these two elements are here combined for the first time, so that before each act a brief instructive scene is performed in which some symbolic *tableau* is presented and subsequently explained. The form of this scene is the same in each case: Ate tells once more what happened in the pantomime and then with a connecting 'So' establishes its relationship with the following act. The spectator's attention is explicitly drawn to the fact that the events in the pantomimes and in the play are in a way parallel, which was not the rule in classical tragedy. Again the train of events is not as important as their deeper meaning. This is stressed by the Latin mottoes with which Ate begins all her explanations. The motto in each case summarizes the significance of the pantomime, and the events of the following act are announced as further illustration of its truth. This method alone shows that the relevance of the dumb shows to the actual play is much more direct and immediately intelligible than in the plays from the Inns of Court. There is no example in which merely the atmosphere of the following act is suggested, as in *Gorboduc* III, but each time a quite definite incident is shown which in the play itself is repeated in a similar form. The figures in the dumb show and the characters in the play also correspond closely, but only the essential and typical characteristics are anticipated in the pantomimes. These do not portray a

[1] Cf. *Tancred and Gismund* and *The Misfortunes of Arthur*.

dramatic situation, but a stylized and meaningful gesture. The dumb show before the fourth act is a good example:

> *Enter Ate as before. Then let there follow Omphale daughter to the king of Lydia, hauing a club in her hand, and a lions skinne on her back, Hercules following with a distaffe. Then let Omphale, turn about, and taking off her pantofle, strike Hercules on the head, then let them depart. Ate remaining, saying:*[1]

> Quem non Argolici mandata seuera Tyranni,
> Non potuit Iuno vincere, vicit amor.

Ate now describes in some detail the incident just shown. This is followed by its application to the plot of the following act:

> So martiall Locrine cheerd with victorie,
> Falleth in loue with Humbers concubine,
> And so forgetteth peerlesse Guendoline.

Here the dumb show is mythological and perhaps not so very different from earlier forms. There are, however, some other dumb shows in this play which are more striking and original, as for instance the pantomime before the first act:

> *Enter Atey with thunder and lightning all in black, with a burning torch in one hand, and a bloodie swoord in the other hand, and presently let there come foorth a Lion running after a Beare or any other beast, then come foorth an Archer who must kill the lion in a dumbe show, and then depart. Remaine Atey.*

Again Ate gives a detailed description of the scene and then continues:

> So valiant Brute the terror of the world,
> Whose only lookes did scarre his enemies,
> The Archer death brought to his latest end.
> Oh what may long abide aboue this ground,
> In state of blisse and healthfull happinesse. *Exit*

The first act then relates the death of Brutus in static rhetoric and declamation.

---

[1] It is interesting to note that the style of these dumb shows bears more resemblance to some stage directions in popular plays than to earlier pantomimes. Thus we have before the second act: '*after a litle lightning and thundring, let there come forth this show:*' Cf. with this the stage directions in Pickering's *Horestes.* One of them is quoted in Chapter 6, p. 88, n. 1.

The form of these dumb shows indicates a strong connection with the Elizabethan emblems.[1] This assumption is supported by the use made of animal figures such as those found in contemporary 'Emblem Books' or pageants. They show in a particularly illuminating way what R. Freeman calls 'the equating of pictorial detail with moral ideas'.[2] The mythological figures, too, are used in an emblematic manner. They are images of certain aspects of moral behaviour and are therefore particularly far removed from the concrete world of the actual play. The playwright was not content with representing the events on one plane and expressing his instructive intention within the play, but he added a living emblem which repeats the moral of the play on another level. Two modes of representation, originating from completely different models, are used side by side, as in the classical tragedies. The two planes are not directly associated. The language of the play is not influenced by the imagery of the pantomimes, although many classical references and comparisons occur in the speeches. This separation is, if possible, even more strictly adhered to than in some classical tragedies, and the dumb shows therefore seem an even less necessary part of the play.

On the other hand there is in *Locrine* no longer the sharp contrast between lively pantomimic action and static dialogue, because the dialogue scenes often further the development of the plot and lively action is included in the play proper, especially in the crude comic subplot. This means that the dumb shows do not have the function of creating a balance between dialogue and action and of satisfying the audience's desire for spectacle, rather they are intended to strengthen the moral and didactic purpose of the play and make it easier to understand. Their strict form also underlines the fact that the play is divided into acts and they mark clearly defined sections, each with its own meaning, so that the continuity of the plot is several times interrupted by such statements of the moral. It seems as if the dramatist consciously sacrificed something of the dramatic effect of the play in order to make his instructive purpose the clearer.

[1] Cf. Chapter 1. See also Spenser's *Ruins of Time*, ll. 568-9, for an exact parallel to Ate's explanation of the first dumb show.

[2] Op. cit., p. 60. On the use of animal figures in the pageants see also Wickham, op. cit., Vol. I, p. 99.

The author of *Locrine*, like Kyd, attempted to transfer the pantomime from the classical drama to the more popular plays. Although they went about this in very different ways it is clear that they endeavoured to bring the dumb shows into closer connection with the rest of the drama and to prevent their becoming mere entertainments between the acts. Kyd's method, however, proved to be by far the more successful one, as can be seen from most of the following examples.

'THE RARE TRIUMPHS OF LOVE AND FORTUNE'

The Rare Triumphs of Love and Fortune and Robert Wilson's plays achieve a very different synthesis of most varied elements of style.[1] They clearly belong to the realm of Court Drama, where the connection with other forms of entertainment, revels, disguisings, and dancing, is particularly close. Drama at Court was only one of the various kinds of amusement which were selected and supervised by the 'Master of the Revels'. Songs, dances, and ingenious stage effects are frequent in these

---

[1] *The Rare Triumphs of Love and Fortune* (*Malone Soc.*, 1930); R. Wilson, *The Three Lords and Three Ladies of London* (*TFT*, 1912); and *The Cobbler's Prophecy* (*TFT*, 1911).

Richard Tarleton's *Seven Deadly Sins*, which has unfortunately been lost, probably belonged to the same type. The second part, of which at least a 'Stage Plot' has been preserved, contained some fairly elaborate dumb shows. Cf. W. W. Greg, *Dramatic Documents from the Elizabethan Playhouses* (Oxford, 1931), *Reproductions and Transcripts*, Plate II; *Commentary*, pp. 105 ff.

The second part of the play shows by means of three *exempla* the disastrous effects of three deadly sins. In this part the poet Lydgate acts as presenter, commenting on the action and introducing the dumb shows like Gower in Shakespeare's *Pericles*. The pantomimes contain telescoped accounts of some important episodes and are very similar to those in some popular plays of adventure. Thus the first part, treating the sin of envy, gives a new version of the story of Gorboduc. In a lengthy pantomime the division of the kingdom and the first quarrel of the two sons is shown (see Appendix II for the text of this pantomime). The following speech by Lydgate, not preserved in the 'Stage Plot', undoubtedly explained the dumb show. It is remarkable that here only the full text of the dumb shows is given and not any speeches or dialogue. One suspects that very often the opposite was the case. (My attention was drawn to this play by the dissertation of L. G. Gibbs.)

plays and are often added at the expense of dramatic unity.[1] The pantomimes in them are therefore only one of many scenic effects and are in no case as isolated between the scenes as in the classical tragedies.

The Rare Triumphs of Love and Fortune belongs among the dramatic *exempla*: it tells in a kind of framework of the contest between Venus and Fortuna, a contest which is afterwards fought out ceremoniously by means of an exemplary love story which is the main subject of the play. The actual plot is therefore a kind of play within a play, with the Gods as spectators who follow the events and comment on them. As in Wilson's play *The Cobbler's Prophecy*, which is in some respects very similarly constructed, the play begins with a solemn procession of the Gods which has almost the character of a dumb show:

> *Enter Mercury, then riseth a Furie: then enter the assembly of Gods, Iupiter with Iuno, Apollo with Minerua, Mars and Saturne, after Vulcan with Venus, the Fury sets debate amongst them, and after Iupiter speakes as followeth.*

The further development of the dispute between Venus and Fortuna is even more interesting. Jupiter, after some preliminary quarrelling, gives orders for the exhibition of some examples of the power of Love and Fortune, and Mercury asks Charon to bring back some famous dead for a short while:

> Transporte the soules of such as may reporte,
> Fortune and Loue and not in open sorte.
> Let them appeere to vs in silent showe,
> to manifest a trueth that we must knowe.
> *Strike with his Rod three times.*

At this, five 'showes' appear one after the other which are briefly introduced by Mercury. Unfortunately the stage directions do not indicate very exactly what is to be shown. See, for instance, the following:

> *Enter the show of Troylus and Cressida.*
> MERCURY: Beholde how Troylus and Cresseda
>   Cryes out on Loue that framed their decay.

---

[1] See especially G. K. Hunter, *John Lyly: The Humanist as Courtier* (London, 1962), pp. 89 ff., where there is also a short discussion of *The Rare Triumphs* and *The Cobbler's Prophecy* (pp. 155 ff.).

It seems quite possible that not only motionless figures were presented, but that the fate of the characters appearing was at least hinted at by means of some typical gestures. Thus it seems likely that in the *Show of Queene Dydo* the suicide which is mentioned by Mercury in his commentary was actually performed in mime. In any case, it is remarkable that the pantomime no longer stands outside the dialogue scene, but is included in it. It is directed at the characters in the play, not at the audience in the theatre. We have here an example of how the dumb show, even at this early stage, could take on completely different forms and was not necessarily isolated between the scenes.

At another point in the same play the close connection can be seen between stage direction and dumb show which makes itself apparent again and again in popular drama and partly explains the varied employment of pantomimes in these plays. At the beginning of one scene (IV, 3) we find the following stage directions:

> *Enter Lentulo with a Ring in his mouth, a Marigolde in his hand, and a faire shute of apparell on his backe: after he had a while made some dum shew, Penulo commeth running in with two or three other.*

The expression 'dumb show' here obviously means a piece of improvised by-play and fooling and has little to do with the dumb shows proper. However, the scene proves that in these plays pantomimic elements in general play a much more important part than in the works treated in the previous chapters. Their style was therefore better suited to the insertion of more extensive dumb shows within the scenes in that it was so much less formal and inflexible than the rhetoric of Senecan drama, offering in consequence a much wider scope for experiment and improvisation. The plays of Peele and Greene show how these new possibilities were seen and exploited.

GEORGE PEELE

George Peele's first play, *The Arraignment of Paris*, reminds one in some respects of *The Rare Triumphs of Love and Fortune*, although artistically it is in a much higher class.[1] As in early Court Drama the most diverse elements are here used side by side to achieve a colourful effect. The highly stylized speech is employed as a kind of independent set-piece (*Oratio*), and the pantomimes, too, seem at first sight only another trick to make the play more effective. They fulfil, however, a dramatic function within a scene of dialogue, similar to that in the previous play. At a certain point in the dialogue one of those taking part discontinues the argument and instead employs a pantomime to convince the other. While in the myth the three Goddesses try to win over Paris by their tempting promises and alluring speeches, here the content of these promises is visibly presented in a series of three 'shows', so that there is a kind of competition between these pantomimes, in which each tries to outdo the other. Naturally enough, the visual elements are strongly emphasized; argument and persuasion are replaced by the attempt to surpass one another by colourful spectacle and splendour.

This intention is borne out by the content of the three pantomimes. The first is only a motionless picture without even actors or plot. It can hardly be termed dumb show and reminds one very strongly of the style of the emblems and pageants. The second, on the other hand, is similar to the pantomime before Act V in *Gorboduc*. Here again there is no complete scene, but a *tableau* with music and dancing, without plot – it is like the simplest type of dumb show. The third pantomime is no more lively than the others and surpasses them only in outward splendour and charm. All three are just as close to the style of the pageants as to the older dumb shows, and are no more than impressive *tableaux*. It is apparent that Peele did not use the dumb show here with any more dramatic effect than did his predecessors. His particular contribution to its development was rather his original way of incorporating it in his play.

Contrary to nearly all examples examined so far, these 'shows' are not directed at the audience, but at some character from the play itself. The three Goddesses act as presenters in

[1] *Malone Soc.* (1910). Cf. W. Clemen, op. cit., pp. 163 ff. On the background of these plays see D. H. Horne, *The Life and Minor Works of George Peele*, being Vol. I of *The Life and Works of George Peele*, ed. Ch. T. Prouty (New Haven, 1952), especially pp. 65 ff.

that they introduce and explain the pantomimes. They have, moreover, a definite aim in view and expect a reply. In his answer to these offers Paris weighs the merits of the three rewards shown to him and decides to accept the last one. The 'shows' thus have a vital connection with the scene and are every bit as important as the speeches. This marks a crucial step towards the incorporation of dumb shows in drama. *The Arraignment of Paris* is of course only a festive pastoral comedy, a masque,[1] but what was achieved in such a play soon had some influence on serious drama as well.[2]

In *The Battle of Alcazar* the pantomime is used in a substantially different manner. As far as its form is concerned, the play is similar to the popular chronicle plays with which it has in common above all a lively plot and a large number of comparatively brief scenes.[3] There is no need here to use dumb shows to make up for any lack of action on the stage. The pantomimes therefore have quite a different function: that previously reserved for the chorus or messenger's report. As in *Locrine*, prologue and chorus are represented by one single figure who in this play for the first time is actually designated 'presenter' and who is even more effective as an intermediary for the play and its audience than Ate is in *Locrine*. The presenter addresses the audience directly and explains the details of the plot. Thus his function is not so much didactic as expository and dramatic. The cause of this innovation lies chiefly in the problem of managing the extensive plot, which could best be accomplished with the help of a presenter. There are many parallels to this device in pre-Shakespearean drama.[4]

---

[1] Cf. E. Welsford, op. cit., p. 278.

The manner of these 'shows' is very similar to that in *The Rare Triumphs*, but they are slightly more elaborate. E.g.: PALLAS SHOW.

Hereuppon did enter 9. knights in armour, treading a warlike Almaine, by drome and fife, & then hauing march't foorth againe, Venus speaketh.

[2] Cf. Kyd's *Spanish Tragedy*.

[3] *Malone Soc.* (1907). Cf. also W. Clemen, op. cit., pp. 171 ff. Peele's *Edward I* also belongs to these chronicle plays. It does not contain any dumb shows proper, but a number of pantomimic stage directions and lively action.

[4] Cf. Doris Fenton, *The Extra-Dramatic Moment in Elizabethan Plays before* 1616 (Unpublished Dissertation, Philadelphia, 1930), pp. 87 ff. See also *Everyman*, Gascoigne's *Supposes*, Preston's *Cambises*, and others.

The 'University Wits'

Unlike earlier examples, Peele uses the dumb show for the purpose of dramatic exposition. Not only does the presenter relate what has happened before the play opens, but he illustrates it as well with a silent scene. The first pantomimes in *The Battle of Alcazar* are not mere *tableaux*, like those in *The Arraignment*, but present lively incidents and have the form of normal scenes. Thus before the beginning of the first act the Moor's murder of his brothers and his uncle is mimed. This is quite an extensive dramatic scene, interrupted only by the explanations of the presenter:

> PRESENTER: . . . this tyrant king, . . .
> Presents himselfe with naked sword in hand,
> Accompanied as now you may behold,
> With deuils coted in the shapes of men.

The first dumbe shew.
Enter Muly Mahamet and his sonne, and his two young brethren, the Moore sheweth them the bed, and then takes his leaue of them, and they betake them to their rest. And then the presenter speaketh.

> Like those that were by kind of murther mumd,
> Sit downe and see what heinous stratagems
> These damned wits contriue. And lo alas
> How lyke poore lambes prepard for sacrifice,
> This traitor king hales to their longest home,
> These tender Lords his yonger brethren both.

The second dumbe shew.
Enter the Moore and two murdrers bringing in his vnkle Abdelmunen, then they draw the curtains and smoother the yong princes in the bed. Which done, in sight of the vnkle they strangle him in his chaire, and then goe forth. And then the Presenter saith.

> His brethren thus in fatall bed behearst,
> His fathers brother of too light beleefe,
> This Negro puts to death by proud command.
> Saie not these things are faind, for true they are,
> And vnderstand how eager to inioy
> His fathers crowne, this vnbeleeuing Moore
> Murthering his vnkle and his brethren,
> Triumphs in his ambitious tyrannie.

Thus the presenter gives a running commentary on the dreadful happenings in the pantomime and explains in detail the background of the plot which the audience cannot deduce from the silent scene alone. The most significant difference between this dumb show and the earlier ones is that it contains an essential part of the plot. But for the absence of dialogue the scene is exactly like all the others in the play. The horror of the subject is even emphasized by the unusual manner of presentation. The audience's attention is drawn only to the actual deed, not so much to the motives behind it. In this way it is immediately engrossed in the plot of the play and requires no further exposition.

The presenter appears before each act and explains what is to come. Here again we can see that classical tragedy served as an example and influenced the structure. Most later chronicle plays are not divided into acts. The influence of classical tragedy can be seen in the pantomimes before the second and fifth acts which are only symbolical and mythological pageants and in their dramatic technique appear only as weak copies of earlier dumb shows. This practice did not, however, survive long, while the type represented by the first dumb show was more influential and determined the further development.

Simultaneously with this new form of dumb show, drama itself underwent some changes. The didactic elements disappeared almost entirely for a time and the habit of illustrating moral lessons by dramatic *exempla* all but died out, while the immediate effect of the dramatic events became the chief concern. In *The Battle of Alcazar* the pantomime leads directly into the plot of the play, introduces the characters taking part, and acquaints the audience with the initial situation. Thus the dramatic complications get under way much more quickly and the first act no longer has to cope with the exposition, but embarks immediately on the first consequences, the arrival of the revengers and the outbreak of war. In this way much is gained in dramatic tension and speed.

The plays of Peele demonstrate two different methods of combining dumb show and play proper: first of all by using dumb show within dialogue, almost instead of speech, second by placing it outside the spoken scenes in order to give a telescoped version of parts of the plot, thus shortening the dramatic exposition. In both cases the dumb show is a genuine dramatic device, not just an addition, and in the period that followed both possibilities were further exploited and developed.

The 'University Wits'

ROBERT GREENE

Robert Greene also made an important contribution to the further development of the dumb show. As a dramatist he knew how to handle the most disparate forms and conventions and he took over from other playwrights whatever he thought would fit into the framework of his own plays.[1] These were meant above all to please and to entertain. Consequently visual effects are rather important in his works and in most of them the stage is full of lively action. The theatre's stage apparatus is exploited to the full and there are several surprising innovations.[2]

All this is particularly true of *James the Fourth*, Greene's only play containing dumb shows in the customary sense. The opening of the play with the dance of the fairies and ghosts and the sudden appearance of Bohan out of the tomb is already unusual. In the dialogue that follows, Oberon and Bohan establish the 'frame' of the play and the audience is, as in *The Spanish Tragedy*, introduced first of all to another audience (Oberon and Bohan) before the actual plot begins. At the same time the meaning of the play and the kind of response expected are explained. Thus the 'frame' fulfils the function of chorus and removes the play proper further away from the audience to some imaginary sphere.[3] As in the plays of Peele and Kyd, the pantomimes are not contrasted in character to the rest of the play, which contains several other pantomimic elements as well. The dumb shows are only one of many other dramatic devices employed by Greene to make his play as many-sided and varied as possible. There are, however, some novel elements in his use of the dumb show.

James the Fourth has in common with Kyd's *Spanish Tragedy* that the dumb shows are within the 'frame' and not in the play itself. While, however, in Kyd's play the content of an act was

---

[1] *The Plays and Poems of Robert Greene*, ed. J. Churton Collins (Oxford, 1905), Vol. II. Cf. also W. Clemen, op. cit., pp. 178 ff.

[2] Cf. the extravagant use of magic and stage effects in *A Looking Glass for London and England* and *Friar Bacon and Friar Bungay* or the following stage direction from *Alphonsus* (V): '*Exit Venus; Or if you can conueniently let a chaire come downe from the top of the Stage and draw her vp,*'

[3] On the 'frame' see E. Welsford, op. cit., pp. 279 ff., and M. C. Bradbrook, *Themes and Conventions of Elizabethan Tragedy* (Cambridge, 1957), p. 45. The play as well as the dumb shows are *exempla* very like those in *The Rare Triumphs*.

hinted at in a brief scene, the pantomimes are here used to prove and illuminate a certain moral statement. They are, as in *The Arraignment of Paris*, built into the dialogue as a means of convincing an opponent and have a definite dramatic function within the spoken scene because they are shown to a character in the play and commented on by him. As in Kyd's play the spectator's first question is 'What meaneth this?', at which Oberon, acting as presenter, explains the incidents. The pantomime becomes the subject of a conversation in the play and is thus very closely integrated.

The content of the dumb shows, too, is clearly connected with the play. Each of the pantomimes presents a short incident which is complete in itself and they are therefore more than just silent *tableaux* like the apparitions in *The Arraignment of Paris*. They are historical pageants depicting the fall of great rulers and are intended to demonstrate the vanity of earthly glory. They are decidedly didactic and in this respect related to allegoric poetry, which often had a similar moralizing tendency.[1] Outwardly they are on quite a different level from the play itself and have no apparent connection with its plot. Nevertheless their didactic tone is greatly modified by the dramatic context.

Bohan's commentary alone takes some of the seriousness from the scene. He appears to have very little interest in the dumb shows and prefers to get on with his own play. The way in which the pantomimes are thus opposed to the play proper shows particularly skilful and effective management on Greene's part. Oberon and Bohan are carrying on a kind of competition in which each tries to outdo the other with his own performance. After Bohan has presented the first act of his play with which he wants to explain and justify his retreat from the world, Oberon lets his three pantomimes appear, to show that he too has some skill in these things and can drive home his moral as well as

[1] Cf. Spenser's *Ruins of Time* where the unstableness of the world is illustrated by a series of pageants (ll. 488 ff.: 'Like tragicke Pageants seeming to appeare.'). Cf. B. Maxwell, op. cit., p. 207, n.31.

The 'pompious shew' in the anonymous play *A Knack to Know an Honest Man* is also a kind of *exemplum*. Although the actual content of this pantomime, as far as we can judge from the text, is 'real' enough, a religious procession of the Venetian aristocracy, it is for Sempronio who watches and, like a presenter, describes it, only an illustration of his statement: *Vanitas vanitatum*. (*Malone Soc.*, 1910, ll. 741 ff.)

Bohan. It is an elaboration of the dispute which begins in the first act where Bohan replies to the dance of the fairies with a 'Scottish jig' performed by his sons. It is this graceful interplay of didactic and comic elements that prevents the play from appearing even for a moment as a purely didactic performance.

In their relation to the frame, therefore, the pantomimes are on the same plane as the actual play of James IV: they are a kind of retort to the first act of it. However, one is struck by the way in which the play presented by Bohan forces the 'frame' and the pantomimes more and more into the background, so that by the end of the play the 'frame' has disappeared completely.

In *James IV*, then, the function of the pantomimes is not to reveal the contents of the play but to confirm and illustrate them by other means. The same moral is simultaneously proved by a series of historical pageants and by a fairy-tale. As a result of this skilful use of different techniques the fairy-tale play has an added depth without being any less entertaining. The 'frame' prevents the different elements from becoming too separate; it strengthens the connection between them and makes them complement each other. Thus the tendency to explain everything repeatedly and unmistakably, so typical of pre-Shakespearean drama, is again apparent. Greene, however, does not use to this end a mere climax of effects, but a genuine interplay and combination of the various artistic means. We rarely find in Elizabethan drama before Shakespeare such a skilful integration of dramatic and pantomimic elements, of stylized rhetoric, realistic comedy, and symbolic dumb show; and in fact few dramatists of the period experimented so daringly as Greene. It was not until the appearance of Shakespeare's early comedies that this light-hearted playing with diverse dramatic techniques was again taken up and surpassed.

The pantomimes in Greene's *Friar Bacon and Friar Bungay* are rather a special case. Here we have on the one hand a kind of play within the play, because the characters whom Friar Bacon shows to Prince Edward through his magic mirror actually speak, but on the other hand the spectators are to assume that these speeches are only audible to themselves, not to the Prince. Thus the Prince sees through the magic mirror a dumb show; he can only guess the words spoken by the persons from their movements and gestures, and Friar Bacon has to act as an interpreter.

The pantomime is here used to present a conjurer's trick, a magic vision, and the two dramatic devices, dumb show and play within the play, are combined in a quite ingenious way.[1]

JOHN LYLY: 'ENDIMION'

Lyly's *Endimion* can only with some reservation be included as an example of the early use of dumb shows, for the pantomime at the end of the second act is not to be found in the earliest editions of the play, but appears for the first time in Blount's *Sixe Court Comedies* of 1632.[2] W. Bond assumed that Lyly used this device in the productions directed by himself and 'did not embody in his original MS. what he could teach orally'; it is also possible, however, that some later adapter added the scene which in its content agrees exactly with Endimion's account in the fifth act. It is rather different from the forms of dumb show dealt with so far:

> *A Dumbe Shew (representing the dream of Endimion).*
> *Musique sounds. Three Ladies enter; one with a Knife and a looking glasse, who by the procurement of one of the other two, offers to stab Endimion as hee sleepes, but the third wrings her hands, lamenteth, offering still to preuent it, but dares not.*
> *At last, the first Lady looking in the glasse, casts downe the Knife. Exeunt.*

[1] There are very similar though on the whole much clumsier pantomimes as magic tricks in the anonymous *John of Bordeaux* (*Malone Soc.*, 1936), W. Rowley's *The Birth of Merlin*, and Marlowe's *Doctor Faustus* (1616), where they are probably a later addition. On the complicated textual history of this play see the edition by John D. Jump in the *Revels Plays* series (London, 1962). It is, by the way, interesting to note that Marlowe does not use dumb shows although his plays are full of impressive stage effects. There seems to be in his plays a particularly close relationship between speech and action which made the introduction of pantomimes unnecessary. See the stimulating article by Bent Sunesen, 'Marlowe and the Dumb Show', *ESts*, XXXV (1954), pp. 241–53. In Chapman's *Bussy D'Ambois* (IV) there is a similar scene in which the characters appearing in a magic vision can be heard by the audience but not by the persons on the stage. For them it is a dumb show.

[2] *The Complete Works of John Lyly*, ed. R. Warwick Bond (Oxford, 1902), Vol. III. Note on the dumb show pp. 508–9. Cf. also G. K. Hunter, op. cit., pp. 154 ff.

Enters an ancient man with bookes with three leaues, offers the same twice. Endimion refuseth: hee rendeth two and offers the third, where hee stands a while, and then Endimion offers to take it.
Exit (the Old Man).

The pantomime is a long scene with several entries and a plot more involved than one would expect in a mere 'show'. The persons taking part are only vaguely characterized, and are very different from those in the play. The incidents presented being made to appear unreal and supernatural, they are on a different plane from the plot of the play itself, although closely connected with it. The sleeping Endimion – his enchantment was shown in the scene immediately preceding – is drawn into the silent scene. He is, even in his sleep, threatened by adverse powers, and his dream reflects the conflict which Cynthia and Tellus fight out over him in symbolic form.

The whole scene is not merely a particularly striking stage effect; it was important for the structure of the play to bring Endimion once more to the fore, because in the following two acts he only makes one brief appearance. The pantomime is, however, not explained by a presenter and only a little light is thrown upon it by Endimion's account and Tellus' confession in the last act. If this dumb show really was part of the first version of the play it would be the earliest example of the representation of dreams and visions by means of pantomimes, a favourite device in later Elizabethan and Stuart drama.[1] It would also be further evidence of the fact, established by all the plays treated in this chapter, that the dumb show had become a very popular and extremely adaptable dramatic convention.

[1] Cf. T. Heywood's *If You Know Not Me, You Know Nobody*; Munday's *The Death of Robert Earl of Huntingdon*, and many others.

6

Popular Plays of Legendary Heroes and Adventure

About the turn of the century and afterwards a large number of plays were written which are very different from the plays of the 'University Wits', although they were probably influenced by them. They are historical-biographical plays presenting the life story of well-known historical or legendary characters or various incidents from Elizabethan London. With their rather loose structure and their colourful sequence of lively scenes they may have partly developed out of the earlier chronicles and interludes, which for their part owe a great deal to the moralities and in contrast to classical drama are characterized by a lively plot and frequent scene-changes. Particularly noticeable is the number of detailed stage directions in these interludes. They strongly emphasize the vivid and dramatic quality of the action and often leave room for improvisation.[1] There is, for instance, in *Appius and Virginia* a short pantomime which has been called a dumb show, although it cannot by any means be compared with the earlier dumb shows,[2] and is not much more than an elaborate stage direction. During one of Appius' monologues Conscience and Justice enter and illustrate with their short mime the fight between the powers of Good and Evil for his soul:

---

[1] Thus we find in Pickering's *Horestes* the following stage direction: *Go & make your liuely battel & let it be longe eare you can win ye Citie and when you haue won it let Horestes bringe out his mother by the arme & let ye droum sease playing & the trumpet, also when she is taken let her knele downe and speake* (*TFT*, 1910, D.j.). On the form of these 'histories', cf. G. Wickham, op. cit., Vol. I, p. 322. See also: Werner Habicht, 'Sénèque et le théâtre populaire pré-shakespearien', in *Les Tragédies de Sénèque et le Théatre de la Renaissance* (Paris, 1964), pp. 175–87.

[2] This is what Pearn does (op. cit., p. 389). He seems to count *Appius and Virginia* among the English classical tragedies with which, however, it has very little in common.

*Here let him make as though he went out and let Consience and Iustice
come out of him, and let Consience hold in his hande a Lampe burning
and let Justice haue a sworde and hold it before Apius brest.*[1]

This is only a kind of allegorical intensification, emphasizing
what is said in the monologue, where Appius describes the
divided state of his mind, and is in its form much like many
other stage directions in these plays. Only some twenty years
later was this form of allegory also used in dumb shows
proper.

From these early plays the authors of popular drama of
adventure took over above all the epic structure and sequence of
scenes, the episodic nature of the plot, and the large number of
characters taking part.[2] The result is in most cases a rough and
ready kind of drama which was quickly written to meet popular
demand and probably often as quickly forgotten. One has the
impression that any story material which appeared at all suitable
was immediately picked on for a play. Dumb shows are
frequently used when some technical difficulty has to be overcome and construction therefore often tends to be weak.
Although hardly any really successful works of art are to be
found among these 'mass-produced' plays, they nevertheless
reveal that technical skill and craftsmanship, that sure theatrical
instinct, which even the lesser dramatists of that period seem to
have possessed. Their works are interesting as spirited attempts
to satisfy the taste of a wide public and at the same time to offer
some moral instruction. They show clearly how the pantomime
could become a handy technical device without being an organic
part of the play.[3] At the same time this free and easy experiment-
ing revealed the various dramatic possibilities of the dumb show
and prepared the way for its use by more discriminating playwrights.

[1] *Malone Soc.* (1911). A very similar 'pantomime' is to be found in
Greene's play *A Looking Glass for London and England* (V, 2).

[2] Consequently one actor often had to play several parts. In Pickering's
Horestes there are twenty-five speaking parts, but there is also a table
showing how these twenty-five parts could be taken over by six actors
only. See D. M. Bevington, *From 'Mankind' to Marlowe* (Cambridge,
Mass., 1962), pp. 68 ff.

[3] F. A. Foster calls the dumb show 'a help to hasty playwrights with
poor craftsmanship' (op. cit., p. 17).

'A WARNING FOR FAIR WOMEN'

The anonymous tragedy *A Warning for Fair Women* is in many ways a particularly interesting example of the type of play we are discussing because in it the tradition of classical drama and the style of the popular histories and interludes are blended in a rather peculiar way.[1] The play shows how a London merchant is murdered by his wife's lover, not without her knowledge and consent, and how the deed is atoned for by their own death. In portraying these events the dramatist introduces some allegoric figures who establish contact between the audience and the characters and are meant to make it easier to understand the meaning of the play and its practical application. This 'frame' gains in dramatic movement through the appearance, at the beginning of the play, of Tragedy, Comedy, and History, who dispute about their relative importance until Tragedy emerges victorious and from then on acts as prologue and chorus. She appears after the first few scenes and at regular intervals, thus dividing the play into units which are the equivalents of acts. Each time she comments briefly on the preceding section and introduces the following one. Thus, after the first part, Tragedy, introducing a dumb show, calls in the Furies who at her bidding prepare a banquet. The passage is well worth quoting:

TRAGEDY: Harke how the gastly fearefull chimes of night
        Do ring them in: and with a dolefull peale
Here some strange solemne musicke like belles is heard within
        Do fill the roofe with sounds of tragedie:
        Dispatch, I say, and be their Ushers in.
The Furies goe to the doore and meete them: first the Furies enter before leading them, dauncing a soft daunce to the solemne musicke: next comes Lust before Browne, leading mistris Sanders couered with a blacke vaile: Chastitie all in white, pulling her backe softly by the arme: then Drewry, thrusting away Chastitie, Roger following: they march about, and then sit to the table: the Furies fill wine, Lust drinckes to Browne, he to Mistris Sanders, shee pledgeth him: Lust imbraceth her, she thrusteth Chastity from her, Chastity wrings her hands, and departs: Drury and Roger imbrace one an other: the Furies leape and imbrace one another.

[1] *TFT* (1912). The play belongs to a similar type as *Arden of Feversham*, *A Yorkshire Tragedy*, and Yarington's *Two Lamentable Tragedies*, in which some notorious murder cases are dramatized.

Tragedy now describes and explains the scene:

> Thus sinne preuailes, she drinkes that poysoned
>   draught,
> With which base thoughts henceforth infects her soule,
> And wins her free consent to this foule deed . . .

Here we have indeed a curious mixture of various elements. While the Furies obviously come from classical drama, the procession of the guests clearly shows the influence of the moralities. As in Pickering's *Horestes* and in *Appius and Virginia*, allegorical figures appear simultaneously with characters from the play: Lust and Chastity try in turn to draw Anne Saunders, the merchant's wife, on their side. The relationship with the moralities is obvious, but such allegories were frequent in the masques and pageants as well; in fact, Tragedy uses the expression 'masque' for this pantomime:

> Here is the Maske vnto this damned murther.

She gives a running commentary on the events in the dumb show, thus fulfilling the role of presenter.

The pantomime which is performed here is rather an extensive scene with a lively content, but it is on a completely different level from the rest of the play. There is a marked contrast between the realistic style of the dialogue, the scenes from the everyday life of London citizens, and the form of allegory used in the dumb shows. This contrast is even more striking than in the classical tragedies, in which the dialogue scenes are also stylized and removed from reality. At the same time, however, the pantomime is, unlike those in the classical tragedies, closely linked with the play because the main characters from the play appear in it. Above all, the plot of the dumb show is part of the play's action. What is so new about this pantomime is the way in which an event which is decisive for the advance of the plot is only represented in the form of an allegorical mime. The first section of the tragedy has dealt with Brown's attempts to meet Anne Saunders and to win her favour. All the time she was strongly opposed to his suggestions. The pantomime thus describes a change of attitude which is hard to believe. Anne's complete change of mind is only staged as an allegory while in another kind of play probably quite a number of scenes would

91

have been necessary to make this development credible. And yet such a task would have given the playwright a particularly good opportunity for exhibiting his skill.[1] The pantomime is a means of evading the difficulty; a crucial part of the plot is practically jumped over and only dealt with in the form of a rather crude morality. Consequently the following events which lead to Brown's murder of the merchant are insufficiently motivated. This inadequate method of handling the dramatic material shows that the mere staging of exciting events was the main concern of the dramatist. The play, like some news report, leaves out all the deeper motives and inner conflicts behind the external action. It contains only scenes in which something really happens. The dramatist tries to present even inner developments as visible actions. While in the moralities all events were usually presented at this level, we have in *A Warning for Fair Women* an attempt to bring the whole play closer to reality. Only in the dumb shows does the dramatist draw on the style of the moralities.

Thus the plot of the play is unfolded simultaneously on two different levels. The realistic dialogue scenes which give no deeper explanation of motives are followed by a morally instructive pantomime in which the characters taking part appear to be only the victims of the virtues and vices struggling for mastery of them. These abrupt changes from one sphere to the other characterize the structure of the whole play.

The first pantomime is followed by a series of lively scenes in which Brown makes some futile attempt to waylay and kill Saunders. Before the actual murder, however, Tragedy appears once more to announce what is going to happen, again introducing a pantomime to portray the event in a particularly vivid manner:

> *The Musicke playing, enters Lust bringing forth Browne and Roger, at one ende mistres Sanders and mistres Drurie at the other, they offering cheerefully to meete and embrace, suddenly riseth vp a great tree betweene them, whereat amazedly they step backe, wherupon Lust bringeth an axe to mistres Sanders, shewing signes, that she should cut it downe, which she refuseth, albeit mistres Drurie offers to helpe her. Then Lust brings the Axe to Browne, and shews the like signes to him as before, wherupon he roughlie and suddenly hewes downe the tree, and then they run togither and embrace. With that enters Chastitie,*

---

[1] Shakespeare seems to have been attracted by such situations which challenge the dramatist's ability. Cf. *Richard III*, I, 2.

*with her haire disheueled, and taking mistres Sanders by the hand
brings her to her husbands picture hanging on the wall, and pointing to
the tree, seemes to tell her, that that is the tree so rashly cut downe.
Whereupon she wringing her hands, in teares departes, Browne, Drurie,
Roger and Lust, whispering, he drawes his sword, and Roger followes
him. Tragedie expressing that now he goes to act the deed.*

> Lust leades togither this adulterous route,
> But as you see are hindred thus, before
> They could attaine vnto their fowle desires.

Again inner developments and moral decisions are translated
into visible events to make them more striking and impressive.
As in the first pantomime Lust and Chastity appear together
with the main characters from the play and a kind of masque is
performed. The tree is a symbol showing that Saunders has a
completely passive part to play as victim of the sinful passion
aroused by Lust.[1]

The second pantomime, however, has a different function from
that of the first because the murder it shows is also presented in
the actual play. The dumb show prepares for what is to come, at
the same time revealing its deeper meaning, as is indicated by
the words with which Tragedy announces the scene:

> Now of his death the generall intent,
> Thus Tragedy doth to your eyes present.

The couplet implies that this is more than a personal tragedy.
The moral application is told before the actual events take place,
in that Tragedy explains in great detail the significance of the
symbolic scene. Thus the incident is successively presented in
two different ways, once in the form of a morality, the second
time as a factual report. The pantomime also emphasizes Anne's
complicity, which is not at first apparent in the play itself. It
works up to a moment of suspense before the actual murder
takes place. In this way the dumb show fulfils a similar dramatic
function to the previous two unsuccessful attempts on Saunders'
life. There is an effective, if primitive, building up of tension,
working to a climax in the murder scene, and the interruption of
Tragedy, giving a last warning of the murder, only increases
this feeling of impending disaster. The events are artificially
dramatized and the visual effects are most impressive.

[1] Cf. the use of a very similar motive in Webster's *The White Devil*, I, 2.

A similar technique is used when the third dumb show is introduced and explained by Tragedy. Again an allegorical pantomime fills a gap in the plot. Justice and Mercy sit in judgment on the murder-case. The accomplices are brought in and sentenced. Only the murderer himself is missing and Diligence is sent out to find him.[1] This dumb show is also an important part of the plot staged by an allegorical pantomime and omitted in the dialogue. The transition is perhaps less abrupt in this case because the plot is immediately continued on a different level. In the following scene we see the murderer actually arrested and led away by the officers of the court in Rochester. Thus a part of the plot is telescoped and the play gains in dramatic speed; at the same time the events are presented and interpreted as a moral lesson.

With the help of these inserted dumb shows the play is also divided into logical units. Although the term 'Act' is not used, the play is made to fall into four parts. The sphere of realistic events and that of moral exegesis are kept distinctly apart. From the actual play we learn little of what the characters are thinking or of the motives for their actions. There is hardly any reflection in the spoken scenes, and the few scattered monologues contribute little to a deeper understanding of the characters. This function is taken over by the pantomimes.

The structure of the tragedy is thus considerably influenced by the dumb shows. The dramatist hardly ever 'burdens' the speeches and dialogue with the explanation of motives. Attempts to convince somebody or to change someone's mind are almost completely absent because this inner dimension of the plot is not dealt with in the actual play. Thus the playwright's technique becomes rather simple. Realistic tragedy and instructive morality alternate in a way not unlike the technique of 'fading in' in films. This is also reflected in the title of the play, which points to its didactic intention while the subtitle describes the factual content.[2] The contrast between the two spheres makes itself felt even in the diction. Tragedy's explanations of the dumb

---

[1] This dumb show is quoted in Appendix II.

[2] *A Warning for Faire Women. Containing, the most tragicall and lamentable murther of Master George Sanders of London Marchant, nigh Shooters hill. Consented vnto By his owne wife, acted by M. Browne, Mistris Drewry and Trusty Roger agents therein with there seuerall ends.*

shows are in their style completely different from the conversations between Brown and Anne Drury. The emphasis in the former is on the moral and didactic aspects, the vocabulary is characterized by abstract nouns and adjectives. There are sententious generalizations and rhetorical periods so that the tone of these speeches stands out in contrast against the scenes of dialogue.[1] Thus, for instance, Tragedy begins her exposition of the third dumb show with a general moralizing sentence:

> Thus lawles actions and prodigious crimes
> Drinke not the bloud alone of them they hate,
> But euen their ministers, when they haue done
> Al that they can, must help to fil the Sceane,
> And yeeld their guilty neckes vnto the blocke.

This is of course very like the style of some crude morality and appropriate for these allegorical mimes, but it is quite different from the factual language of the dialogue, in which only the present situation is discussed without any concern for its general application.

In hardly any other Elizabethan play are the connections between dumb show and morality so obvious and the inner conflicts so clearly separated from the actual dramatic plot. Here we see something of the unconcerned way in which Elizabethan dramatists exploited the most diversified elements of style in order to achieve novel and startling effects. The play combines the sensational and topical with the didactic and moral. All the apparent realism of the dialogue scenes and the whole plot cannot disguise that the murder is, above all, meant to be a warning example. The spectator is again and again torn from the world of the play by the figure of Tragedy and reminded of the application of the lesson to his own life. The dumb shows provide an effective balance to the realism of the dialogue scenes and prevent the creation of any lasting illusion on the part of the audience.

It must, however, be noted that the form of allegory used in *A Warning for Fair Women* was already somewhat out of date by

---

[1] 'The murky rhetoric in which Tragedy expounds the meaning of these "Shows" is in uneasy contrast with the homely dialogue of the main action which follows with pedantic closeness the details of the pamphlet which was the dramatist's source.' (F. S. Boas, *An Introduction to Tudor Drama*, pp. 108–9.)

the turn of the century and was not used by more discerning dramatists. New and more subtle ways of pointing the moral for the audience were found and the dumb shows were given other functions, as can be seen in some plays of adventure written about the same time.[1]

ANTHONY MUNDAY: THE ROBIN HOOD PLAYS

One of the earliest examples of the biographical plays of adventure is Anthony Munday's tragedy in two parts about the life and death of Robert, Earl of Huntingdon.[2] As in most plays of this type, no complete, rounded-off development is presented, but a rather loosely connected series of episodes, a kind of historical panorama. The dramatist is obviously more interested in the lively and colourful events than in the psychology of the characters taking part. The structure of the two plays is somewhat diffuse, the divisions into scenes irregular and almost accidental. The mass of subject-matter would be very confusing were it not for the 'presenter' who is particularly necessary here and helps the audience sort out the large number of characters and unravel the plot.

Munday connects the figure of the presenter very skilfully with the rest of the play. The 'frame' within which the whole tragedy takes place portrays the preparations for the performance. The players discuss their parts and the stage directions indicate that the whole scene is to be as natural and vivid as possible. E.g.:

> *At euery doore all the Players runne out, some crying where? where? others welcome sir Iohn, among other the boyes and Clowne.*

Among the players is the poet John Skelton whose job it is to act as interpreter between the play and the audience. After a short conversation he sends the actors off to prepare for the pantomime while he himself remains to explain the initial situation. As in *A Warning for Fair Women*, the silent scene is con-

---

[1] A similar, rather primitive use of dumb shows is to be found in Dekker's early play *The Whore of Babylon* where, however, allegory is not confined to the dumb shows.

[2] *The Downfall of Robert, Earl of Huntingdon*, and *The Death of Robert, Earl of Huntingdon* (*TFT*, 1913).

nected with the play by a presenter and is not placed in isolation
before the first act. It is a vital part of the play and introduces
the audience directly to the somewhat complex historical
situation. It presents a rather detailed scene with several entries
and exits, which only differs from the other scenes of the play by
the absence of dialogue, because those taking part are all
characters from the play itself. Richard's departure for the
crusade, the handing over of the government to Ely, and the
first beginnings of the conspiracy are shown. The emphasis is
not so much on the visual effects, as in most allegorical and
symbolic dumb shows, but on the factual content. What is
presented is a considerable part of the plot and gives the
audience definite information about the individual characters and
their part in the story:

SKELTON: Goe in, and bring your dumbe scene on the stage,
          And I, as Prologue, purpose to expresse
          The ground whereon our historie is laied.

Exeunt, manet Skelton.
*Trumpets sounde, enter first king Richard with drum and Auncient,
giuing Ely a purse and scepter, his mother, and brother Iohn, Chester,
Lester, Lacie, others at the kings appointment doing reuerence. The
king goes in: presently Ely ascends the chaire, Chester, Iohn, and the
Queene part displeasantly. Enter Robert, earle of Huntingdon, leading
Marian, followes him Warman, and after Warman the Prior, Warman euer flattering and making curtsie, taking gifts of the Prior
behinde, and his master before. Prince Iohn enters, offereth to take
Marian. Queene Elinor enters, offering to pull Robin from her; but
they infolde each other, and sit downe within the curteines, Warman
with the Prior, sir Hugh Lacy, Lord Sentloe, & sir Gilbert Broghton
folde hands, and drawing the curtens, all (but the Prior) enter, and
are kindely receiued by Robin Hoode. The curteins are againe shut.*

SKELTON: Sir Iohn, once more, bid your dumbe shewes come in;
          That as they passe I may explane them all.

Thus the play begins with a silent state scene, a historical
pageant, which explains straightaway the whole situation and
introduces the main characters. After Peele's *Battle of Alcazar*
this is one of the first examples of such an introductory use of the
dumb show. The form of the scene shows that the desire to make
it easy for the audience to understand the play was the main
consideration. For, after the pantomime has finished, Skelton

asks the performers to repeat the whole scene again so that he can explain everything at his leisure. The dumb show is therefore acted a second time, divided into short separate scenes, and interrupted by Skelton's description. He gives an involved explanation of everything and introduces each character in turn. This form of exposition is reminiscent of the pageants and other primitive types of drama. It saves the dramatist having to give all these details in the first dialogue scenes. The task of exposition is thus not left to the actual play, but given to the dumb show and presenter, a considerable simplification of dramatic technique. While in later Elizabethan plays the tension of the first scenes often lies in the gradual unfolding of previous events, here the point is clearly to present as much action and movement as can possibly be fitted into a single play with the least technical effort.[1] All important incidents are enacted on the stage in a kind of historical panorama, thus relieving the dialogue considerably, but at the same time weakening it, as we have also noticed in *A Warning for Fair Women*. This technique is of course the exact opposite to that of classical tragedy where all incidents are translated into epic reports or declamation. For instance, John's wicked passion for Marian and that of his mother for Robert are only hinted at in eloquent gestures, not gradually revealed in dialogue scenes. The dramatist does not describe the gradual growth of such an emotion. Rather he represents it in symbolic form and later in his play shows its effect on the plot. We have here the same tendency as in *A Warning for Fair Women*, to portray mental processes and inner developments in terms of outward gestures and actions. The play is not concerned with the deeper thoughts and feelings of the characters taking part, but only with their colourful adventures and careers. The characterization is extremely primitive and flat. Monologues of reflection or persuasive dialogue are lacking almost completely. The spectator is not, as in Shakespeare's plays, made to understand and to sympathize with the various characters, each with his own distinct personality, but is only to be diverted by their exciting fate.

This new attitude of the dramatist to his subject-matter is shown particularly clearly by the manner in which the play is

[1] Cf. I. R. Green, *The Development of a Technique of Exposition in the English Drama* 1588–94 (Unpublished Dissertation, New York, 1935).

concluded and the second part introduced. The first part ends with a general reconciliation after Richard's return home. Skelton, however, announces the continuation of the history up to Robert's death. It is Skelton again who introduces the second play, *The Death of Robert, Earl of Huntingdon*, and, by his explanations, connects it with the previous one. Once more an epic report, this time without a dumb show, is substituted for a dramatic exposition. Apparently, however, the material was not sufficient for a complete second play, so that Skelton, when after Robert's death he is about to ask the audience's pardon for the brief performance, is interrupted by Chester and asked to present the remainder of Mathilda's fate as well:

> Nay Fryer, at request of thy kinde friend,
> Let not thy Play so soone be at end.
> Though Robin Hoode be deade, his yeomen gone,
> And that thou thinkst there now remaines not one,
> To act another Sceane or two for thee:
> Yet knowe full well, to please this company,
> We meane to end Mathildaes Tragedie.

The tragedy is only complete when all the main characters are dead. This passage, quite impossible in classical drama, shows clearly how author and audience are chiefly interested in the bare plot of the play. The apparently improvised conversation about the continuation of the performance makes the scene appear rather informal and life-like.

At this point in the play a completely new beginning is made. Skelton invokes the Muses and announces a tragedy of calamity and mourning. A Chorus in black enters and a dialogue follows in which, again by means of extensive accounts, a long development is summarized, and the illusion is created that the audience is experiencing the making of a new play. In the course of the dialogue Skelton's explanations are supplemented by the Chorus. Here it is also noticeable that the language of the prologue is different in tone from that of the rest of the play. There is plenty of moralizing. The simple rhymes and the prolix style bring to mind some of the older moralities while the florid rhetoric tries to imitate classical drama. Here, as in many Elizabethan plays, the prologue and dumb show follow older conventions while the play proper tries to explore new ways. The 'frame' seems

H   99

archaic in comparison with the rest of the play, an impression confirmed by the following dumb shows which, by means of three visions, illustrate John's state of mind.

In Lyly's *Endimion* we have already seen how a dream was visibly presented on the stage in the form of a pantomime and thus clearly elevated to another sphere so that it stands out from the dialogue scenes. The same applies here. The characters appearing are meant to come from some other world. In John's first vision Austria and Ambition enter, and historical events are presented in allegoric form. The pantomime is similar to those in *A Warning for Fair Women* where allegoric figures appear together with characters from the play itself. Here, however, it is not inner conflicts and decisions which are made visible in pantomimic form, but historical events which are abridged. In this way the dramatist manages to skip over longer periods of time and to take for granted the audience's knowledge of certain situations without having to give a detailed account of them. It was particularly in history plays that this possibility was used because the wealth of material often forced the dramatist to look for a briefer method of presentation than that of elaborate dialogue scenes.[1]

The second vision is very similar. It also summarizes a long development in a brief scene and again an allegoric figure (Insurrection) appears which reminds one of the moralities and shows how long such elements still kept their place in English drama, although by the turn of the century they were hardly to be found in dialogue scenes any more:

> *Enter Constance, leading young Arthur: both offer to take the crowne; but with his foote he ouerturneth them: to them commeth Insurrection, ledde by the F.K. and L. menacing him, and lead the childe againe to the chaire: but he only layeth hand on his sworde, and with his foote ouerthroweth the childe, whome they take vp as deade: and Insurrection flying, they mournefully beare in the bodie.*

SKELTON: The Ladie and the childe that did ascend,
Striuing in vaine to take the crowne from Iohn,
Were Constance, and her sonne the Duke of Britaine,
Heire to the elder brother of the king.[2]

---

[1] Cf. M. C. Bradbrook, op. cit., pp. 36 and 44.
[2] See Shakespeare's completely different handling of the same story in *King John*.

The third vision is of a different kind from the two previous ones: it does not advance the plot, but rather throws light on John's state of mind. His passion for Mathilda makes him see imaginary figures; the visionary character of the apparition is underlined by the fact that John tries in vain to address her while the courtier standing nearby can see nothing:

> . . . *Enter Matilda, in mourning vaile, reading on a booke, at whose comming he starteth, and sitteth vpright: as shee passeth by, hee smiles, and foldeth his armes, as if hee did embrace her; being gone, he starts sodainly, and speakes.*

KING: Matilda, stay Matilda, doe but speake:
Whoes there? Intreate Matilda to come backe.

This pantomime brings a new sphere within the scope of drama, the presentation of something which only takes place in the imagination of some character on the stage. The spectator can thus take a look into his inner being and learn more than the other characters in the play. The pantomime carries out a function which was otherwise frequently fulfilled by the mono-logue. Visual intensification is achieved at the expense of dramatic speech.

Thus the three dumb shows present the historical situation and at the same time describe John's state of mind. Both functions are necessary for an understanding of the following tragedy. The pantomime is above all a technical means of managing an abundance of subject-matter and has no essentially dramatic function. In neither of the two plays do the dumb shows contribute anything which could not be achieved by other dramatic means. On the whole, therefore, they have a detrimental effect on the dramatic technique and help make the play appear extremely primitive. The dialogue is usually without tension because it only develops external events and neither creates a dramatic exposition nor reveals anything about the characters taking part.

Through dramatists like Anthony Munday the dumb show became an easy way out wherever the management and dramatic structure of the plot became difficult for the playwright. This applies to almost all those plays which do not deal with a clearly defined story, but in which a series of episodes and adventures follow one upon the other. Dumb show is employed particularly frequently in such plays, but in many cases its use is so simple and unoriginal that we need not discuss each of these works in detail. It is, I think, sufficient to mention one or two characteristic examples.

'CAPTAIN THOMAS STUKELEY'

Captain Thomas Stukeley belongs to a group of popular plays about the fantastic adventures of brave and daring Englishmen in various parts of the earth.[1] These plays are characterized by a large number of lively scenes, colourful processions, and spirited battles. The stage directions indicate that the performance must have been a rather loud and varied spectacle.[2] The spoken word often seems of secondary importance because all the main events are shown on the stage, not merely reported. Here also the pantomime was a convenient and suitable means of accommodating large sections of the plot.

The play falls into two parts, of which the first shows the rise of the hero and the second his fall. The gap in the plot is bridged by a chorus which gives a detailed report and introduces a lengthy pantomime.[3] In it we see how Stukeley, contrary to his original plans, makes up his mind to go with Sebastian to fight the Turks, eventually meeting his death in the battle of Alcazar:

> *Enter at one doore Phillip King of spaine, Alua and souldiors they take their stand: then Enter another way, sebastian, Don Antonio, Avero with drumes and ensines they likewise take their stande. After some pawse Antonio is sent forth to Phillip, who with obeysance done approching away againe very disdainfully: and as the spanish souldiors are about to follow Antonio Phillip with his drawn sword stops them and so departs. Whereat sebastian makes showe of great displeasure, but whispering with his lords each incoraging other as they are about to depart. Enter stukly and his Italian band: who keping aloof, sebastian sends Antonio to him, with whom stukley drawes neere towarde the king, and hauing awhile conferd, at last retirs to his souldiors, to*

---

[1] *TFT* (1911). Heywood's *The Four Prentices of London*, J. Day's *The Travails of the Three English Brothers* and R. Daborne's *A Christian turned Turk* belong to the same type. Cf. Appendix I.

[2] For instance: *Alarum is sounded, diuers excurtions, Stukly persues, shane Oneale, and Neale Mackener, And after a good pretty fight his Lieftenannt and Auntient rescue Stuklie, and chace the Ireshe out.*

[3] Cf. the similar structure of Shakespeare's *Winter's Tale* where, however, no pantomime is used.

whom he makes show of perswading them to ioyn with the portugeese: at first they seeme to mislike but last they yeelde and so both armie meeting imbrace when with a sudden Thunder-clap the sky is one fire and the blazing star appears which they prognosticating to be fortunat departed very ioyfull.

The action in the pantomime is different from most earlier examples because we are presented with typical dialogue situations, which are of course not very effective in a dumb show. While the majority of earlier dumb shows only contained obvious incidents and gestures, here we have silent consultation and persuasion. Stukeley's decision, which finally leads him to his end, is hardly substantiated; thus a turning point in the plot loses much of its effect. The play merely dramatizes the biographical details without making any attempt to reveal much about Stukeley's personality. Everything is presented in terms of picture and movement even when the material is most unsuitable for this kind of presentation. The dumb show only consists of a series of brief separate scenes and does not achieve any striking visual effect, except, perhaps, for the appearance of the 'blazing star'. The principle that the dumb shows should show *tableaux* or processions which would probably be less effective in a spoken scene is here abandoned. The pantomime is much more like an ordinary scene, only lacking dialogue. In this way it is of course closely connected with the play itself, but it also loses its characteristic quality and seems somewhat out of place, because its function could be much better fulfilled by a dialogue scene. Such a haphazard use of diverse technical devices is typical of popular Elizabethan drama in which the main consideration was often to bring a well-known and perhaps topical story on to the stage as quickly as possible; little attention seems to have been paid to the way in which this was done. The dumb show thus became a device which could certainly make the playwright's job easier. *Captain Thomas Stukeley* is a particularly good example of how indiscriminately pantomimes were often employed in these popular plays of adventure.

'THE WEAKEST GOETH TO THE WALL'

As far as its structure is concerned, this play is very similar to the ones we have dealt with so far in this chapter, although the plot is of a slightly different kind.[1] It belongs to a group of romantic plays of adventure in which members of a family are torn apart and then, after long wanderings and dangerous misunderstandings, are united again. The play has a certain coherence because only the last part of the history is dealt with while the first part is merely shown in a pantomime. There is no presenter to announce the pantomime, but a prologue in which the events are briefly related. Thus a long time-gap in the play itself is unnecessary and what happens in it could take place in a few weeks or months.

The play begins immediately with the dumb show:

> *A dombe showe.*
> *After an Alarum, enter one way the Duke of Burgundie, an other way, the Duke of Aniou with his power, they encounter, Burgundie is slaine. Then enter the Dutches of Burgundie with young Fredericke in her hand, who being pursued of the French, leaps into a Riuer, leauing the child vpon the banke, who is presently found by the duke of Brabant, who came to aid Burgundie, when it was too late.*

The pantomime presents the moment of separation to which the play, in a way, returns. Only characters from the play take part, although they are several years younger than in the main play. Thus the pantomime is an indispensable part of the play because its content is necessary to explain the following complications; it is repeated at the end in narrative form. Only then do the characters concerned learn about the family relationship, whereas the spectators have this knowledge from the beginning. Without the pantomime the audience would remain in the dark about these basic facts until the very end, and the play would make much less sense to them. The dumb show is here far more skilfully used than in *Captain Thomas Stukeley* because it does not break the continuity of the play, but rather contributes to it. It shows a scene which is rightly detached from the main play and serves as a lively prologue to it.

THOMAS HEYWOOD

Most of Thomas Heywood's plays are also of the popular entertaining type and he, too, uses dumb shows as an easy way

---

[1] *Malone Soc.* (1912). Cf. also Mary L. Hunt, *Thomas Dekker* (New York, 1911), pp. 42 ff.

of managing his often rather extensive plots.[1] However, he selects the scenes to be presented as pantomimes far more skilfully than do many of his contemporaries. Thus, for instance, in the early play *The Four Prentices of London* a presenter appears after the departure of the four brothers from home and with the help of four dumb shows explains where the shipwreck has driven them.[2] The following parts of the play in which the fate of each brother is pursued individually seem therefore much clearer and more comprehensible than they would otherwise have been.

In the two historical plays *If You Know Not Me, You Know Nobody*, two elaborate state scenes and a dream of Queen Elizabeth, that is, scenes particularly suitable for silent presentation, are staged as dumb shows. An example is Elizabeth's vision which, we are to understand, is visible only to the queen and not to her attendant. The dumb show is rather like John's dreams in *The Death of Robert, Earl of Huntingdon*. It is particularly interesting for its resemblance to the pageant of 1558, quoted in the first chapter:

> *A dumb show.*
> *Enter Winchester, Constable, Barwick, and Fryars: at the other dore 2. Angels: the Fryar steps to her, offering to kill her: the Angels driues them back. Exeunt. The Angel opens the Bible, and puts it in her hand as she sleepes, Exeunt Angels, she wakes.*
>
> ELIZABETH: O God, how pleasant was this sleepe to me!
> Clarentia, saw'st thou nothing? (Part I, Sc.XIV)

She finds the Bible in her hand, opened at some appropriate passage.

Heywood employs dumb shows particularly frequently, however, in the so-called *Ages*. These plays attempt, following undoubtedly the popular drama of adventure and the tragicomedy which had just then become fashionable,[3] to present in

---

[1] The best and most complete edition is still that of R. H. Shepherd (London, 1874), in six volumes.

[2] Cf. the passage quoted above, p. 23.

[3] Cf. Chapter 11. On the *Ages* cf. A. M. Clark, *Thomas Heywood* (Oxford, 1931), pp. 222-3; C. W. Hodges, *The Globe Restored*, pp. 74 ff.; Ernest Schanzer, 'Heywood's "Ages" and Shakespeare', *RES, NS*, XI (1960), pp. 18-28. Dr Schanzer suggests that the dumb shows were inspired by those in Shakespeare's *Pericles*.

dramatic form the whole field of Greek myths about Gods and heroes, from the fight of the Titans down to the destruction of Troy. As in the historical and biographical plays, the structure in the *Ages* is clearly epic. The plot is a long string of episodes and does not attempt to rise to any climax, nor does it even present a continuous development. As in Shakespeare's *Pericles*, each act is introduced by a chorus-figure (Homer) and the story is several times helped along by a pantomime. Thus a kind of 'frame' is established and pauses are inserted between the acts. The plot unfolds in single sections which are divided by explanations and, in most cases, by dumb shows. In *The Silver Age*, for instance, a completely new episode, usually even a new set of characters, is dealt with in each act. The play contains the legends of Perseus, Amphitryon, Hercules, Semele, and Persephone. Homer provides the transitions and introduces the new characters by means of a dumb show. Thus we almost get the impression of seeing five complete one-act plays, each opened by a prologue and a pantomime. In the second act, for example, the whole history of Amphitryon is staged. The dumb show enables the dramatist to compress the story into one brief act. The opening situation is described in a few words and the pantomime serves as an exposition:

HOMER: Lend vs your wonted patience without scorne,
        To finde how Hercules was got and borne.

> *Enter Amphitrio with two Captaines and Socia with drum and colours: hee brings in the head of a crowned King, sweares the Lords to the obeysance of Thebes. They present him with a standing bowle, which hee lockes in a casket, and sending his man with a letter before to his wife, with news of his victory. He with his followers, and Blepharo the maister of the ship, marcheth after.*

This is followed by a detailed explanation by Homer and a dramatic version of the further developments. The next act tells the story of Hercules' birth and his first heroic deeds.

The use of the pantomime to manage an excessive mass of subject-matter can be found in a whole series of plays, usually of a rather popular and primitive kind. In some of them, as in *The Four Prentices of London*, the audience is asked to pardon this method of accelerating time, as for instance in the later play *Herod and Antipater* by Markham and Sampson:

Let mee now
Intreat your worthy Patience, to containe
Much in Imagination; and, what Words
Cannot haue time to vtter; let your Eyes
Out of this dumbe shew, tell your Memories.[1]

The same excuse is made in Heywood's *Brazen Age* before the
fifth act, where Homer says:

Our last Act comes, which lest it tedious grow,
What is too long in word, accept in show.

The extensive use and the long popularity of this type of dumb
show with many different dramatists seem to suggest that the
audience did not take offence at such requests for indulgence and
enjoyed such pantomimes.

We have seen how in the popular plays of legendary heroes
and adventure the pantomime was less bound to any definite
form than before. It can be part of a prologue, occur between the
acts, or be used within a dialogue scene. In this way the dumb
shows became a generally available technical device which every
playwright could use and vary as he liked. Their use is no longer
confined to a certain type of play: they are found in serious
plays as well as in tragicomedies. The fact that the dumb show
could take on so many different functions accounts for its wide
use by Elizabethan dramatists.

However, all the dumb shows dealt with in this chapter have
in common the fact that they are directly connected with the
plot of the play in which they occur and often contain quite an
important part of it. Most of the characters in them are the same
as those in the play and there is no longer a striking contrast
between the two levels of action. Thus the dumb shows had

[1] Gervase Markham and William Sampson, *The true Tragedy of Herod
and Antipater* (London, 1622). Two of the four dumb shows present visions
of a more symbolic kind, which confirm Antipater in his wicked plans (Cf.
Appendix I and II). The other two dumb shows serve to telescope parts of
the play's plot.

Similar pantomimes which summarize parts of the action can be found in
B. Barnes' *The Devil's Charter*, R. Daborne's *A Christian turned Turk*,
J. Day's *The Travails of the Three English Brothers*, Heywood's *The Fair
Maid of the West* and *A Maidenhead Well Lost*, and in the anonymous plays
The Valiant Welshman, *The Bloody Banquet*, *The Two Noble Ladies*.
Cf. Appendix I for a list of these plays.

become an organic part of the play and even more careful and critical dramatists did not hesitate to make use of them. The following chapters are therefore concerned with the work of individual playwrights and their special contribution to the development of the dumb show.

7

William Shakespeare

In considering Shakespeare's plays one is struck by the fact
that there are so few dumb shows in them, only about six in all,
if we do not count the more transitional forms. It is particularly
interesting to see that no pantomimes are to be found in any
of his earlier plays which in other respects show the marked influence of the 'University Wits' and *The Spanish Tragedy*. The
only exception is *A Midsummer Night's Dream* and here, too,
the dumb show is very unlike any of the earlier forms. What
makes it so original is the fact that it is part of a play performed
within the drama and as such seems to imply a certain negative
criticism of the whole convention of the dumb show. This in
turn connects it with *Hamlet* where the pantomime serves a
rather similar purpose.

'A MIDSUMMER NIGHT'S DREAM'

The pantomime in this play is not explicitly described and can
therefore only be conjectured from the text. I feel, however,
fairly certain that the play performed by the craftsmen was to
be preceded by a brief dumb show in which the plot of the play
was acted while the Prologue gave his account of it. Hamlet's
scornful criticism of the players who 'must tell all' would be
particularly appropriate here because the substance of the play
is told in some detail before the actual performance begins.
When Quince introduces the actors with his:

> The Actors are at hand; and by their show,
> You shall know all, that you are like to know.

this could of course refer to a mere procession round the stage
in the manner of popular drama, but the following prologue
sounds in places very much like a description of a pantomime
performed at the same time:

> Gentles, perchance you wonder at this show,
> But wonder on, till truth make all things plaine.

One by one the characters are introduced and the main events in which they are to be involved are outlined:

> Anon comes Piramus, sweet youth and tall,
> And findes his Thisbies Mantle slaine;
> Whereat, with blade, with bloody blamefull blade,
> He brauely broacht his boiling bloudy breast,

Assuming that here the action is anticipated in the pantomime as well as in the prologue,[1] we can say that this is the only play before *Hamlet* in which dumb show is used with this function. As in *Hamlet*, this repetition of the plot could be explained as a conscious attempt to make the spectator familiar with the content of the play before it actually begins so that he is free to give more of his attention to the spectators on the stage who comment on the performance. At the same time the clumsy habit many popular dramatists had of introducing a play by a lengthy and circumstantial pantomime is effectively satirized. Shakespeare does not use the dumb show 'in earnest', but employs it to characterize the crude dramatic style of the craftsmen. His own brilliant handling of various contrasting modes in this play is only emphasized by this inclusion of a more primitive technique which considerably widens the range of the comedy and is cleverly set off against the high-flown rhetoric of the lovers and the fairy world of Oberon and Puck. Thus the pantomime in *A Midsummer Night's Dream* has much in common with that in *Hamlet* which we must now consider.

'HAMLET'

Of all the dumb shows in Elizabethan drama the one performed before the court of Elsinore is by far the most famous and most frequently discussed. Its form and its function within the whole play has been the subject of much scholarly argument and contro-

---

[1] As far as I know Theobald was the first to suggest this. J. D. Wilson makes the same assumption in his edition (Cambridge, 1924). See also the editions by F. C. Horwood (*The New Clarendon Shakespeare*, Oxford, 1939) and W. Clemen (*The Signet Classic Shakespeare*, New York, 1963), pp. 112–13.

versy,[1] but comparatively few studies have taken into account the earlier dumb shows. I do not propose here to discuss all the problems posed by this intriguing scene, nor do I really wish to add another variety to the large and ever growing number of existing interpretations, but it is perhaps possible to indicate in what manner Shakespeare took over and modified the tradition of the dumb show and what conclusions can be drawn from this for our understanding of the play scene.

First of all the pantomime has to be seen as part of the play which it precedes and introduces.[2] It has often been remarked how skilfully *The Murder of Gonzago* is in its style differentiated from and contrasted to the main play.[3] Its language is highly stylized and epigrammatic, as is emphasized by the jingling rhymes. There are hardly any run-on lines; each line or couplet seems to be a unit in itself, again reminding one of pre-Shakespearean drama. Everything is said in a rather general and impersonal manner; hardly any names of characters or places are mentioned and there is no proper exposition. In the speeches there is often a deliberate play on certain pairs of words (love – fear; joy – grief; love – fortune),[4] a liberal use of rhetoric 'figures', and some archaic vocabulary. This peculiarity of style is of course emphasized by Hamlet's prose comments, which very clearly mark the sharp contrast between the two planes of action and heighten the tension of the scene effectively. The language of this inserted play recalls in many ways Shakespeare's early comedies, strongly influenced by Euphuism, while Hamlet's prose in comparison sounds rather down to earth and

[1] See especially the editions by H. H. Furness (*New Variorum*, Philadelphia, 1877), E. Dowden (*Arden*, London, 1899), A. W. Verity (Cambridge, 1904), J. Q. Adams (Boston, 1929), J. D. Wilson (Cambridge, 1934), G. Rylands (*New Clarendon*, Oxford, 1947), L. L. Schücking (English and German, Wiesbaden, 1949). The most important studies of the play scene are quoted in the following footnotes.

[2] This is also suggested by Pearn who does not, however, go into any detail. His results have several times been referred to. Cf. Moody E. Prior, 'The Play Scene in *Hamlet*', *ELH*, IX (1942), pp. 188–97, and W. W. Lawrence, 'Hamlet and the Mouse-Trap', *PMLA*, LIV (1939), pp. 709–35.

[3] Cf. M. C. Bradbrook, op. cit., p. 103; L. L. Schücking, op. cit., pp. 400 ff.; H. Granville-Barker, *Prefaces to Shakespeare* (London, 1958), pp. 84 ff.

[4] See Harry Levin, *The Question of Hamlet* (New York, 1959), pp. 49 ff.

unrefined. This pointed contrast is not only a help to the audience in the theatre, who can thus more easily distinguish the play within the play from the tragedy itself, but it also stresses the somewhat antiquated character of the performance, which is clearly meant to come as from some earlier period and is thus further removed from the audience in the theatre. In this way it becomes apparent that throughout the scene Hamlet, Claudius and the Court are spectators and that their reactions are for us just as important as the inserted play itself.

The dumb show is part of this performance and it serves by its strange character to distinguish the play from the rest of the scene.[1] Whereas in *Hamlet* it is mainly the indirect and round-about way of acting and talking which is so typical of the tone and style of the play,[2] *The Murder of Gonzago* is characterized by directness and lack of ambiguity, especially in the primitive and straightforward pantomime. At first sight it seems to be anything but 'inexplicable'. There is no allegorical and symbolic disguise as in the older dumb shows. A lengthy story in several movements is presented. It is perhaps worth noting that in the second Quarto and in the Folio only general terms are used for the characters (*a king, a queen, a fellow*), while the first Quarto is more specific and mentions Lucianus' name.[3] It seems probable, however, that the characters in the dumb show were – presumably by their costumes – clearly identified with those in the play itself. In the dumb show they introduce themselves by some typical gestures and mime the plot of the whole play that is to follow. Even some less important details, like the protestations of the queen, are here anticipated.[4] I quote the text of the Folio:

[1] This is emphasized by W. W. Lawrence. Cf. 'Hamlet and the Mouse-Trap'.

[2] Polonius' expression 'by indirections find directions out' is, in an ironic way, rather typical of the play's dramatic style. It characterizes not only Polonius, but Claudius and Hamlet as well. For Hamlet the whole performance of the actors is such an 'indirection'.

[3] On the different versions see J. D. Wilson, *The Manuscript of Shakespeare's 'Hamlet' and the Problems of its Transmission* (Cambridge, 1934).

[4] An exact comparison is, of course, impossible as only part of the play is actually performed. The rest has to be gathered from Hamlet's hints and from the dumb show. It is interesting to see that, as in some plays of adventure (e.g. *Captain Thomas Stukeley*), typical dialogue situations are presented in the pantomime, like the wooing of the poisoner.

William Shakespeare

Hoboyes play. The dumbe shew enters.
Enter a King and Queene, very louingly; the Queene embracing him.
She kneeles, and makes shew of Protestation vnto him. He takes her vp,
and declines his head vpon her neck. Layes him downe vpon a Banke of
Flowers. She seeing him asleepe, leaues him. Anon comes in a Fellow,
takes off his Crowne, kisses it, and powres poyson in the Kings eares,
and Exits.
The Queene returnes, findes the King dead, and makes passionate
Action. The Poysoner, with some two or three Mutes comes in againe,
seeming to lament with her. The dead body is carried away: The
Poysoner Wooes the Queene with Gifts, she seemes loath and vnwilling
awhile, but in the end, accepts his loue. Exeunt.

It has rightly been claimed that there are no other examples of this directly anticipatory use of the dumb show in Elizabethan drama.[1] There are, of course, many plays where the content of the dumb show is repeated in the dialogue, but in all these the dumb show is allegorical or symbolic and does not exactly anticipate the particular plot of the play. This new form of pantomime can be accounted for by the fact that here dumb show and play are themselves parts of a very complex drama. To make the pantomime allegorical might have detracted too much from the actual play and puzzled the spectators unnecessarily. Instead it contributes to the effect of the play within the play by drawing the attention of the audience to its plot, that plot which is Hamlet's means of probing the conscience of the king. At the same time this rather clumsy and long drawn-out introduction delays the beginning of the actual performance and thus heightens the dramatic tension, not only for Hamlet, who eagerly waits for the play to begin, but also for the audience, which expects something decisive to happen soon. Here again, as in many other scenes of *Hamlet*, delay and suspense are deliberately employed as structural devices.[2]

[1] The only exception seems to be *A Midsummer Night's Dream*. Cf. J. D. Wilson, *What Happens in Hamlet* (Cambridge, 1951), pp. 145-6; L. L. Schücking, op. cit., p. 403; S. L. Bethell, *Shakespeare and the Popular Dramatic Tradition* (London, 1944), pp. 158 ff.; E. Th. Sehrt, op. cit., pp. 21 ff., and the excellent chapter on *Hamlet* in A. Righter, op. cit., pp. 154 ff.

[2] Cf. W. Clemen, 'Zum Verständnis des Werkes' in his edition of *Hamlet* (*Rowohlts Klassiker*, Hamburg, 1957), p. 242.

The previous chapters have shown that it is not quite true, as is sometimes said, that dumb shows were already out of fashion by the time *Hamlet* was written.[1] On the contrary, they were still enjoying an ever increasing popularity. It must, however, be admitted that they had by the turn of the century almost completely disappeared from more refined plays and were mainly to be found in the type of popular drama that is ridiculed by Hamlet. Only after *Hamlet* were they used again by more ambitious dramatists like Marston, Webster, and Middleton. In *Hamlet* the dumb show contributes to the archaic tone of the play and associates it with those popular hack-plays to which Hamlet in his address to the players takes exception. In its form, the dumb show, though immediately intelligible, is very like some of those 'inexplicable dumb shows', scathingly referred to by Hamlet, and his comments during the performance make clear that he does not think very much of it. As part of the play which it precedes, the pantomime, then, does not serve any useful purpose and is in this respect similar to some of the earlier examples. Within the context of the whole tragedy, however, it is extremely important and has a very definite function.

This, of course, applies to the whole drama of Gonzago. On the surface it is just another of those courtly entertainments so frequent in Elizabethan plays.[2] At the same time, however, it is part of Hamlet's revenge or at least preliminary to it. The main purpose of the performance is to achieve an immediate and visible effect on the spectators in the Danish court. It seems certain that for most Elizabethans the stage was a kind of moral institution and the drama was expected to produce visible results.[3] The play scene derives its particular effect and tension from the fact that here the moral purpose of drama is deliberately exploited and that actors and spectators are on the stage simul-

---

[1] Cf. the edition of J. Q. Adams, pp. 264–5, and L. L. Schücking, *The Meaning of Hamlet* (Oxford, 1937), p. 128. For the opposite opinion cf. J. D. Wilson, *What Happens in Hamlet*, pp. 146–7.

[2] Cf. Kyd's *Spanish Tragedy* and Marston's *The Malcontent*.

[3] Cf. M. C. Bradbrook, op. cit., p. 75:'the drama had not only a general moral purpose; immediate results were expected'. See also M. Doran, *Endeavors of Art* (Madison, 1954), pp. 93 ff. On the play within the play see Wolfgang Iser, 'Das Spiel im Spiel. Formen dramatischer Illusion bei Shakespeare', *Archiv*, 198 (1961–2), pp. 209–26, and my article quoted above in the introduction, pp. 143 ff.

taneously. In no other play before *Hamlet* is the relationship between audience and play so effectively portrayed and made the subject of a dramatic scene as it is here.[1] This relationship alone connects the play and the dumb show very closely with the rest of the tragedy.

The content of the play, too, is skilfully fitted into the whole tragedy. In *Hamlet*, as in the so-called 'analytic drama' of Ibsen and his followers, an important event (the murder of King Hamlet) has taken place before the actual play begins. This event, although it is the cause of all the ensuing complications, is at first only reported by the ghost, but so ambiguously that Hamlet's doubts as to the ghost's trustworthiness have even been shared by modern critics.[2] The ghost's story, however, is the strongest impulse behind Hamlet's actions and behind his reaction towards the environment. A large part of the play is occupied by his efforts to find out what really happened and how far the ghost is to be trusted.[3] Thus the exposition of the play has not given us a reliable account of all the antecedents of the plot or, conversely, the exposition takes up more than the first half of the play because only in the third act is the murder of old Hamlet established as an undeniable fact. It is therefore important that what at first was only reported by the ghost should now be visibly presented in some detail in the pantomime.[4] The audience is thus most forcefully reminded of the play's real issue and Hamlet's obsession. The following play describes for the third time the murder, or at least part of it, so that the poisoning can be truly called a *leitmotif* which is stressed by the lan-

[1] A rather similar though exaggerated situation is portrayed in Massinger's *The Roman Actor*. There is a famous description of how a murderess was moved to betray herself by a play in *A Warning for Fair Women* (H 2, *recto*).

[2] Cf. W. W. Greg, 'Hamlet's Hallucination', *MLR*, XII (1917), pp. 393–421.

[3] See R. A. Foakes, '*Hamlet* and the Court of Elsinore', *ShS*, 9 (1956), pp. 35–43: 'Hamlet has to fight continually to see what lies behind appearances, behind the court formality, in order to find out the truth about his father's death' (p. 42).

[4] Cf. C. J. Sisson, 'The Mouse-Trap Again', *RES*, XVI (1940), pp. 129–36. The pantomime is described as 'flash-back'. This is how it appears to the spectator, although the murder acted is that of Gonzago, not of Hamlet's father.

guage and imagery of the play.[1] The pantomime also indirectly points to the king's guilt, which during the first part of the play is only vaguely presented, but from the prayer-scene onwards is more in the centre of the play.

This method of describing the murder several times and in different ways is typical of the manner in which events are presented from different angles in this play. Just as the forward and resolute Laertes is presented as a foil to the reflective and hesitating prince, so the main part of the tragedy, slow-moving and many-sided, is contrasted with the swift and direct *Murder of Gonzago*, in which a similar plot without any deeper motivation is acted by itinerant players who have nothing to do with the characters in *Hamlet* and are completely ignorant of the real significance of their play. The spectators, too, vary in the depth of their perception. The King and Gertrud recognize their own guilt in this performance, for the Court it is only a harmless amusement whose real meaning remains obscure, while Hamlet and, with less insight, Horatio, pay more attention to the reaction of the King than to the play itself, which for them is only a means to an end and has no value as an entertainment.

It is easy to see that some very conventional devices have here, with consummate craftsmanship, been adapted and integrated. Dumb show and drama are on the one hand very sharply contrasted, but at the same time closely linked; the one throws light on the other. The pantomime is seen and commented on from different angles, Hamlet acting as a kind of presenter in a way typical of him and his part in the tragedy. For him, as some of his ambiguous replies to Ophelia reveal, the play of Gonzago is not the only performance whose meaning is obscure. His answer to her, 'You are as good as a chorus, my lord,' shows that for him many of his fellow-creatures are 'puppets', like the actors. However, he hardly ever provides a direct explanation of the performance and the audience in the theatre can probably make as little of his cryptic remarks as can the Court of Elsinore. The other characters, too, do little to illuminate the play; rather they detract our attention from it and direct it at the spectators on the stage, whose response is more important for the development of the tragedy than is the performance.

[1] Cf. W. Clemen, *The Development of Shakespeare's Imagery* (London, 1951), pp. 112 ff.

Ophelia's puzzled reaction to the pantomime indicates that its significance was not immediately obvious to an Elizabethan audience. Her enquiry, 'What meanes this, my lord?' is, from all we know about previous dumb shows, perfectly justified, because it was by no means clear from the dumb show what kind of play was to follow. Her tentative guess, 'Belike this show imports the argument of the play', may be intended as a hint for the audience, but neither Ophelia nor the King can be certain that the play will only be a more elaborate repetition of the same incident. E. Dowden was one of the first to see this[1] and some critics have drawn far-reaching conclusions from it, especially M. E. Prior, who, recognizing the unusual form of the dumb show, suggested that it was deliberately employed by Hamlet to deceive the King and lull him into a sense of false security because he would, after seeing the dumb show, assume that the play itself would take quite a different turn.[2] This interpretation seems to me rather far-fetched and perhaps over-ingenious, crediting Hamlet with more subtle cunning than is warranted by the text, but it is quite true that probably no contemporary spectator would have been surprised to hear Claudius ask about the argument of the play after the dumb show. Without an explanatory prologue or presenter – Hamlet's commentaries as presenter do not in any way contribute to the enlightenment of the audience – the significance of the pantomime for the play that is to follow could not be immediately intelligible.[3]

---

[1] 'The King, on the other hand, does not recognize in the dumb-show the argument . . . he might suppose that the dumb-show presented, in English fashion, action which was not to be developed through dialogue.' (Op. cit., p. 116.)

When Ophelia uses the word argument this could as well apply to an allegorical presentation of the plot. Claudius, however, wants to know the exact plot. In this connection it is particularly interesting to turn to the play scene in Middleton's *Women Beware Women* where the King is watching the play with a written 'argument' in his hand and notes every deviation from it in the actual performance. It seems to have been a general practice to inform the monarch about the content of the play beforehand. Cf. also *A Midsummer Night's Dream* for this practice.

[2] 'The whole point of this tense scene is that the king asks his question not because he did not see the dumb show, but because he did.' (Op. cit., p. 195.)

[3] This is stressed by J. H. Walter, 'The Dumb Show and the *Mouse Trap*', *MLR*, XXXIX (1944), pp. 286–7: 'If Claudius does speculate on the

Admittedly, the parallels to the actual event, the murder of Hamlet's father, are striking, especially the unusual manner in which the murder is carried out, but this does not give a very definite indication of the contents of the following play. It must also be taken into account that the way in which these dumb shows were acted was probably so different from the rest of the play and from real life that it would be surprising indeed if Claudius betrayed himself at this early point.[1] It was not for nothing that most of these pantomimes, especially in popular plays of the type parodied here, were accompanied by long and detailed explanations by the chorus, as can be seen from *A Midsummer Night's Dream*. The meaningless prologue ('or the posy of a ring') here is therefore almost more unusual and astonishing than the actual pantomime and is undoubtedly intended to provide an even better reason for the bewilderment of the spectators, expressed in Ophelia's question. The audience in the theatre alone can recognize the true meaning of the dumb show and therefore keeps an eye not only on the play, but also on the King and Hamlet.

All this suggests very strongly that it is rather unnecessary to assume that Claudius cannot have seen the pantomime because he would in that case have interrupted the performance earlier.[2] The King, who knows nothing of Hamlet's share in the play, has very little reason to grow suspicious only because some incidents could remind him of his own guilt. It has been remarked that he does not leave until he is certain of Hamlet's knowledge of the murder and until Hamlet's behaviour provides him with a

---

meaning of the dumb show, he may well decide that the changeableness of woman's love is the theme' (p. 287).

[1] I find myself in complete agreement with S. L. Bethell here: 'The behaviour of Claudius is now quite understandable: he has seen the dumb-show, but he has only seen a symbolic reference to murder . . . a dumb-show is, after all, only a dumb-show, the darkest hint at what is to follow.' (Op. cit., p. 160); for a similar view see A. Hart, 'Once more the Mouse-Trap', *RES*, XVII (1941), pp. 11–20.

[2] This is the well-known theory of J. D. Wilson. Cf. J. D. Wilson, 'The Parallel Plots in *Hamlet*. A Reply to Dr W. W. Greg', *MLR*, XIII (1918), pp. 139–56, and *What Happens in Hamlet*, pp. 144 ff. Cf. also G. Rylands, op. cit., p. 212. Elizabethan stage conditions are quoted in support of this theory by C. J. Sisson (op. cit.) and Richard Flatter, *Hamlet's Father* (London, 1949), pp. 40 ff.

good reason for withdrawing.[1] Nor are there in the text any
convincing proofs that the dumb show is an unpleasant surprise
for Hamlet and makes him fear for the success of his plan, as
Professor Dover Wilson assumed,[2] or even less, that Hamlet
has carefully prepared the pantomime in order to administer a
well-dosed shock to Claudius.[3] Such theories seem to contain a
stronger element of modern psychology than is justified in the
interpretation of Elizabethan drama.

On the other hand, it cannot be disputed that many of these
problems become irrelevant when the scene is acted on the stage
and that it does not present so many difficulties there. As often
in Shakespeare's plays, the immediate dramatic effect is more
important here than strict psychological consistency.[4] The dumb
show increases the suspense and tension of the scene considerably by presenting the murder and its consequences visibly on
the stage in exaggerated gestures whereas the play itself breaks
off half-way. The hideous and unnatural character of Claudius'

[1] Cf. John W. Draper, *The Hamlet of Shakespeare's Audience* (Durham
N.C., 1938), p. 144, and W. W. Greg, op. cit.

[2] Cf. J. D. Wilson's edition, pp. 200–1. Hamlet's 'miching mallecho'
which is quoted by J. D. Wilson to support his interpretation refers, I am
sure, to the content of the pantomime, the poisoning, not to the actors. The
rather archaic character of this expression would seem to support this.
Similarly Hamlet's scornful remark about the actors who 'cannot keep
counsel' does not mean this particular situation, but the general habit
popular dramatists had of explaining everything circumstantially in
prologues and pantomimes.

[3] Cf. A. J. Green, 'The Cunning of the Scene', *ShQ*, IV (1953), pp. 395–
404: 'in an affair that concerned him so deeply Hamlet cannot have planned
carelessly' (p. 400). Similar views are expressed by M. E. Prior (op.
cit.), J. H. Walter (op. cit.), and J. M. Nosworthy, 'A Reading of the
Play-Scene in Hamlet', *ESts*, XXII (1940), pp. 161–70.

[4] Cf. L. L. Schücking, *Character Problems in Shakespeare's Plays* (Lon-
don, 1922), pp. 111 ff. and *passim*. See also W. W. Lawrence, 'The Play
Scene in Hamlet', *JEGP*, XVIII (1919), pp. 1–22, and 'Hamlet and the
Mouse-Trap'; J. M. Nosworthy, op. cit.; G. R. Elliott, *Scourge and
Minister* (Durham N.C., 1951), p. 90; Bertram Joseph, *Conscience and the
King, A Study of Hamlet* (London, 1953): 'all that the author does is
imagine a scene which keeps us in a state of tension, wondering if the King
will stay till the right moment, wondering when the moment will come,
wondering whether he will or will not show himself guilty when it does'
(p. 86). A very similar interpretation is given by H. Levin, op. cit.,
pp. 87 ff., and Irving Ribner, *Patterns in Shakespearian Tragedy* (London,
1960), pp. 74 ff.

crime and the suddenness of the Queen's change of heart could not have been better brought out than by this kind of grotesque puppet-show.[1]

Thus Shakespeare has in *Hamlet* exploited and modified a well-worn dramatic convention in a most brilliant and original manner. The pointed use of the pantomime is a particularly good example of the play's rich and complex structure. The primitive spectacle which on the surface is only a courtly amusement serves as a foil for tragic guilt, suffering, and suspicion. The shallow and antiquated play becomes a test for all those who watch it. For Hamlet it is a means of penetrating the inscrutable mask of the King, for Claudius and the Queen it is a mirror in which they can discover their own guilt. Within the structure of the whole play, however, this performance is only another of those devious turns and subterfuges which avoid the real issue and do not bring Hamlet much closer to the accomplishment of his task.[2] It does not rouse him to any immediate action, but is partly the cause of his own destruction. For him the only result of the scene is that now he is quite convinced of Claudius' guilt and believes in the words of the ghost. His own exultation and the dramatic tension of the whole scene stand in rather ironic contrast to this meagre result. In fact, the tragedy as a whole shows a certain contrast between the outward form of the revenge play and its deeper, quite different meaning. Needless to say, this is a supreme example of the brilliant handling and transforming of traditional material that is so typical of Shakespeare's art.[3]

'MACBETH'

Among the plays of Shakespeare's early and middle period there are no other examples of the use of dumb show. This may

---

[1] Most modern scholars seem to agree in rejecting J. D. Wilson's reading of the play scene. See C. Leech, 'Studies in *Hamlet* 1901–1955', *ShS*, 9 (1956), pp. 1–15.

[2] This is strongly emphasized by L. L. Schücking, *The Meaning of Hamlet*, pp. 135–6.

[3] On *Hamlet* and the tradition of the revenge play see F. T. Bowers, *Elizabethan Revenge Tragedy 1587–1642* (Gloucester, Mass. 1959), pp. 85 ff., and J. C. Maxwell, 'Shakespeare: The Middle Plays', *The Age of Shakespeare* (*Pelican Guide to English Literature*, Vol. II, Harmondsworth, 1960), pp. 209 ff. The wide-spread practice of leaving out the pantomime altogether in modern performances is therefore regrettable.

perhaps be explained by the fact that in most of his plays there is such a perfect balance between word and gesture, dramatic speech and action, that such a comparatively simple and one-sided device as the pantomime would not easily have fitted into their complex structures. Dumb show is only used for particular stage effects and where it is precisely the contrast and the unusual technique that are wanted, as has been seen in *Hamlet*.[1]

The famous 'Show of Kings' in *Macbeth* is a very different kind of pantomime. It belongs to those conjured-up apparitions we find in some plays of the 'University Wits' and in several popular plays. There is here no plot, but a simple procession round the stage, the strange effect probably being heightened by some music and by the weird appearance of these figures.[2] The 'Show of Kings', moreover, is not the only spectacular effect in this scene. There are three other, similar apparitions, like the 'Armed Head' and the 'Bloody Childe', which, however, cannot be considered dumb shows.

Prophecy and foreboding play an essential part in the tragedy of Macbeth and are particularly prominent in this scene. The show in which Macbeth's future is forecast marks a turning point in his fate. It is a definite indication that he will not enjoy the fruits of his crime for long and that his tragic end is imminent. Thus the content of the dumb show is closely related to the substance of the play and it is far more than just a theatrical effect like many of the earlier dumb shows, although *Macbeth* was here undoubtedly influenced by some popular plays of witchcraft and magic.

Particularly effective and appropriate is the way in which Macbeth himself, who is most affected by these apparitions, acts as a kind of presenter and describes in a very dramatic way the figures as they pass:

> Thou art too like the Spirit of Banquo: Down:
> Thy Crowne do's seare mine Eye-bals. And thy haire
> Thou other Gold-bound-brow, is like the first:
> A third, is like the former. Filthy Hagges,
> Why do you shew me this? – A fourth? Start eyes!

[1] Shakespeare's last plays belong to quite a different type and are therefore treated in a later chapter (see Chapter 11).

[2] On such apparitions in earlier plays see Chapter 5. On the 'Show of Kings' see A. Venezky, op. cit., pp. 123–4.

What will the Line stretch out to th'cracke of Doome?
Another yet? A seauenth? Ile see no more:
And yet the eight appeares, who beares a glasse,
Which shewes me many more: and some I see,
That two-fold Balles, and trebble Scepters carry.
Horrible sight: Now I see 'tis true,
For the Blood-bolter'd Banquo smiles vpon me,
And points at them for his. What? is this so?

The similarity between these shapes, not indicated in the stage direction, is forcefully impressed on the spectator because it is just this similarity that arouses Macbeth's horror and apprehension. The speech is not only remarkable as a description of the pantomime, but because of the effective manner in which Macbeth's emotion is expressed at the same time. It is a particularly felicitous modification of the traditional presenter's account. Macbeth describes each figure as it enters, his fear and terror increasing at every new appearance, until he refuses to see any more and yet cannot turn his eyes from the disturbing sight. The remainder of the play reveals how strongly Macbeth is influenced by this show and how much his actions from now on are governed by the impression it makes on him.

Thus the pantomime is, in spite of its conventional character, an integral part of the play and of the scene in which it occurs. It adds to the spectator's feeling of sinister expectation in a way that would perhaps not have been effected by any other dramatic device.

8

John Marston

Hardly any other dramatist of the period succeeded so well in making dialogue and speech subservient to dramatic plot and action as Marston did. In reading his plays one feels that the writer had a practical experience of the theatre and knew how to make use of it.[1] In Marston's plays the rhetorical element, though very strong, only contributes to the dramatic movement of the incidents on the stage. At the same time stage directions are used much more frequently and consciously than in the work of many other dramatists to make the spoken word more effective and expressive. Pantomime often serves the same purpose and he uses it several times and in a variety of forms. It is significant that he only devised comparatively few elaborate dumb shows of the traditional kind, but preferred to include silent action in spoken scenes. It is in this respect particularly that he made an important contribution to the development of the dumb show and to the interplay of dramatic speech and visible action.

'ANTONIO AND MELLIDA'

Even Marston's first play, *Antonio and Mellida*, contains a typical example of his original use of the pantomime. There are here no dumb shows as we have understood them so far, but a special form of silent scene such as hardly occurs in earlier plays. In one scene of the first act several characters appear on the

[1] See Harvey Wood's introduction ('Marston as a Dramatic Author') in his edition of the plays (Edinburgh, 1934–9), Vol. III, where this point is emphasized. Cf. also T. S. Eliot, *Elizabethan Dramatists* (London, 1963), pp. 152 ff.; Una M. Ellis-Fermor, *The Jacobean Drama* (London, 1936), pp. 77 ff.; Robert Ornstein, *The Moral Vision of Jacobean Tragedy* (Madison, 1960), pp. 151 ff.

It is important to remember that Marston wrote for the Private Theatre and could therefore, on the whole, count on a more select and educated audience than most of the 'popular' dramatists.

main stage while others appear on the upper stage at the same time. Such scenes are frequent in Elizabethan drama and are used particularly to indicate such localities as balconies, city walls, or galleries. However, in almost all these cases there is an exchange of words between the two parties, whereas Marston combines this form of scene with the convention of the eavesdropper, also a favourite dramatic device. What is new here is that only one of the two groups is speaking while the other performs a kind of mime. This situation is all the more curious because the silent scene takes place on the main stage, the dialogue in the gallery:

> *The Cornets sound a Cynet. Enter above, Mellida, Rossaline and Flavia: Enter belowe, Galeatzo with attendants; Piero meeteth him, embraceth; at which the Cornets sound a florish: Piero and Galeatzo exeunt: the rest stand still.*
> MELLIDA: What prince was that passed through my fathers guard?
> FLAVIA: Twas Galeatzo, the young Florentine.

The same arrangement is repeated when the second suitor, Matzagente, is received with some pomp by Piero. Thus the spectator sees a kind of pantomime which is commented on from the gallery. The conversation between Mellida and the two maids fulfils the function of presenter. It gives the audience all the information that is necessary, without detracting from the main action of the play.

In both scenes only characters from the play itself take part. The effectiveness of the silent scene lies chiefly in the pointed gestures and the musical accompaniment; it seems likely that the pompous atmosphere of the court was indicated by the presence of servants and the whole style of acting. Piero's triumph (he has just won a victory over Andrugio) and his intention of marrying Mellida off to some powerful prince are impressively portrayed, and at the same time they are shown in a particular light because of the dramatic method employed. The use of silent action alone for such an incident could, especially if accompanied by exaggerated gestures, give the whole scene an unnatural and slightly comic character. That this was the author's intention is emphasized by the simultaneous conversation in the gallery which reveals Mellida's opinion of her father's schemes quite clearly. The spectator thus sees the scene through

Mellida's eyes because she makes her scornful remarks about the two suitors as the events on the stage are explained to her.

The whole scene is a very skilful continuation of the exposition. Two different groups of persons are introduced and characterized at the same time. The silent scene throws a somewhat sarcastic light upon life at the court and on the two suitors. Mellida's commentary heightens this effect and reveals her own attitude to the events. Thus the entrance of Antonio is prepared in a very striking manner: after the Duke has withdrawn with his followers and Mellida's remark, 'The tryumph's ended', has again made it clear that for her it was only an empty show, Antonio, who is to be the third suitor, enters. He also remains silent at first and is described from the gallery until the girls decide to descend and address him. Then he begins his monologue and a new scene follows.

Thus Marston rather skilfully combines the pantomime with the device of the play within the play, at the same time telescoping part of the action. From the earlier dumb shows he takes over the idea of a silent scene on the main stage, but he replaces the chorus or presenter by a group of characters from the play. The pantomime is completely incorporated in the play and is no longer an independent element outside the plot; its specific effect is fully exploited. The absence of the spoken word serves a special dramatic purpose and the silent scene no longer appears as a foreign element in the play. This is true to some extent of all pantomimes in Marston's plays, although the particular form used in *Antonio and Mellida* does not recur.[1]

'ANTONIO'S REVENGE'

The dumb shows in Marston's second play, *Antonio's Revenge*, stand more outside and are not completely drawn into the dramatic action like the pantomime in *Antonio and Mellida*. As in the earlier classical tragedies they are placed before the individual acts. Three of the play's five acts are introduced by a dumb show. Nevertheless, there are important differences

[1] The second pantomime in *The Spanish Tragedy* is slightly similar. Pearn does not include this dumb show in his list, perhaps because of its close connection with the play.

between the handling of the pantomimes here and in earlier examples.

The dumb show before the second act begins with the traditional motif of the funeral procession, obviously a favourite effect, which could be made very striking by means of suitable dress, gestures, and music.[1] Unlike the earlier examples, however, this pantomime is closely connected with the rest of the play:

> *The Cornets sound a cynet.*
> *Enter two mourners with torches, two with streamers: Castilio &*
> *Forobosco, with torches: a Heralde bearing Andrugio's helme &*
> *sword: the coffin: Maria supported by Lucio and Alberto, Antonio*
> *by himselfe: Piero, and Strozzo talking: Galeatzo and Matzagente,*
> *Balurdo & Pandulfo: the coffin set downe: helme, sworde and*
> *streamers hung up, placed by the Herald: whil'st Antonio and Maria*
> *wet their handkerchers with their teares, kisse them, and lay them on*
> *the hearse, kneeling: all goe out but Piero. Cornets cease, and he speakes.*

The pantomime here does far more than create a suitable atmosphere for the following act. First of all it shows a very particular funeral procession: the spectator knows whose body lies in the coffin and the identity of the murderer, while the other characters on the stage know nothing. The scene is of dramatic importance because several characters express their attitude to the dead by their gestures: Maria and Antonio are weeping while Piero whispers to his confidant. At the same time the scene is an impressive preparation for the role of Andrugio as the ghost who asks for revenge. He appears twice in the following act inciting Antonio to avenge him. Andrugio's death is in fact the starting point of the whole tragedy. The way in which Marston presents it visually in the form of a funeral procession reveals his instinct for good theatre. Again the effect of the scene is heightened by the absence of the spoken word. It contains nothing that would make dialogue necessary and is hardly different from the other scenes of the play. The question is whether such an introduction can really be called a dumb show at all; the word at least is not used here and Pearn's definition would hardly apply to the scene.[2] It is often very difficult to draw the line between dumb

[1] Cf. *Gorboduc* (III), *Jocasta* (II), and many later examples.
[2] See Introduction.

show and a particularly festive procession. Marston's plays provide some interesting examples of how an originally independent element gradually becomes part of the play, increasing its visual effect, closely linked with the dialogue. The spectator does not miss dialogue in this scene nor would he consider the pantomime a separate performance like most of the earlier dumb shows. Nevertheless, it is clearly related to those earlier pantomimes and is separated from the following scene in so far as all the characters taking part, except Piero, leave the stage without having spoken. This clearing of the stage distinguishes the pantomime from the ceremonious processions which frequently in Elizabethan drama introduce big state scenes.[1] Marston's technique resembles rather the 'introduction' in Wilmot's *Tancred and Gismund*,[2] where also the pantomime leads directly into the dialogue at the beginning of some acts. This artistic device is intensified by Marston. Piero's outburst:

> Rot ther thou cearcloth that infolds the flesh
> Of my loath'd foe; moulder to crumbling dust:

as soon as the others have left is a direct commentary on the pantomime. His monologue has a particularly striking and immediate effect because it grows out of the preceding scene and after the formal procession of mourners reveals the true face of the murderer. The visual and the rhetorical are contrasted with conscious artistry and as a result both become more dramatically effective. Similarly, in Shakespeare's plays, a monologue is sometimes prepared for by a brief scene and thus placed in a definite dramatic context, a technique which often heightens the dramatic effect considerably.[3]

While the pantomimic scene before the second act is so much part of the play that one can doubt whether the term dumb show is justified at all, real dumb shows are used before the third and fifth acts of the tragedy and given that name by the dramatist

---

[1] There are good examples of such processions in *Look About You* (1600) and *The Stately Tragedy of Claudius Tiberius Nero* (1607). Cf. also the beginning of Dekker's *The Honest Whore*, Part I, with the mock-funeral of Infelice.

[2] See Chapter 3.

[3] Cf. Shakespeare's *Hamlet*, IV, 4. The monologue derives some of its effect from the contrast to the preceding scene.

himself.[1] The silent scene which precedes the third act is considerably longer and livelier than the previous one. It contains a definite piece of action with several entries and exits, but, what is more important, it contains some elements which make the absence of dialogue particularly noticeable:

> *A dumbe showe. The cornets sounding for the Acte.*
> *Enter Castilio and Forobosco, Alberto and Balurdo, with polaxes: Strozzo, talking with Piero, seemeth to send out Strotzo. Exit Strozzo. Enter Strotzo, Maria, Nutriche, and Luceo. Piero passeth through his guard, and talkes with her with seeming amorousnesse: she seemeth to reject his suite, flyes to the toumbe, kneeles, and kisseth it. Piero bribes Nutriche and Lucio: they goe to her, seeming to solicite his suite. She riseth, offers to goe out, Piero stayeth her, teares open his breast, imbraceth and kisseth her, and so they goe all out in State.*

Here a rather complicated part of the plot is presented which could have been far more convincingly portrayed with the help of dialogue. Five times in succession a wish, request, or order is conveyed by different persons, situations which are far less easy to put over in pantomime than in speeches. This difficulty is most noticeable in Piero's attempt to convince Maria of his love and to persuade her to accept him, obviously a dramatic situation calling for dialogue and persuasive rhetoric. As a pantomimic scene it loses all dramatic effectiveness and conviction. Maria's change of heart is not very credible and seems particularly sudden. On the whole, extensive dramatic conflicts and scenes in which various characters influence each other by eloquent arguments and powerful speeches are not Marston's strong point. He consciously seems to avoid persuasion by dialogue in this scene by presenting it as a dumb show. The silent scene is necessary for the course of the plot because in the previous act Piero reveals his plan to marry Maria, and in the following act it is assumed that she has already consented to his wishes. We have here a scene, in all other respects like the rest of the play, presented as a pantomime, although it loses greatly by this method of presentation. There are hardly any examples of this kind of dumb show in earlier plays.[2] Although in several

---

[1] Marston does not use the term in other plays.

[2] See, however, *Captain Thomas Stukeley* (cf. Chapter 6) and, in a different manner, *The Murder of Gonzago* in *Hamlet*.

plays of the period parts of the plot are abridged by dumb shows
these parts were usually less important, or else longer periods of
time had to be jumped over by a pantomime.

It is not, however, mere lack of dramatic skill which makes
Marston use dumb show here. He obviously employs it to increase the tempo of the action and to shift the point of emphasis
within the play. With the help of the pantomime he ensures that
the audience does not pay too much attention to Piero, who in
the second part of the tragedy fades somewhat into the background. Piero dominates the first two acts and his wicked plans
are at first the centre of interest; the pantomime at the beginning
of the third act is his last big scene before the court scene in the
fourth act; from the third act onwards Antonio and his desire for
revenge predominate and he takes part in nearly every scene.
The pantomime before the third act therefore marks a turning
point in the play, immediately preceding the scene in which
Antonio is roused to revenge by his father's ghost. Thus the
dumb show fulfils an important dramatic function and is not just
a convenient means of tying up the plot.

The same is true, if in a slightly different manner, of the
pantomime before the fifth act. It is not so much a silently performed section of the plot as a kind of pageant with some
typical gestures, in which almost all characters in the play take
part:

> *The Cornets sounde for the Acte.*
> *The dumbe showe.*
>
> *Enter at one dore, Castilio and Forobosco, with halberts: foure Pages
> with torches: Luceo bare: Piero, Maria and Alberto, talking: Alberto
> drawes out his dagger, Maria her knife, ayming to menace the Duke.
> Then Galeatzo betwixt two Senators, reading a paper to them: at which
> they all make semblance of loathing Piero, and knit their fists at him;
> two Ladies and Nutriche: All these goe softly over the Stage, whilst at
> the other doore enters the ghost of Andrugio, who passeth by them,
> tossing his torch about his heade in triumph. All forsake the Stage,
> saving Andrugio, who speaking, begins the Acte.*
>
> ANDRUGIO . . . The fist of strenuous vengeance is clutcht,

The form of the dumb show here is particularly suitable for expressing visually the differences and enmities between the two
parties. The characters are divided into two groups. The threaten-
ing gestures of Maria and Alberto show how the plans for

revenge are progressing and how far Maria is concerned in them. A direct confrontation of the two sides could hardly have been presented more impressively by a scene with dialogue. The same is true of the second part of the scene in which Galeatzo's appeal to the Senate is shown. Here again the simultaneous presence of both parties on the stage is a very effective, if somewhat primitive, means of dramatic presentation. The spectator can see clearly how the net tightens round Piero without him being aware of it. Without a pantomime the unfolding of such a situation would probably take several scenes. The dumb show thus contributes to the dramatic acceleration of the action before the final catastrophe. It gives a great deal of information to the audience in a brief space. The end is also prepared for by the renewed appearance of Andrugio's ghost, who has a double part to play. On the one hand he is the ghost of the murdered man come to demand revenge, a familiar figure in revenge tragedies; at the same time he has the function of a presenter because he explains the meaning of the pantomime to the audience.[1] In doing so he does not relate a long tale, but describes very briefly the events which are necessary for an understanding of the last act. Here as at the beginning of the second act the monologue follows the pantomime without a break. Andrugio's speech is a direct outcome of the incidents shown in the silent scene, not a detached commentary; it is he who is most satisfied to see all these forces uniting to bring about Piero's destruction. Even more than Kyd's ghost of Andrea in *The Spanish Tragedy* Andrugio is a kind of 'ideal spectator' who watches the last stage of the tragedy with open approval and pleasure:

> Here will I sit, spectator of revenge,
> And glad my ghost in anguish of my foe. (V, 5)

In this tragedy Marston has revived the old custom of introducing most acts by a dumb show. The first pantomime brings the murderer and the family of his victim face to face. At first there is complete harmony, at least outwardly, until Piero's monologue shows how completely he has shut himself out from their circle. The presence of the murderer himself at the funeral of his victim is a new effect not found in early tragedies of

[1] Cf. Skelton in Munday's Robin Hood plays and the different handling of the victim's ghost by Kyd in *The Spanish Tragedy*.

revenge. The pantomime thus marks the first climax of the play. The second dumb show presents Piero at the height of his career. He has banished Pandulfo, seeks Antonio's life, and woos Andrugio's widow. He seems to have no dangerous opponent yet. It is significant that Antonio does not appear in this pantomime; the stage is dominated by Piero and his supporters. Nevertheless Marston seems to hint at the hollowness of Piero's triumph by turning such an important and lively incident into a dumb show, thus pushing it into the background and making it appear particularly artificial and insincere. Immediately afterwards Antonio enters and from then on dominates the play.

The third pantomime is also placed at an important point in the play, immediately before the catastrophe. It shows in a short and unambiguous scene how Piero is threatened and hated from all sides, thus preparing the way for the last act which contains the traditional masque of revengers and the bloody end.

One can therefore say that the dumb shows in this tragedy present or give warning of special climaxes, although they usually consist only of incidents which are not decisive for the plot. Antonio only appears in one pantomime and then has a rather small part to play. On the other hand, Piero and his followers take part in all three dumb shows. Thus the silent scenes are chiefly a means of presenting the court, with its empty ceremony and false appearance, whereas the more psychological and human problems of the action are left to the dialogue scenes. It seems as if the contrast between the two parties is reflected in the choice of dramatic technique. The dumb show has become an instrument of satire, to expose deceptive splendour and false harmony. Although no really comical effects are produced by the pantomimes, the incidents presented are sometimes shown in an unfavourable or even ridiculous light.

At the same time Marston connects the pantomimes with the other dramatic techniques employed in this play. The contrast between mimic action and dramatic speech is exploited for increased effect. Each of the three dumb shows is followed by a soliloquy. This device probably originated from the tradition of presenter, as becomes clear from the fifth act where Andrugio's ghost remains on the stage to explain the meaning of the pantomime. Piero's monologue in the second act, too, is a direct commentary on the pantomime, whereas in the third act a completely new scene begins after the dumb show. Nevertheless, Antonio's monologue is an effective dramatic contrast to the preceding state scene. After his mother has received Piero favourably he appears to be left completely on his own. It is only then that the task of avenging his father's murder is given him[1] and he begins to overcome his isolation.

Thus all the pantomimes in this play are deliberately contrasted with the spoken scenes and give the play a novel and increased dramatic effect. The organic union between pointed pantomime and dramatic speech is Marston's particular contribution to the development of the dumb show. This can also be seen in several of his other plays although none of them contain such extensive dumb shows as *Antonio's Revenge.*

CYRIL TOURNEUR: 'THE REVENGER'S TRAGEDY'

The Revenger's Tragedy may be briefly dealt with here as another example of the revenge play and for its similarity to *Antonio's Revenge.*[2] The dramatist's ability to fuse different dramatic techniques and combine influences as far apart as the morality play and the Court Masque has been one of the strongest arguments for Tourneur's authorship of the play.[3] Indeed the first scene, so often quoted, is in itself a highly effective mixture of primitive morality and sophisticated masque:

> *Enter Vendici, the Duke, Dutchesse, Lusurioso her sonne, Spurio the bastard, with a traine, passe ouer the Stage with Torch-light.*

VINDICI: Dvke: royall letcher; goe, gray hayrde adultery,
And thou his sonne, as impious steept as hee:
And thou his bastard true-begott in euill:
And thou his Dutchesse that will doe with Diuill,
Foure exlent Characters –

[1] The situation here is very similar to that in *Hamlet,* I, 2, where the contrast between the state scene and Hamlet's isolation is also particularly effective.

[2] Cf. the edition by Allardyce Nicoll (London, 1929). On *The Revenger's Tragedy* see especially T. S. Eliot, op. cit., pp. 107 ff.; M. C. Bradbrook, op. cit., pp. 165 ff.; R. Ornstein, op. cit., pp. 105 ff.; Irving Ribner, *Jacobean Tragedy: The Quest for Moral Order* (London, 1962), pp. 72 ff.

[3] This is very well argued by Inga-Stina Ekeblad, 'On the Authorship of *The Revenger's Tragedy*', *ESts*, XLI (1960), pp. 225–40.

Vendice here acts as presenter, introducing the main characters of the play as they pass in dumb show. At the same time he is closely involved in all the proceedings and becomes the most important character of the tragedy. The very first line is suggestive of royal corruption, one of the main themes of the play, and it reminds of a more primitive type of drama in which characters are only presented as embodiments of moral virtues or vices.

Throughout *The Revenger's Tragedy* we find recurring references to masques, revels, and other courtly entertainments as particularly sinister manifestations of the depravity of the rich.[1] It is only fitting in this play that the installation of the profligate Lussur oso as Duke should be presented as a dumb show. It is a hollow triumph, full of outward 'show', but doomed from the beginning. The ghastly double-masque of murderers and avengers, ending in wholesale carnage, is a deliberate dramatic effect, showing at the same time the superficial splendour of the court and its deceptive and transitory character. The favourite device of combining the execution of revenge with a masque is here closely woven into the play with its masque-imagery, its vivid depiction of worldly vanity and its grim juxtaposition of revels and death. It is in plays like this that the tradition of the dumb show seems most appropriate.

'SOPHONISBA'

Marston's next play, *Sophonisba*, is rather different from the two earlier ones. It clearly reveals the influence of Jonson and Chapman, although Marston in his preface 'To the Generall Reader' expressly refers to himself as an independent poet.[2] In spite of some obvious similarities in the choice and management of the subject-matter, *Sophonisba* is in its whole style and structure

---

[1] See Antonio's account of the revels during which his wife was ravished (I, 4) and Vendice's references to such revels (III, 4) while he himself is preparing a most macabre masque of his own devising. The importance of the 'masque' in the action and imagery of the play is stressed by L. G. Salingar, '*The Revenger's Tragedy* and the Morality Tradition', *Scrutiny*, VI (1937–8), pp. 402–24, and Peter Lisca, '*The Revenger's Tragedy*: A Study in Irony', *PQ*, XXXVIII (1959), pp. 242–51.

[2] 'Know, that I have not labored in this poeme, to tie my selfe to relate any thing as an historian but to inlarge every thing as a Poet.'

very different from the Roman plays of Jonson. It has been noticed that Jonson and Chapman seem to avoid dumb shows consciously.[1] Pantomimic elements disappear in favour of ceremonious speeches and witty debate. Thus in *Sejanus* the execution of the hero takes place off stage and is only described later by an eye-witness. In Marston's play, however, visual impressions take up much room on the stage and there are plenty of surprising effects and stately processions, although Marston appears to apologize for some of these effects at the end of the play.[2] Two of the five acts are introduced by dumb shows, but these are far less elaborate than those in *Antonio's Revenge*.[3]

An example is the beginning of the first act, where Marston is apparently following the tradition of popular history plays in which often a dumb show replaces the exposition. At the beginning of the play the hostile troops march on to the stage and take their stand on opposite sides of the stage. Almost all characters taking part are on the stage before the action proper begins. The prologue, standing between the two parties, explains in full detail what the play is about. Here the simplest kind of exposition and one of the oldest forms of dramatic prologue are backed by an impressive *tableau* to which the speaker of the prologue can point during his account.[4] This technique is of course rather unrefined in comparison with Shakespeare's far more complex ways of unfolding previous events, but it succeeds in drawing the audience immediately into the dramatic situation. Both partners, whose quarrel takes up the greater part of the play, are introduced and unmistakably differentiated.

There are also other places in the tragedy where impressive rhetoric and primitive stage effects are used side by side without being in any way blended. Marston had too much theatrical instinct to follow the strict rules of classical tragedy even as far as

[1] Cf. F. A. Foster, op. cit., p. 17, and L. L. Schücking's edition of *Hamlet*, p. 403.

[2] 'After all, let me intreat my Reader not to taxe me, for the fashion of the Entrances and Musique of this Tragidy, for know it is printed onely as it was presented by youths, and after the fashion of the private stage.'

[3] It is interesting to note that, with the only exception of *Antonio and Mellida*, Marston never uses pantomimes within a scene, but always at the beginning of a new scene or an act.

[4] 'The Sceane is Lybia, and the subject thus . . .' Cf. the prologue to Shakespeare's *Romeo and Juliet*.

Jonson did. This is why he attempts to relieve the dialogue by striking effects, although a real unity between pantomimic elements and rhetoric is not always achieved.

The second pantomime, however, shows that Marston did try to bring those two elements together and was often successful. It is little more than a set of stage directions; the characters are the same as those in the following scene and remain on stage all the time, so that the transition from the silent scene to the dialogue is hardly perceptible. As in Wilmot's *Tancred and Gismund*, the pantomime only prepares for the dialogue, which consequently gets more swiftly under way:

> *Whil'st the Musicke for the first Act soundes Hanno, Carthalon, Bytheas, Gelosso enter: They place themselves to Counsell, Gisco th' impoisner waiting on them, Hanno, Carthalon, and Bytheas, setting their hands to a writing, which being offer'd to Gelosso, he denies his hand, and as much offended impatiently starts up and speakes.*

GELOSSO: My hand? my hand? rotte first, wither in aged shame!

By this method it is possible to begin the dialogue with such a lively exclamation.

This particular form of pantomime is used several times in Marston's plays and with different modifications, which shows how much he kept the stage in mind in his writing; for only there the full effect of this technique becomes apparent.

A similar use of pantomime is found in *The Malcontent*, written shortly before. Here again the dumb show makes a good starting point for a scene without itself being a very extensive scene. The first act of this tragicomedy shows how a whole series of intrigues are set afoot. With his skill and cunning, Mendoza succeeds in averting the suspicion that he is having an affair with Pietro's wife. The young Farnese, who also has designs on the Duchess, is suspected instead and Mendoza offers to catch him red-handed. The second act begins with a pantomime in which Farnese is received by the bawd Maquerelle and shown into the rooms of the Duchess. Mendoza, who has watched the scene, remains on the stage after the others have left and the monologue which follows is an immediate commentary on what has happened:

> Hee's caught, the Woodcockes head is i'th noose.

Again the silent scene adds dramatic significance to the spoken one that follows.

This technique can be seen as Marston's attempt to develop a new way of beginning a scene. Whereas the modern theatre can give the audience the impression that it is being shown a scene already in progress by a quick raising of the curtain, on the Elizabethan stage all characters had to enter in full view of the audience and then begin their dialogue.[1] Marston achieves a similar effect to the modern producer by quickly bringing a scene (by means of a pantomime) to a point where the dialogue can begin with more dramatic tempo and immediacy.

This device is skilfully used in the Induction to the comedy *What You Will.* The pantomime merges almost imperceptibly into the spoken scene:

> *Before the Musicke sounds for the Acte: Enter Atticus, Doricus &*
> *Phylomuse, they sit a good while on the Stage before the Candles are*
> *lighted, talking together, & on suddeine Doricus speakes.*
> *Enter Tier-man with lights.*

> DORICUS: O Fie some lights, sirs fie, let there be no deeds of darknesse done among us—

The lighting of the candles has the same function here as the raising of the curtain in modern playhouses. The pantomimic introduction provides a starting point for the dialogue and increases the pace of the first scene.

In the first act of the same play there is also a more extensive pantomime. Here a complete little scene is presented as a dumb show and, contrary to most of the other examples, it contains an important part of the plot. Celia's brothers decide to hand the Duke a petition to prevent the forced marriage of their sister. The result is shown in a pantomime:

> *The Cornets sound.*
> *Enter the Duke coppled with a Lady, two cooples more with them,*
> *the men having tobacco pipes in their hands, the woemen sitt, they*
> *daunce a round. The Petition is delivered up by Randolfo, the Duke*
> *lightes his tobacco pipe with it and goes out dauncing.*

---

[1] Only the back-stage was probably concealed by a curtain which could be drawn back. This is why in many Elizabethan plays we find the stage direction '*draws a curtain*'. Usually, however, only *tableaux* or smaller episodes are presented in such a way, not extensive scenes with dialogue.

RANDOLFO: Saint Marke! Saint Marke!
IACOMO: Did not I tell you? loose no more rich time;
 What can one get but mier from a swine?

This pantomime is probably far more effective than a spoken scene would be. The Court's preoccupation with shallow amusement and the contemptuous gesture of the Duke are vividly portrayed. The pantomime is an instrument of biting satire and comedy as it very seldom was in earlier plays. Again the two parties are placed in sharp contrast to each other. The brothers who have handed over the petition find themselves spectators of a mime and only when the Duke and his followers have withdrawn do they begin to speak and discuss what has happened. Thus, although the most important part of the scene is presented as a dumb show, it is by no means separate from the play or pushed into the background, but rather more effective for this method of presentation. After the pointed mime the anger of the brothers seems only too natural and justified.

Almost all Marston's plays exemplify this organic linking of dramatic speech and silent action.[1] Marston as a practical man of the theatre seems to have attached particular importance to dramatic openings of scenes and acts. Even when he does not use a pantomime to this end he tries to make a striking first impression and to begin the dialogue at full speed.[2]

Marston does not normally use the term dumb show for all his mimes. The characters taking part in them are always the same as those in the actual play and the silent action nearly always leads straight into the dialogue. As a result the pantomime never appears as an independent element or an additional effect, but always as an integral and necessary part of the whole play. This skilful merging of the pantomime into the spoken scene makes Marston particularly important for the development of the dumb show.

---

[1] There is no need to discuss all the other examples. See Appendix I for a list of them. The pantomimes in *The Fawn* (V) and *The Insatiate Countess* are very similar to that in *The Malcontent*. Similar scene-openings in N. Field's *A Woman is a Weathercock* (V, 2) and *Look About You* (Sc. 2).

[2] Cf. *What You Will* (II) and *The Malcontent* (I, IV).

9

John Webster

Webster, too, tried to achieve a synthesis between popular drama, high classical style, and drama intended for reading, but he did this in a bolder and more ambitious way than most of his predecessors and contemporaries[1] and he succeeded better than Marston or Tourneur in moulding various dramatic conventions and styles into an organic whole. His preface to *The White Devil* suggests that he was a very conscientious artist who, although writing for the rather mixed audience of the Red Bull, still endeavoured to produce a kind of drama that could be read and enjoyed by more discriminating minds. It has been claimed that his is an 'impure art' because throughout his tragedies we find conventional and 'realistic' elements used side by side;[2] but the mixture of these two tendencies is achieved in such a way that the one illuminates the other and the result is not just a piling on of stage effects, but a convincing unity, though this has not always been recognized.

In using pantomimes Webster also explores new possibilities, achieving startling show effects with them, while still relating them closely to the rest of his play. The character and structure of his two major tragedies make the use of dumb shows seem natural enough because he employs such a large variety of artistic conventions, utilizing everything he found in the plays of his contemporaries to accomplish novel effects and express

[1] Cf. F. L. Lucas, *The Complete Works of John Webster* (London, 1927). The two tragedies were reprinted from this edition in 1958. On Webster cf. especially M. C. Bradbrook, op. cit., pp. 186 ff.; U. Ellis-Fermor, op. cit., pp. 170 ff.; F. T. Bowers, op. cit., pp. 179 ff.; Clifford Leech, *John Webster: A Critical Study* (London, 1951); R. Ornstein, op. cit., pp. 128 ff.; I. Ribner, op. cit., pp. 97 ff.; Ingeborg Glier, *Struktur und Gestaltungsprinzipien in den Dramen John Websters*. This study also contains a good section on the dumb shows.

[2] See the excellent article by Inga-Stina Ekeblad, 'The "Impure Art" of John Webster', *RES*, *NS*, IX (1958), pp. 253–67, where this aspect is particularly well treated.

the 'meaning' of his own plays in a unique and forceful manner. Songs, dances, ceremonial processions, stage properties, and apparitions play an important part. The visual element is always predominant, even in the dialogue scenes, so that the spectator does not feel the dumb shows to be independent additions, contrasted with the character of the play proper; there are natural transitions and the strange technique of the pantomimes is very well accounted for by their dramatic context. This happens in a rather similar way in both of Webster's tragedies.

In *The White Devil* the two dumb shows occur within a normal spoken scene. They are an integral part of the play in that they are surrounded by dialogue and cannot be left out. Their content is also closely related to the rest of the scene because a part of the plot is here portrayed that is not separated from the events in the play by a long period of time. The spectator who has already been prepared for the murder of Isabella and Camillo learns from the first sentence that the event has actually taken place, so that the emphasis in the following scene is mainly on the manner in which the crimes have been carried out. Each of the two pantomimes shows an incident in two parts, the preparation for and the execution of a murder. There are several entrances and exits and an important part of the plot, complete in itself, is thus performed. Marston, whose dramatic technique in other respects approaches that of Webster most nearly, hardly ever (except, perhaps, in *Antonio's Revenge*) used dumb shows in this way. To find a closer parallel to this type of presentation we have to go back to the popular plays of adventure. In these plays fairly long portions of the plot are often presented as pantomimes, but it is usually a character outside the play who takes over the role of presenter.[1] Probably Webster got the idea of telescoping certain episodes in pantomimic form from this type of play. At the same time, however, he tried to connect such dumb shows even closer with the rest of the play. In doing so he made use of a second device which can also be found in several pre-Shakespearean plays. A character from the play introduces a pantomime which is, however, directed at the other players on the stage, not at the audience in the theatre. In this way the two

---

[1] See Chapter 6. In most of these plays the dumb show is a mere technical device. The pantomime in Greene's *Friar Bacon and Friar Bungay* is perhaps nearest to Webster's method.

planes of action no longer appear side by side, but a second make-believe world, a play within a play, is created. This happens, though in a much simpler form, even in Kyd's *Spanish Tragedy* and in Peele's *The Arraignment of Paris*.

Webster is one of the first to combine these two techniques, so that we have in *The White Devil* a play within a play whose subject is part of the actual plot of the tragedy. The murder of Isabella and Camillo is presented and watched as a play by two other characters from the tragedy. The magician who has been bribed by Brachiano fulfils the role of presenter and explains the apparition he has conjured up at his request. It is indeed a weird scene, most typical of Webster's 'impure art':

CONJURER: Put on this night-cap sir, 'tis charm'd, and now
I'le shew you by my strong-commanding Art
The circumstance that breakes your Dutchesse heart.
A Dumbe Shew.

Enter suspiciously, Julio and Christophero, they draw a curtaine wher Brachiano's picture is, they put on spectacles of glasse, which cover their eyes and noses, and then burne perfumnes afore the picture, and wash the lips of the picture, that done, quenching the fire, and putting off their spectacles they depart laughing.

Enter Isabella in her night-gowne as to bed-ward, with lights after her, Count Lodovico, Giovanni, Guid-antonio and others waighting on her, shee kneeles downe as to prayers, then drawes the curtaine of the picture, doe's three reverences to it, and kisses it thrice, shee faints and will not suffer them to come nere it, dies, sorrow exprest in Giovanni and in Count Lodovico, shees conveid out solemnly.

BRACHIANO: Excellent, then shee's dead –
CONJURER: She's poysoned,
By the fum'd picture –
. . . now turne another way,
And veiw Camillo's farre more polliticke fate –
Strike louder musicke from this charmed ground,
To yeeld, as fits the act, a Tragicke sound.
The second dumbe shew

The following pantomime shows Camillo's equally ingenious murder. The idea of the world being a stage, so frequent in Elizabethan drama, is given pointed expression here. Brachiano is watching his own machinations like a play in the theatre. His complacent comments, spoken without any feeling or sympathy, make the contrast between the two planes of action particularly clear. A similar effect is often achieved in the eavesdropping scenes, also a favourite device with many dramatists of the period, where certain incidents on the stage are commented on simultaneously by other characters from the play.[1] This technique of presenting vivid scenes and at the same time providing a pointed commentary to them is particularly frequent in Webster. The figure of Flamineo is typical of it.[2] On the one hand he is actively involved in what is going on and is the driving force behind much of the play's action, but on the other hand he often sees himself as a detached onlooker. This shifting viewpoint characterizes many scenes of the play. It also partly explains the dumb shows. Brachiano is not simply an eavesdropper or an unwilling witness, but he eagerly watches the two murders which he himself has instigated. His comments do not, of course, express the reaction of the audience and therefore he does not function as a chorus who reveals the opinion of the author. Rather the audience is intended to turn against Brachiano even more after his cynical remarks and recognize him as the guilty one. The natural response is, however, not expressed in the drama, only perhaps in the silent grief of Lodovico and Giovanni in the pantomime.

The strange character of the dumb shows, probably heightened by the music and the manner of performance, is skilfully exploited. The absence of dialogue in the murder scenes makes them seem like cynical demonstrations of two particularly interesting and ingenious methods of getting unwanted people out of the way, an impression supported by Brachiano's approving remark: "'Twas quaintly done.' All human sympathy is excluded by this method of presentation and this technique in itself is an indirect comment.

Thus the two pantomimes are not only a mere technical device, but an important contribution to the specific meaning and effect of the scene. They increase the tempo of the performance by telescoping the plot. They also stress Brachiano's guilt

[1] See Shakespeare's *Troilus and Cressida*, V, 2, for a particularly striking example of this technique.

[2] Cf. C. Leech, op. cit., p. 49. John Russell Brown in his edition of *The White Devil* (*The Revels Plays*, London, 1960) also comments on this aspect of Webster's art (pp. xliv ff.).

and the hideousness of his crime. The figures in the dumb show appear to be entirely his creatures who carry out his plans,[1] while Vittoria's share in the crime remains rather vague and ambiguous.

Looking at the play as a whole we see how the dumb show is surrounded by scenes in which the chief interest lies in the dialogue, another example of Webster's conscious use of contrasting artistic means. The first part of the tragedy closes with a striking visual effect. The following scene, which prepares for the great trial, introduces a new section of the plot. As in the classical tragedies the dumb shows mark points of emphasis, so the pantomimes here come at the end of the first 'movement' of the play.[2]

In Webster's second tragedy, *The Duchess of Malfi*, pantomime is used in quite a similar way. Here also we find many scenes in which the action on the stage is commented on by detached onlookers. The third scene of Act III is a good example. Although the expression dumb show is not used here, the scene is a kind of pantomime which is commented on by three characters from the play in an exchange of dialogue. The reader of the tragedy only learns what is happening on the stage through indirect description and comment. The reaction of the two brothers to the news of their sister's pretended pilgrimage to Loretto is at first conveyed only by the expression on their faces, but at the same time this is observed and explained by those standing by:

PESCARA: Marke Prince Ferdinand,
              A very Salamander lives in's eye,
              To mocke the eager violence of fire.
SILVIO: That Cardinall hath made more bad faces with his
              oppression
              Then ever Michael Angelo made good ones,
              He lifts up's nose, like a fowle Por-pisse before
              A storme—
PESCARA: The Lord Ferdinand laughes.
DELIO: Like a deadly Cannon,
              That lightens ere it smoakes.

[1] Cf. C. Leech, op. cit., p. 45, and M. C. Bradbrook, op. cit., p. 188.
[2] On the connection between the structure of the play and the division into acts see I. Glier, op. cit., pp. 21 ff.

PESCARA: These are your true pangues of death,
The pangues of life, that strugle with great
states-men –
DELIO: In such a deformed silence, witches whisper
Their charmes.
(III, 3, ll. 58 ff.)

The tense and pregnant atmosphere before the two brothers
begin to strike could not have been more effectively evoked than
by this pantomime and the scared comment.[1]

In the following scene there is a more extensive dumb show.
Again the pantomime is drawn into the play by the surrounding
dialogue and by its content. An important part of the plot in
which most of the leading characters of the play are involved is
telescoped to accelerate the dramatic tempo and to introduce
a new section. In contrast to *The White Devil* the horrible and
grotesque are absent; instead there is a solemn ceremony which
takes place simultaneously with the rest of the scene. The two
pilgrims are only by coincidence witnesses of the scene which
unfolds before their eyes. No presenter appears to explain the
pantomime, which instead is prepared for by the dialogue of the
two pilgrims and afterwards briefly commented on by them.
The situation rather resembles an eavesdropping scene. In this
scene, however, a tragic-ironic effect is achieved by the way in
which the pilgrims, who are not directly involved, learn about
the banishment of the Duchess:

SECOND PILGRIM: The Cardinall of Arragon
Is, this day, to resigne his Cardinals hat,
His sister Duchesse likewise is arriv'd
To pay her vow of Pilgrimage – I expect
A noble Ceremony.
FIRST PILGRIM: No question: – They come.

Here the Ceremony of the Cardinalls enstalment, in the habit of a
Souldier: perform'd in delivering up his Crosse, Hat, Robes, and Ring,
at the Shrine; and investing him with Sword, Helmet, Sheild, and
Spurs: Then Antonio, the Duchesse, and their Children, (having
presented themselves at the Shrine) are (by a forme of Banishment in
dumbe-shew, expressed towards them by the Cardinall, and the State
of Ancona) banished: During all which Ceremony, this Ditty is sung

[1] See the chapter on 'Kommentiertes Spiel', I. Glier, op. cit., pp. 70 ff.

143

The Elizabethan Dumb Show

(to very sollemne Musique) by divers Church-men; and then Exeunt.

. . .

FIRST PILGRIM: Here's a strange turne of state –

In the second part of the scene the pilgrims have the function of a chorus. They do not appear in any other scene of the play and remain apart from the plot. Their commentary is thus particularly revealing, coming from two apparently quite un-biased peakers. The audience is made to see the episode as it must appear to an outsider. The real motives of the characters involved have been partly shown in the previous scenes, but they are not touched upon in the pantomime. This is why the implied criticism of both parties in the dialogue of the pilgrims becomes an important hint for the audience.

As in *The White Devil*, the pantomime in *The Duchess of Malfi* occurs at a turning point in the play. In the previous scene the two brothers learn of their sister's intended flight and make their first preparations for revenge. The banishment is the first stage on the Duchess' path of suffering; the following scene shows her arrest and the separation from Antonio. In both of Webster's tragedies, therefore, the actual revenge-plot is introduced by a dumb show. In the first the crime is shown which is subse-quently avenged, whereas in the second the beginning of the revenge itself appears as a pantomime.

In both plays the use of the pantomime illustrates that shift-ing of perspective which is so typical of Jacobean drama and of Webster in particular. The audience is invited to watch the events sometimes from a very short distance, with the eyes of characters who are immediately involved, or, at other times, from a seemingly objective point of view, but is never quite sure which is supposed to be the 'true' perspective: the dramatist himself seems to refrain from any clear judgment.[1] He does not content himself with a simple presentation of certain incidents

---

[1] See Wylie Sypher, *Four Stages of Renaissance Style* (New York, 1955), pp. 116–7 and *passim* for some perceptive criticism on these lines, which is not invalidated by the fact that the main thesis of the book is somewhat questionable. For a treatment of Shakespeare's use of shifting viewpoint see the valuable study by Ernest Schanzer, *The Problem Plays of Shakespeare* (London, 1963). The controversial nature of most criticism of the 'Problem Plays' is in itself evidence of some shifting perspective in these plays.

and characters, but shows them, sometimes simultaneously, in different lights. Webster does this in a particularly effective manner by using the technique of the play within the play, which we find in both tragedies, and by combining it with other devices: the telescoping dumb show, the eavesdropping scene, and the magic apparition. In both plays an incident which could have been portrayed in an ordinary dialogue scene is detached from the action and removed further away from the spectator, a technique not to be found in earlier drama. Thus the convention of the dumb show is fitted into the structure of the play in a novel and particularly successful way. It does not only help to create some striking scenic effects, but it also contributes substantially to the particular style and meaning of Webster's two masterpieces.

10

Thomas Middleton

Of all Jacobean dramatists Thomas Middleton is perhaps the one whose plays have in dramatic style and character-portrayal most in common with the works of Shakespeare.[1] Characterization is particularly important in his plays and the didactic element rather fades into the background compared with Marston, Tourneur, or even Webster. Like Shakespeare, Middleton often does not seem to take sides, but to throw light on situations from different angles without committing himself to a final judgment. Consequently his major works are particularly difficult to interpret conclusively.

Middleton's plays are especially rich in elements that betray the strong influence of the pageants and masques in which he showed great interest. Indeed, he himself was the author of several masques which were written and performed during the same years as his plays.[2] Masque-like performances can be found at various points within his plays and the visual element has altogether a very important role in them.

The comparatively early comedy *Your Five Gallants* is a characteristic example of this particular aspect.[3] Whereas in early Elizabethan drama dumb shows are almost invariably confined to tragedy, in this play pantomime is used with comic and satirical effect. This, of course, also happens in Shakespeare's *A Midsummer Night's Dream*, where the style of classical tragedy is parodied, but there the dumb show is, as in *Hamlet*, quite definitely a part of a tragedy, i.e. the play of Pyramus and Thisbe,

[1] Cf. Samuel Schoenbaum, *Middleton's Tragedies: A Critical Study* (New York, 1955); R. H. Barker, *Thomas Middleton* (New York, London, 1958); M. C. Bradbrook, op. cit., pp. 213 ff., and the works by Ornstein and Ribner, cited in the previous chapter. There is as yet no modern complete edition of Middleton's plays. I have used the edition of A. Dyce (London, 1840) in five volumes, and modern editions of individual plays.

[2] See Vol. V of Dyce's edition.

[3] Cf. R. H. Barker, op. cit., pp. 42 ff.

and made fun of as such. The same does not apply to Marston's and Middleton's comedies.

Your Five Gallants is a comedy of disguise and intrigue of a type frequent in Elizabethan drama after 1600. These plays are, as far as their structure is concerned, superficially like the tragedies of revenge.[1] The whole of the plot works up to the final act, in which all the threads of the action are disentangled, the villains unmasked and punished. In a disguise which gives him a better opportunity for studying his surroundings than the other characters in the play have, Fitsgrave takes part in nearly all incidents and learns to see through all deceptive appearances. Thus the whole plot is seen from a certain perspective and is continually commented on. The hero in a way lives two separate existences, because he can only reveal his true character in monologues, asides, or in conversation with those he trusts. The play consists of a series of pretences and confusions of identity. Only the audience always knows the real state of affairs. It is told about the true nature of the 'gallants' right at the beginning, whereas Fitsgrave has to acquire this knowledge in the course of the play and Katherine's eyes are only opened at the very end.

The pantomime before the first scene is employed purely for purposes of exposition. A presenter opens the play by introducing the five gallants. The way in which this is done seems at first rather awkward and reminds one of some late medieval allegory. Each figure is characterized by a gesture which is typical of him:

> *Presenter, or Prologue, passing over the stage; the bawd-gallant (Primero), with three wenches gallantly attired, meets him; the whore-gallant (Tailby), the pocket-gallant (Pursenet), the cheating-gallant (Goldstone), kiss these three wenches, and depart in a little whisper and wanton action. Now, for the other, the broker-gallant (Frippery), he sits at home yet, I warrant you, at this time of day, summing up his pawns. Hactenus quasi inductio, a little glimpse giving.*

[1] Cf. Shakespeare's *Measure for Measure*, Marston's *The Malcontent*, *The Phoenix*, and *Parasitaster*, Jonson's *Bartholomew Fair*. A comparison between *Antonio's Revenge* and *The Malcontent* in particular reveals the similarities in structure between this type of comedy and the tragedies of revenge.

This technique is continued in the first scene of the following act, in which Frippery is shown 'summing up his pawns'[1] and receiving his customers. Thus the play is immediately characterized as a comedy of 'types' in which each of the five gallants embodies a particular form of depravity and corruption. In the pantomime the gallants are shown as they really are; it is an 'objective' scene, clearly directed at the spectator in the theatre. From the first scene it is made clear that characterization is more important than the plot, which serves almost only to give the characters various opportunities for revealing themselves; the spectator knows from the start that all these villains are to be unmasked eventually. The dumb show lends a deliberately archaic colouring which leads one to expect a kind of morality play, in ironic contrast to what is actually presented.[2]

The masque at the end of the comedy in particular is sharply contrasted with the rather stiff beginning. As in many tragedies of revenge, a colourful series of disguises crowns all the intrigues. The general pretence reaches a climax as the gallants try to stage a performance which completely contradicts their true character, and in doing so are exposed. What is especially striking is the way in which emblems and Latin mottoes are used to achieve a comic effect. The comedy lies in the contrast between the learned 'show' and the actual ignorance of the five gallants for whom Latin is only a sequence of well-sounding but meaningless syllables. The scene takes the form of a courtly wedding masque in which the five suitors reveal themselves without realizing it and are exposed to the laughter of the onlookers. The device of the play within the play is used in a particularly skilful way here. It serves, like the pantomimic introduction, to represent satirically the five vices. An artistic convention, originally confined to tragedy, is transferred to comedy and very suitably adapted.

Pantomime is used rather similarly in the comedy *A Chaste*

---

[1] See the beginning of Marlowe's *The Jew of Malta* and Jonson's *Volpone*.

[2] 'The characters are not so much human beings as illustrations – illustrations of various underworld tricks and swindles.' R. H. Barker, op. cit., p. 43. This, however, applies only to the first part of the play. In the second part the 'gallants' appear slightly more human and not just 'types'.

Maid in Cheapside. Here, too, it presents a situation which before had been used in tragedy only, a funeral procession. The convention is, moreover, exaggerated by the effect of two coffins brought on to the stage from two sides, and two different groups of mourners. The music also follows the tradition of tragedy, so that for a contemporary audience the whole scene must have seemed like the last act of a particularly sad tragedy:

> *Recorders dolefully playing, enter at one door the coffin of Touchwood junior, solemnly decked, his sword upon it, attended by many gentlemen in black, among whom are Sir Oliver Kix, Allwit, and Parson, Touchwood senior being the chief mourner: at the other door the coffin of Moll, adorned with a garland of flowers, and epitaphs pinned on it, attended by many matrons and maids, among whom are Lady Kix, Mistress Allwit, and Susan: the coffins are set down, one right over against the other; and while all the company seem to weep and mourn, there is a sad song in the music-room.*

At this point, however, there is a surprising and comic denouement. The two lovers have decided to resort to pretended death as a last way out of their difficulties in order to escape their angry parents. The funeral celebration is carried out with all the pomp of high tragedy,[1] the pantomime contributing to this effect. In contrast to *Your Five Gallants,* however, the audience does not know that this is only a mock funeral, until the two lovers rise up from their coffins and obtain the blessing of their parents. As in the previous play the pantomime is the climax to which the whole play leads up.

While this adaptation of a motif from tragedy for comedy is on the one hand an effective dramatic device and produces some very amusing scenes, it shows on the other hand that the decline and a certain devaluation of the dumb show was beginning. As a means of achieving tragic effects pantomimes are after Middleton used only in popular plays and hardly ever by more discriminating dramatists.

Middleton himself still employs dumb shows in his tragedies, most effectively perhaps in *Women Beware Women,* though here the term dumb show is only partly justified. The pantomimic element, however, is very important and is more closely inter-

[1] Cf. the mock-funeral at the beginning of Dekker's *The Honest Whore,* Part I.

woven with the dialogue than in most other plays of his.[1]

Within the main plot complications arise chiefly out of the contrast between the simple conditions in the house of Leantio and the splendid world of the Court. Bianca is by degrees drawn from one sphere into the other. While the special atmosphere in Leantio's house is conveyed by means of the language, by dialogue and description, the world of the Court is presented by magnificent 'show'. This contrast can be seen right at the beginning of the play, as Bianca and her mother-in-law watch the procession of the Duke and his Court. The splendour and ceremony is emphasized by the stage direction:

> *They pass over the stage in great pomp, and exeunt.*

MOTHER: How like you, daughter?
BIANCA: 'Tis a noble state;

The natural dialogue of the two women is contrasted with the silent pomp of the court. All further developments arise out of this first encounter. It is the first indication that Bianca is attracted by the deceptive lustre of the court. The way in which this alluring world breaks in on the sphere of the unsophisticated citizens is obvious enough and is underlined by the deliberate choice of artistic means.

The same contrast pervades the second act, where Bianca is brought into the presence of the Duke. Here again it is the visual impression that has most effect on her. While on the main stage Livia and Leantio's mother play a game of chess and carry on a merry conversation, Guardiano leads Bianca to a curtain behind which the Duke has hidden himself. The curtain is then suddenly drawn back and Bianca is left alone with her seducer. It is significant that he tries to blind her above all by his outward appearance, comparing himself to the sun:

> Pish, look not after him; he's but a vapour,
> That, when the sun appears, is seen no more.

Bianca is overcome by the sight of him and succumbs.

The visual element has a different function in the scene in which Leantio has to stand by and see how his wife is courted

---

[1] Cf. M. C. Bradbrook, op. cit., pp. 224 ff.; R. H. Barker, op. cit., pp. 131 ff.; S. Schoenbaum, op. cit., pp. 102 ff.

by the Duke. This scene takes the form of a great banquet with music, dancing and general animation. Leantio is shown in the role of a spectator for whom all the magnificence and gaiety of the court only stands for breach of faith and seduction. In a series of asides he expresses his suffering and disgust. Thus the audience sees the whole scene with his eyes and partly shares his point of view.[1] We have almost the same situation as that of a play within a play. It is just these various perspectives and reflections which make Middleton's plays similar to Shakespeare's.

The pantomimic element also contributes largely to the effect of the final scene. Here again, as in most earlier revenge tragedies, a masque is introduced, if in a particularly grotesque form. Guardiano, Isabella, and Bianca prepare, each independently, a deadly trick to remove their personal enemies out of the way. Thus the masque, which is very artistically performed, really consists of a series of ingenious traps. Horrible death comes from all sides and lurks in almost every stage-property that is used. Bianca has prepared a kind of 'antimasque' in which Hymen appears with the intention of handing the Cardinal a goblet of poison. The Cupidos shoot with poisoned arrows, deadly fumes rise from the censer. All the traditional paraphernalia of the Court Masque here become instruments of death. Even more than in Middleton's comedies, well-worn theatrical conventions are here employed in a way that makes them appear almost absurd.[2] Dialogue and pantomime complement each other in a very effective manner.

The way in which the plot of the masque unfolds at different levels is very striking. The irony of the performance lies not only in the fact that Livia, who has acted as a procuress, now embodies the Goddess of marriage and that Hippolito and Guardiano, disguised as shepherds, compete for Isabella's favours, but it colours the whole plot and lurks behind many utterances. Each of the actors represents his own fate and character, as we have seen in *Your Five Gallants*. Thus the Duke, describing the final disaster, makes use of images from the sphere of the masques:

[1] Cf. M. C. Bradbrook, op. cit., p. 231.

[2] Cf. M. C. Bradbrook, op. cit., pp. 233 f.; S. Schoenbaum, op. cit., pp. 130 f., and my article quoted above (Introduction), pp. 140 ff.

> Upon the first night of our nuptial honour
> Destruction play her triumph, and great mischiefs
> Mask in expected pleasure!

Needless to say, he himself dies shortly afterwards having taken a poisoned drink intended for someone else. This acting at different levels is also reflected in the frequent asides. The players' attention to their roles is only half-hearted because each is eagerly waiting for some hidden trap to work and several are frustrated by their own machinations. No dramatist before Middleton achieved such a grotesque juxtaposition of reality and play within a play. The general confusion at the end is surely not a sign of the dramatist's incompetence, but a deliberate device.

In this tragedy one can see very clearly how the pantomime by degrees merges completely into the dialogue. Even the allegories are integrated into the spoken scene, providing an ironic commentary on the surrounding 'reality'. The transitions are so smooth that it is hardly possible to speak of dumb shows in the traditional sense, although the pantomimic element plays such an important part, probably more so than in most plays that contain conventional dumb shows.

The use of pantomime in the tragedy *The Changeling*, on the other hand, is at first sight far less original and dramatically efficient. The dumb show in this play is above all a means of managing the rather extensive plot, although at the same time it is carefully motivated and fitted into the structure of the play, which is too compact to admit of any digressions and in which the dialogue serves mainly to further the action without ever becoming independent as it sometimes appears to do in the plays of Marston and Jonson. The dumb show here does not bring out a particular scene by making it peculiarly striking, but it summarizes a certain part of the plot which, although important as a preliminary for the following complications, would not contribute much to the central idea of the play. While De Flores' murder of Alonzo, his relationship with Beatrice, and her marriage to Alsemero are described in great detail, the actual result of De Flores' crime, the choice of Alsemero as the new suitor, is only presented in the form of a dumb show:

> *Enter Gentlemen, Vermandero meeting them with action of wonderment at the disappearance of Piracquo. Enter Alsemero, with*

*Jasperino and gallants: Vermandero points to him, the gentlemen
seeming to applaud the choise. Alsemero, Vermandero, Jasperino, and
the others, pass over the stage with much pomp, Beatrice as bride
following in great state, attended by Diaphanta, Isabella, and other
gentlewomen; De Flores after all, smiling at the accident: Alonzo's
ghost appears to him in the midst of his smile, and startles him,
sheweing the hand whose finger he had cut off.*

The incident could easily have been made into a great state-
scene, but this would probably have contributed nothing to the
characterization of the main personages. The brief pantomime
accelerates the dramatic tempo and introduces some rather more
interesting turns of the plot, thus preparing for the final catastrophe.

This pantomime, unlike that in *Women Beware Women*, is not
incorporated in a scene, but stands on its own and is directed
at the audience in the theatre. It is like the other scenes of the
play, except for the absence of dialogue, and is thus similar in
form to the dumb shows in Marston's *Antonio's Revenge* or
Tourneur's *The Revenger's Tragedy*. It is only a shallow sum-
mary of events and avoids all deeper motivation. The part of
the plot dealt with seems to have interested the dramatist rather
less and therefore remains in the background, whereas the actual
play is mostly taken up with character-portrayal. At the same
time such a mode of presentation implies some oblique comment. Bianca's wedding superficially appears as a personal
triumph, but further developments reveal the emptiness of what
she has gained. By presenting her wedding in dumb show her
downward change of fortune is in a subtle way prepared for.[1]
We notice a clear change of perspective which is partly brought
about by the pantomime.

Like Marston, Middleton experimented over and over again
with the form and convention of the dumb show.[2] He tried to

[1] See the edition by N. W. Bawcutt (*The Revels Plays*, London, 1958,
repr. 1961), pp. lvi f., where this is suggested, but not explicitly applied to
the dumb show.
[2] It is not necessary to discuss the other two plays by Middleton that
contain dumb shows. In *The Mayor of Queenborough* (ed. R. C. Bald, New
York, London, 1938) three extensive dumb shows are introduced by a
kind of presenter (Raynulph, a monk). They summarize parts of the plot
which the dramatist obviously wanted to pass over quickly. Bald (p. xlv)

make it suit his own particular purposes. His use of pantomimes is more varied than Marston's or Webster's, but there are in his plays, too, many transitional forms which often make it difficult to distinguish clearly between dumb show and dialogue scene, as for instance in *Women Beware Women*. These transitional forms suggest the end of the dumb show as an independent element in drama. In most later plays dialogue and pantomime are no longer kept strictly separate, but overlap, thus blurring the exact line of demarcation.

---

thinks that the pantomimes are used very skilfully here. They are, however, very conventional and only a technical device.

In *A Game at Chess* (ed. R. C. Bald, Cambridge, 1929) a short episode is described in a dumb show and thus takes up little time in performance. It does not contribute much to the play as a whole.

11

Romantic Tragicomedy

Although it may not be possible to draw up a precise chronological list of Elizabethan plays from the available material, it can nevertheless be said with a fair amount of certainty that audiences' tastes and with them the style of dramatic productions of the period varied considerably. Certain types of plays enjoyed great popularity for a time and then disappeared almost completely from the stage, often only to be fashionable again a few years later. The same is true of particular elements of style, of particular subjects and characters, of the use of chorus, prologue, and epilogue.[1] It also applies, as we have seen, to the dumb show.

Of the types of play which were most enjoyed throughout the Tudor and Stuart periods the romantic drama of adventure is perhaps the most typical. It is not a very clearly defined genre, having much in common with the early chronicle plays on the one hand, and dramatic fairy tales like Peele's *The Old Wife's Tale* on the other, often combining elements from legend, history, and pastoral literature. We find before the turn of the century a whole series of plays presenting the adventures of well-known historical and legendary characters, often without logical development of plot or climax in the action, and usually with a rather rambling and loose structure. Some of these plays have been treated in an earlier chapter.[2]

Although this type of drama never disappeared completely it seems to have lost some of its appeal after the turn of the century, only to regain popularity towards the end of the first decade. The revival of *Mucedorus* is often mentioned as a sign of this change in literary taste.[3] This play combines almost all

---

[1] See for instance: Clifford Leech, 'Shakespeare's Prologues and Epilogues', *Studies in Honor of T. W. Baldwin*, ed. D. C. Allen (Urbana, 1958), pp. 150–64.

[2] Cf. Chapter 6.

[3] Cf. Shakespeare's *Cymbeline*, ed. J. M. Nosworthy (*New Arden*, London, 1955), Introduction.

characteristic elements of a romantic drama of adventure and seems to have been one of the most popular pieces of the whole period. In many of the plays written about that time we find a return to earlier techniques and structural devices, though these are often employed to new purposes and effects.

At the same time as this revival a new type of play began to emerge which, it is true, took over numerous characteristics from earlier examples, but was in many respects very different from anything that had gone before. The most interesting examples of this new type are Shakespeare's last plays and, on a different level, the exceedingly successful tragicomedies of Francis Beaumont and John Fletcher.[1] Unlike the popular plays of adventure these tragicomedies were mostly written for the more exclusive and discriminating audiences which gathered in the 'Private Theatres', although this distinction was probably less clear-cut than has often been assumed.[2] There is about most of these plays a certain primitiveness in dramatic technique and character-portrayal as well as a noticeable refinement and artificiality of tone and language. Thus Shakespeare in his last plays employs certain elements of style which he himself had ridiculed in his earlier plays. This change only reflects a general tendency of that time in which even the masque rose from a popular entertainment to an aristocratic pastime.[3] The sophistication of primitive techniques and genres seems particularly typical of the Jacobean period.

This is not the place to discuss all the various problems which arise in connection with Shakespeare's last plays and their

[1] See particularly: E. M. Waith, *The Pattern of Tragicomedy in Beaumont and Fletcher* (New Haven, 1952); M. T. Herrick, *Tragicomedy: Its Origin and Development in Italy, France, and England* (Urbana, 1955), pp. 215 ff.; C. Leech, 'The Structure of the Last Plays', *ShS*, 11 (1958), pp. 19–30; C. Leech, *The John Fletcher Plays* (London, 1962), Chapter 2. I follow Leech in using the label 'Fletcher', not 'Beaumont and Fletcher', throughout the following chapter, even in those cases where collaboration is certain.

[2] Cf. G. E. Bentley, 'Shakespeare and the Blackfriars Theatre', *ShS*, 1 (1948), pp. 38–50. For a different view see A. Nicoll, 'Shakespeare and the Court Masque', *ShJ*, 94 (1958), pp. 51–62, and C. Leech, *The John Fletcher Plays*, pp. 7 ff. Shakespeare's *Pericles* and *Henry VIII* at least were acted at the Globe and thus seem to belong to a more popular type.

[3] E. Welsford calls the Court Masque a 'sophistication of a popular custom' (op. cit., p. 30).

possible influence on Fletcher's style (or vice versa). It is, however, important for our own study that with the return to an earlier form of drama the pantomime also plays a more important part again and the influence of the earlier pageants as well as that of the court masque, just becoming fashionable again, is more prominent. Only three of Shakespeare's five 'last plays' contain genuine dumb shows, but in all of them masque-like elements, impressive processions, and other visual effects such as hardly occur in his earlier plays are to be found. The reason lies partly in their loose structure, which leaves more room for the inclusion of all sorts of semi-dramatic devices, and also in the great importance of the supernatural and unearthly, common to them all. The gods often take part in the action and even determine the outcome. Thus the appearance of Jupiter in *Cymbeline*, Apollo's oracle in *The Winter's Tale*, and the masque conjured up by Prospero in *The Tempest* are important parts of the drama in which they occur and by no means additional effects, as for instance the fantastic apparitions in W. Rowley's *The Birth of Merlin*.

'PERICLES'

Pericles, the first play of this group, and perhaps the clumsiest (in comparison with *The Winter's Tale* and *The Tempest*), shows the new form in many ways and has little in common with the earlier plays of adventure.[1] The whole play seems at first sight rather rhapsodic and loosely constructed. The introduction of a chorus-figure (Gower), who appears before each act to explain the plot and to fill out the gaps in the action, is a new element though certainly influenced by earlier plays, and one which was not taken over in the later romances. Professor Leech has noted that Gower's speeches are written in the metre of the *Confessio Amantis*, just as Skelton in Munday's Robin Hood plays speaks

[1] Cf. the thorough editions by J. C. Maxwell (*New Cambridge*, Cambridge, 1956) and F. D. Hoeniger (*New Arden*, London, 1963) for the problem of authorship and dramatic style.

Most relevant criticism on Shakespeare's last plays is quoted in Vol. 11 of the *Shakespeare Survey* and in the *New Arden* editions of *Pericles*, *Cymbeline, The Winter's Tale*, ed. J. H. P. Pafford (London, 1963), *The Tempest*, ed. F. Kermode (London, 1954), *Henry VIII*, ed. R. A. Foakes (London, 1957).

in 'Skeltonics'.[1] This observation, too, points to a connection between these tragicomedies and the earlier plays of adventure. The same applies to the three dumb shows which fill in the gaps between some sections of the plot. They are of the same type as most of the pantomimes we discussed in Chapter 6. Part of the action is summarized in a silent scene to keep the scope of the play within a certain limit. Nevertheless the employment of the dumb shows here betrays great skill. The first two show how Pericles, who just appears to have found a new home, receives letters which send him on his way again and expose him to the dangers of a sea journey. The voyage itself and its result are in each case the subject of the following act. Thus a very convenient link is established between the separate episodes, which would otherwise be rather disconnected.

The third pantomime shows Pericles before the statue of Marina in Tharsus. Gower's explanation is significant:

> See how beleefe may suffer by fowle showe.

Pericles' grief is only the result of a deception which is thus (by a dumb show) made particularly impressive while taking up only a very small section of the play. Considering the structure of the play, the dumb shows are an effective means of connecting the separate parts of the plot and making them a whole. The chorus, appearing after each episode, provides a firm framework. It does not, as in some earlier plays of adventure, come on at points selected more or less at random, but at regular intervals, introducing some new event. Shakespeare had already used a similar technique successfully in *Henry V* where, however, there are no pantomimes.[2] The position of the pantomimes between the acts of the play is also strongly reminiscent of the classical tragedies with their formal dumb shows. Even though they fulfil a completely different function in *Pericles*, it is nevertheless interesting to see Shakespeare returning to this older technique, deliberately separating his dumb shows from the rest of the play.

---

[1] Cf. C. Leech, 'Shakespeare's Prologues and Epilogues', p. 163.

[2] I recently saw a production of *Henry V* in which the speech of the Chorus before the second act was accompanied by a dumb show. This seems rather superfluous, but it may well be that similar dumb shows were inserted in other plays in contemporary performances without being included in the printed text.

In spite of this separation they do not seem to be a foreign element. There is not, as in the classical tragedies, an abrupt contrast between the dramatic technique of the pantomimes and that of the rest of the play; rather there is a certain harmony with the particular tone of the play and its episodic structure. It is not a history play and does not at any point pretend to truth in a realistic sense. The whole story is presented as a kind of fairy tale by Gower, as an old song whose fleeting and imaginary character is strongly emphasized. No importance is attached to probability or consistency in the portrayal of events and characters, but, as the title page promises, 'strange and worthy accidents' are depicted. To this end most diversified means are used, as in the older chronicle plays. Gower's narratives form a kind of framework, providing the outline of the story.[1] The most important parts of the plot are then picked out and represented as scenes with dialogue. The play derives its specific tone and quality from the skilful combination of these various forms of presentation. The dumb shows, so well in keeping with the rhapsodic and airy structure of the play, contribute to this effect.[2]

'THE TEMPEST'

The influence of the pageants and masques is particularly obvious in Shakespeare's last romance. It pervades, as has often been noticed, not only the dramatic technique and the variety of stage effects, but is also apparent in the imagery of the play, particularly in Prospero's famous speech (IV, 1, ll. 148 ff.) where he refers to the 'insubstantial pageant' and appears to describe the artificially constructed scenery of some 'Royal Entry'.[3]

Thus, for instance, a masque is performed as a kind of play

[1] As in earlier plays the audience is asked to co-operate and to pardon this kind of plot-presentation:
> . . . be attent,
> And Time that is so briefly spent,
> With your fine fancies quaintly each,
> What's dumbe in shew, I'le plaine with speach. (III)

This is very similar to the plays discussed in Chapter 6.

[2] A similar interpretation is given by John Arthos, '*Pericles, Prince of Tyre*: A Study in the Dramatic Use of Romantic Narrative', *ShQ*, IV (1953), pp. 257-70.

[3] See especially A. Venezky, op. cit., pp. 167 ff.

within a play, and at another point a pantomime is used which also has the air of some refined entertainment for the characters in the play. This is the banquet conjured up by Prospero (III, 3) in which the decorative and masque-like elements are again particularly striking, especially when compared with Shakespeare's earlier use of such 'shows'. As in *Macbeth* the pantomime is connected with magic; whereas, however, in *Macbeth* the scene has an immediate dramatic effect because the content of the dumb show has a direct bearing on the plot, here the need for some ingenious stage effect, a convincing demonstration of Prospero's power, seems to be the main reason for the magic apparition. The unusual and supernatural character of the scene is emphasized in the stage direction:

> *Solemne and strange Musicke: and Prosper on the top (inuisible:)*
> *Enter seuerall strange shapes, bringing in a Banket; and dance about*
> *it with gentle actions of salutations, and inuiting the King, &c. to*
> *eate, they depart.*

Shortly afterwards it says: '*with a quient deuice the Banquet vanishes*'. As in earlier plays of the type of Greene's *Friar Bacon and Friar Bungay* the whole machinery of the stage comes into action to create an atmosphere of the miraculous and extraordinary. This effect is here emphasized by the reaction of the spectators, whose comments express their astonishment and apprehension. Alonso's speech is particularly revealing, because it draws attention to the absence of speech as a typical mark of this apparition:

> I cannot too much muse
> Such shapes, such gesture, and such sound expressing
> (Although they want the vse of tongue) a kinde
> Of excellent dumbe discourse.

The dumb show expresses something which could not be presented in a spoken scene. The silent figures obviously belong to some lower order of nature which has not yet been given the gift of speech. They can be connected with the 'wilde men' of earlier pageants, who also used to appear without speaking and were often intended to represent some earlier stage of man's development.[1] Here, however, they are part of the world of the

[1] See Chapter 1. The 'wilde men' in the pageants sometimes represented the first inhabitants of Britain.

play in which the contrast between wild nature and cultivated nature plays such an important part. Prospero, who freed the island from the thralls of the witch Sycorax, brought at the same time human language with him and taught it to Caliban, who until then had been dumb also (I, 2, ll. 354 ff.). The 'strange shapes' which appear in the dumb show similarly embody nature only partly civilized. They are subject to Prospero, but are not in any way 'educated' by him as Caliban and Ariel are. By presenting actual speechlessness the pantomime is here of course much more than just a stage effect. It is a particularly skilful variation and adaptation of earlier forms of dumb show.

'HENRY VIII'

The supernatural also plays an important part in the pantomime in Shakespeare's last play.[1] Although *Henry VIII* differs from the romances in many respects, especially in the choice of subject-matter and in structure, it is nevertheless more closely related to them than to Shakespeare's earlier history plays. The purely historical and national aspects of the story seem to have receded into the background in favour of a more general picture. The play is less dominated by the figure of the King than are most other histories of Shakespeare. As in the romances there are plenty of elaborate visual effects. The prologue announces that 'those who come to see only a show or two' will not be disappointed and Henry Wotton's description of that memorable performance, during which the Globe went up in flames, emphasizes specifically that the external splendour and expenditure was remarkable.[2] Much space is given to elaborate court ceremony and pompous state scenes, as can be seen from the detailed stage directions. Most striking is Anne's coronation, which is presented as a kind of dumb show. The festive proces-

---

[1] On the authorship see Marco Mincoff, 'Henry VIII and Fletcher', *ShQ*, XII (1961), pp. 239–60; C. Leech, *The John Fletcher Plays*, pp. 153 ff., and the introduction by R. A. Foakes to his edition. Foakes emphasizes the similarities between *Henry VIII* and the romances. See also John P. Cutts, 'Shakespeare's Song and Masque Hand in *Henry VIII*', *ShJ*, 99 (1963), pp. 184–95. Cutts thinks that the pantomimes were written by Shakespeare.

[2] Quoted in P. Alexander's edition of the histories (Glasgow, 1951), p. 611 (Vol. II of the *Collins Tudor Shakespeare* in four volumes).

sion, exactly specified in the stage direction, moves silently across the stage; the dialogue in the scene consists only of the comments of the impressed spectators. It is a purely visual effect, a magnificent historical pageant.

The contrast with the following scene, in which Katharine, robbed of her earthly crown and nearing her death, sees in a vision her own coronation in heaven, is the more effective. By means of this contrast Anne's coronation loses in retrospect some of its lustre, while Katharine's celestial coronation gains its effect partly from the preceding pageant which it surpasses.[1] This contrast is also revealed in the structure of the two scenes. In both the dialogue is for the most part carried on only by two outsiders who have no importance for the plot. While at Anne's coronation the two spectators unite in admiring exclamations and are later joined by a third who gives further news of the festivities, Katharine's coronation is only a vision which is not shared by anyone else. The two bystanders can see nothing and can only feel the transformation which takes place in Katharine.

The idea of presenting dreams and visions in the form of a pantomime does of course go back to earlier drama,[2] but here again an old tradition has been skilfully adapted to the play; it does not appear as a merely added theatrical effect, but performs an important function in the series of state scenes. It also does not stand in contrast to the other dramatic devices used in this play. Again it is the absence of dialogue which makes the scene more effective than it would be otherwise. The pantomime is also one of the various elements which relate the play to the romances and give it a certain spiritual quality.

The Two Noble Kinsmen, possibly written in the same year as *Henry VIII*, is of a similar type as the romances and romantic tragicomedies. Its beginning and end have repeatedly been ascribed to Shakespeare.[3] Here also the gods have an active

[1] 'Anne's earthly coronation is set against the spiritual coronation of Katharine – in which lies the importance of her vision.' (R. A. Foakes, op. cit., p. l.)

[2] Cf. the similar use of dreams in Heywood's *If You Know Not Me, You Know Nobody*, Part I.

[3] See Marco Mincoff, 'The Authorship of *The Two Noble Kinsmen*', *ESts*, XXXIII (1952), pp. 97–115; Kenneth Muir, 'Shakespeare's Hand in *The Two Noble Kinsmen*', *ShS*, 11 (1958), pp. 50–59; C. Leech, op. cit., pp. 145 ff.

hand in the course of events, and the festive procession which opens the play as well as the end before the altar of the gods, point emphatically to this close connection between the earthly happenings and the governance of the gods. There is a lavish and deliberate use of visual elements which makes the resemblance with Shakespeare's last plays particularly strong. There are, however, no dumb shows in the strict sense of the word.

THE TRAGICOMEDIES OF FLETCHER

As has often been noticed, Fletcher's tragicomedies are of a rather similar type to Shakespeare's last plays. However one tries to interpret the relationship between the two dramatists, there is little doubt that it does exist and has to be reckoned with.[1] Fletcher did of course develop a dramatic style very different from Shakespeare's and never reaches the depth and many-sidedness of *Cymbeline* or *The Tempest*, but the similarities, particularly in technique, are also striking. A frequent use of scenic effects and surprising devices and a sometimes rather ingenious juxtaposition of diverse artistic means can be found in the plays of both writers, just as in the plays of adventure of some years earlier.

A peculiar example of Fletcher's often experimental style is *Four Plays or Moral Representations in One*, written sometime between 1608 and 1612. It includes within a conventional 'frame' four different short performances, of which the second, *The Triumph of Love*, belongs to that type of tragicomedy just coming into fashion. In condensed form the play contains all the important features of this new genre, and it is interesting to see that it is precisely here, where only little time is available for the unfolding of a complicated love story, that the pantomimes become a technical aid. Only with the help of three dumb shows can the whole plot be compressed into such a brief play. At the same time no longer only comparatively incidental and sub-

---

[1] Cf. Una Ellis-Fermor, op. cit., pp. 201 ff., and C. Leech, op. cit., pp. 144 ff. On Fletcher's dramatic style see particularly the studies by E. M. Waith and C. Leech. Some perceptive criticism is also to be found in John F. Danby, *Poets on Fortune's Hill* (London, 1952), M. T. Herrick's study quoted above, and William W. Appleton, *Beaumont and Fletcher: A Critical Study* (London, 1956).

ordinate episodes are presented in this fashion, as in most earlier examples, but often the very climax of the plot. This suggests that with the rising popularity of the masques and related elements in drama particular care was given to the elaboration of the dumb shows, while dialogue often had a minor part to play. How far this can go may be illustrated by the first dumb show. It consists of a succession of scenes all of which would be more intelligible and moving if they were accompanied by dialogue. The dramatist, however, seems to have thought differently:

> *Dumb Shew.*
>
> *Enter Violanta at one door, weeping, supported by Cornelia and a Frier; at another door, Angelina weeping, attended by Dorothea. Violanta kneels down for pardon. Angelina shewing remorse, takes her up, and cheers her; so doth Cornelia. Angelina sends Dorothea for Gerrard. Enter Gerrard with Dorothea: Angelina and Cornelia seem to chide him, shewing Violanta's heavy plight: Violanta rejoyceth in him: he maketh signs of sorrow, intreating pardon: Angelina brings Gerrrad and Violanta to the Frier; he joyns them hand in hand, takes a Ring from Gerrard, puts it on Violanta's finger; blesseth them; Gerrard kisseth her: the Frier takes his leave. Violanta makes shew of great pain, is instantly conveyed in by the Women, Gerrard is bid stay; he walks in meditation, seeming to pray. Enter Dorothea, whispers him, sends him out. Enter Gerrard with a Nurse blindfold; gives her a purse. To them Enter Angelina and Cornelia with an Infant; they present it to Gerrard; he kisseth and blesseth it; puts it into the Nurses arms, kneels, and takes his leave. Exeunt all severally.*

This must be one of the most eventful dumb shows in the history of Elizabethan drama. It contains as much incident as the spoken scenes of the play and demonstrates how much dramatic speech has now declined in importance.

The other three *Triumphs* in this curious play consist almost entirely of outward theatrical effects and showy processions.

The remaining plays of Fletcher which contain dumb shows are all of a similar type and in each the pantomime seems to mark a particular climax. *The Prophetess* is the only one in which a chorus appears to comment on the dumb show and to give an often quoted justification for it:

> So full of matter is our Historie,
> Yet mixt I hope with sweet varietie,

Romantic Tragicomedy

The accidents not vulgar too, but rare,
And fit to be presented, that there wants
Room in this narrow stage, and time to express
In Action to the life, our Dioclesian
In his full lustre.
(IV, 1)

The passage is particularly interesting because it does not only,
as do some other such apologies,[1] mention the shortage of time
which makes some summarizing of the plot necessary, but particularly hints at the splendour and magnificence of the scene
that is to follow. The dumb show is therefore not only a means
of shortening the performance, but is on the contrary used to
give prominence to a certain incident and make it dramatically
effective by forceful gestures and theatrical 'show', rather than
by dialogue. The description of the pantomime demonstrates
this quite clearly:

> *Loud Musick.*
> *Dumb Shew.*
> *Enter, at one Door, Delphia, Ambassadours. They whisper to-*
> *gether; they take an Oath upon her hand; She circles them (kneeling)*
> *with her Magick-rod; they rise and draw their Swords. Enter, at the*
> *other door, Dioclesian, Charinus, Maximinian, Niger, Aurelia,*
> *Cassana, Guard; Charinus and Niger perswading Aurelia; She offers*
> *to embrace Maximinian; Diocles draws his sword, keeps off Maximin-*
> *ian, turns to Aurelia, kneels to her, lays his Sword at her feet, she*
> *scornfully turns away: Delphia gives a sign; The Ambassadours and*
> *Souldiers rush upon them, seize on Aurelia, Cassana, Charinus, and*
> *Maximinian; Dioclesian, and others offer to rescue them; Delphia*
> *raises a mist; Exeunt Ambassadours and Prisoners, and the rest*
> *discontented.*

In this way a rather extensive scene is shown as a pantomime,
not only telescoping a large section of the plot, but also giving
particular emphasis to a climax of the play, the intervention of
the prophetess, which is actually the turning point in the story.
On the other hand, the dumb show is not very skilfully incorporated in the play. It is primarily a striking visual effect and
expresses nothing that could not have been presented with equal
effect in a dialogue scene. Similarly in the other two plays by

[1] Cf. pp. 23 and 107.

Fletcher, *The Queen of Corinth* and *The Faithful Friends*,[1] turning points in the plot are presented as dumb shows. A similar use of pantomimes can also be found in some tragicomedies by other authors in which Fletcher's style is partly emulated.[2] The descriptions of the dumb shows in these plays are usually very circumstantial and emphasize the spectacular. They do not merely consist of brief encounters or processions round the stage, but of momentous scenes, including a large number of characters and probably taking up more time in performance than most of the earlier dumb shows. In most cases outward pomp plays some part and the scenes performed as dumb shows have some importance for the plot. Thus the dumb show has become a special theatrical effect and is not just an easy way of managing large stretches of plot as in the earlier popular plays of adventure.

After these tragicomedies (and the tragedies of Middleton) the tradition of the dumb show came to an end. There are no dumb shows in Restoration drama.[3] The latest examples are probably Richard Brome's plays, *The Queen and Concubine* and *The Love-sick Court*,[4] which closely follow the tradition of Fletcher and continue the type of romantic tragicomedy. Here again, particularly in *The Queen and Concubine*, a climax of the play is presented as a pantomime. However, these scenes are more directly incorporated in the play and usually go over into

[1] This play should, I believe, be included in the canon of the Fletcher Plays. It seems to be particularly similar to some of Fletcher's tragicomedies in style and subject-matter. See my article 'Beaumont and Fletcher's *The Faithful Friends*', *Anglia*, 80 (1962), pp. 417–24.

[2] Cf. for instance Dekker's *Match Me in London*, Heywood's *A Maidenhead Well Lost* and *The Thracian Wonder*, sometimes ascribed to Webster and Rowley. It is possible, however, that this play was written much earlier.

[3] There is a late but distinctly ironic example in William Congreve's *The Old Bachelor* of 1693:

Bellmour. Faith Madam, I dare not speak to her, but I'll make Signs. (*Addresses* Belinda *in dumb shew.*)

Belin. O foh, your dumb Rhetorik is more ridiculous, than your talking Impertinence; as an Ape is a much more troublesome Animal than a Parrot (II, 9).

(*Comedies*, ed. Bonamy Dobrée, London 1925, *The World's Classics*).

This seems only to suggest that dumb shows were by then completely obsolete and ridiculous.

[4] In *Five new Playes* (London, 1659).

the dialogue without a break. In *The Queen and Concubine*, as in Shakespeare's *Henry VIII*, a dream of the rejected queen is performed as a dumb show and explained by a 'Genius'. On the whole these later examples do not add anything new to the history of the dumb show. They betray, as Fletcher's plays and Shakespeare's romances did, a strong influence of the masques which is not confined to the pantomimes and the appearance of gods, but makes itself felt in a general loosening of dramatic structure and a heavy reliance on visual elements even in the dialogue scenes.

Thus, by way of conclusion, one can say that the dumb shows, as Foster noticed, did not just disappear; they were merged into the play proper and only lost their character as an independent device,[1] without ceasing to influence the dramatic style. Their decline can perhaps be connected with the emergence of a certain realism in drama, already noticeable before 1642, but more obvious in Restoration drama. In Shakespeare's last plays as well as in the tragicomedies of Fletcher the unrealistic and anti-illusionary elements of Elizabethan drama had once more predominated. It is important to bear in mind that the increasingly elaborate stage-machinery and the striving for strong visual effects in these plays was by no means intended to imitate reality, but to stimulate the imagination of the spectators and to show them a world of make-believe which had little to do with the surrounding actuality.[2] This applies to the dumb shows as well. They are, with very few exceptions, only appropriate and successful in plays which appeal to the imagination and intellectual co-operation of the audience[3] and they disappear as soon as the dramatist attempts to develop a more realistic style.[4]

[1] Op. cit., pp. 16–17.

[2] This is emphasized by A. Nicoll ('Shakespeare and the Court Masque'): 'if any of Shakespeare's dramas need to be divorced from the actuality of the scenic, these plays are his last works.' (p. 61). See also the works quoted on p. 61, n. 1.

[3] Several speeches announcing dumb shows contain such appeals to the imagination of the audience, which has to supply the deficiencies of the presentation. Cf. the passages quoted pp. 107, 159, n. 1, and 198.

[4] The term dumb show has of course survived, though with a more general meaning. Cf., for instance, the pantomime in *Oliver Twist*: 'Mr Sikes contented himself with tying an imaginary knot under his left ear, and jerking his head over on the right shoulder; a piece of dumb show which the Jew appeared to understand perfectly' (Chapter XII).

One can, of course, as Foster did, welcome the development away from the pantomime, because the dumb shows were often no more than a clumsy technical device and stood in the way of more refined techniques. On the other hand, it must be admitted – and I hope that this book has succeeded in proving it – that a skilful use of this convention often heightened the particular effect of a play in a remarkable way and that many dumb shows appear to be by no means inessential or interchangeable parts of a play. The varied, often surprisingly original, and nearly always extremely effective use of the dumb show is only new proof of the versatility and creative vitality of Elizabethan drama.

Conclusion

This book has attempted to show that the development of the dumb show has to be studied in relation to the general history of Elizabethan drama, because its use by various dramatists throws light not only on the particular style of the individual author, but at the same time reveals something of the general tendencies of dramatic writing during this period.

The introduction of pantomimes into classical tragedies alone is evidence of the manifold influences which made their impact on Elizabethan drama. This is also why these early dumb shows cannot simply be accounted for by reference to the Italian *intermedii* or other models. It seems beyond doubt that they owe at least as much to native popular traditions as to any foreign influences. The deciding factor for the inclusion of such elements in rhetorical tragedy was certainly the need to relieve the strict form of these plays and to give the audience more than just static declamation without action. At the same time the pantomimes were intended to help express the deeper significance and moral 'message' of the plays' action and impress them forcefully upon the minds of the spectators by visual presentation. Unlike the plays themselves, the dumb shows presented only rather abstract incidents, general outlines of episodes or parables without real characters. Nevertheless, they had a clear connection with the plot of the play proper. Thus they were on the one hand closely linked with the play, and on the other stood out in sharp relief against it, because they remained outside the acts and had a completely different set of characters.

In the later classical tragedies a certain convergence of the two planes, of dialogue and pantomime, is already apparent, and the more popular plays of Kyd and the 'University Wits' take another decisive step in this direction. The dumb shows, instead of being allegorical pageants between the various acts, have now become scenes within the play itself, although usually still in clear contrast to it. The final integration was brought about in the popular plays of adventure where the pantomime soon proved to be an excellent aid when it came to reducing extensive sections of the plot and telling a long story in a few words without having to be content with the plain explanation of a chorus. This form of dumb show was widespread in popular drama and undoubtedly contributed much to the liveliness and magnificence of the performances.

At the same time, however, the pantomime found its way into the more pretentious and sophisticated drama, especially the tragedy of revenge, where after Kyd the dumb show became an established tradition. In these plays some important turning point is often presented as a pantomime, not so much as a means of shortening the play, but to achieve a striking visual effect and to make dynamic scene-beginnings possible, as in several of Marston's plays. It is usually the villain and his party who are thus presented, as can be seen in the plays of Marston, Tourneur and Webster, and to some extent in Shakespeare's *Hamlet* where also, if in an oblique way, the depravity and the triumph of the hero's opponent is revealed in the dumb show. This tradition continued as late as Middleton who made use of it in *The Changeling*. In most of these plays the pantomime is not just a convenient technical stopgap, but an artistic device used with some skill and effect.

On the other hand, subsequent development was also influenced by the romantic plays of adventure, and the revival of this type around 1608 led to a new popularity of dumb shows, which were used once more in plays written for more select and discriminating audiences. There seems, therefore, to have been an interesting fluctuation in the reputation of the dumb shows. While around the turn of the century they were mostly confined to popular and often rather crude plays, they now became again more sophisticated and elaborate. Almost all later dumb shows are of this type. At the same time particular importance came to be attached to external 'show' and scenic effects, partly because of the influence of the Court Masques. The pantomimes often presented particular climaxes and had the character of extensive and eventful scenes without dialogue. They are sometimes only a means of achieving spectacular effects and seem to have no particular dramatic function, like many of the earlier dumb shows.

The introduction of dumb shows into the early classical

tragedies added an important dimension to serious drama, that of lively and visibly presented action on the stage, which had been up till then almost completely confined to comedy. The dumb shows played a far from negligible part in making the stage the scene of exciting movement and incident where speech and gesture complemented and interpreted each other. They are at their best where they are not only effective pantomimic scenes, but at the same time enrich the spoken word and express something by visual means which could not have been conveyed with equal effect through dialogue. It is typical of the versatile and often experimental character of Elizabethan drama that its authors were always trying to discover new ways and dramatic devices and were seldom satisfied with the conventional means of presentation. This striving for powerful effects, for a multiplicity of diverse impressions and, at the same time, for the visualization and intensification of moral ideas and concepts, found particularly original expression in the dumb shows.

List of Plays Containing Dumb Shows

The following list is intended as a brief guide to the large number of extant dumb shows and their function in the plays in which they occur. It also gives the editions from which I have quoted. The dates of the plays are those suggested by Alfred Harbage in his *Annals of English Drama, 975–1700* (New Edition, Revised by Samuel Schoenbaum, London, 1964). I have not included such early forms as Skelton's *Magnificence* nor plays that only contain festive processions or pantomimic stage directions, but I have tried not to be dogmatic and therefore a number of plays will be found here which are not mentioned in the preceding chapters.

There are similar lists in the studies of Pearn and Gibbs, but they give only the titles and say nothing about the form and number of the various dumb shows. I have also listed some examples that have not been noticed before, although they are for the most part more transitional forms.

BARNABY BARNES

The Devil's Charter: a Tragedy (1607)
TFT (1913)
> One Dumb Show. The play opens with the appearance of Francis Guicchardine, who introduces and explains the following dumb show. It presents some action necessary for the understanding of the play. The characters are the same as those in the play.

FRANCIS BEAUMONT, *see* JOHN FLETCHER

RICHARD BROME

The Love-sick Court, or *The Ambitious Politic* (1639)
Five new Playes (London, 1659)
> Two Dumb Shows, leading up to dialogue. Parts of the plot are presented as pantomimes.

The Queen and Concubine: a Comedy (1635)
Five new Playes (London, 1659)
> Two Dumb Shows, introducing dialogue. The first contains some important part of the plot; the second, introduced and explained by a 'Genius', shows a dream.

ROBERT DABORNE

A Christian Turned Turk (1610)
Ed. A. E. H. Swaen, *Anglia*, 20 (1898)
> Two Dumb Shows, introduced and explained by a Chorus. They summarize parts of the plot. Only characters from the play appear.

The Poor Man's Comfort (1617)
Ed. A. E. H. Swaen, *Anglia*, 21 (1899)
> One Dumb Show at the beginning of an act. Festive procession which is, however, not described in great detail.

JOHN DAY

The Travails of the Three English Brothers (1607)
The Complete Works of John Day, ed. A. H. Bullen (Reprint, London, 1963)
> Three Dumb Shows, introduced and explained by a Chorus 'attired like fame'. They summarize parts of the action. There are also several pantomimic stage directions which in performance may have assumed the character of proper dumb shows.

THOMAS DEKKER

Match Me in London: a Tragicomedy (1611)
The Dramatic Works of Thomas Dekker, ed. F. Th. Bowers, Vol. III (Cambridge, 1958)
> One Dumb Show. A section of the plot is summarized in a fairly extensive pantomimic scene.

The Whore of Babylon (1606)
Bowers, Vol. II (Cambridge, 1955)
> Five Dumb Shows. The first is introduced by a Prologue. Some episodes from the play are presented as pantomimes.

Appendix I

Apart from the characters of the play allegorical figures like Time, Truth, Plaine-dealing appear in the dumb shows.

The Wonder of a Kingdom (1631, 1623?)
Bowers, Vol. III.
> Three Dumb Shows. They are like festive processions at the beginning of some scenes and do not advance the plot significantly.

NATHANIEL FIELD

A Woman is a Weathercock: A New Comedy (1609)
The Plays of Nathan Field, ed. W. Peery (Austin, 1950)
> One Dumb Show. It makes a lively beginning for a new scene before dialogue begins, but does not contribute much to the action of the play.

JOHN FLETCHER

The Faithful Friends (1614)
The Works of Beaumont & Fletcher, ed. A. Dyce (London, 1843–46), Vol. IV.
> One Dumb Show, containing a festive procession, but not very important for the action of the play.

Four Plays or Moral Representations in One (1612)
The Works of Francis Beaumont and John Fletcher, ed. A. Glover and A. R. Waller (Cambridge, 1905–12), Vol. X
> Three Dumb Shows. They all occur in the second 'Triumph' (*The Triumph of Love*) and telescope large sections of the plot.

The Prophetess: a Tragical History (1622)
Glover & Waller, Vol. V
> One Dumb Show, introduced and explained by a Chorus. An important part of the plot is summarized.

The Queen of Corinth: a Tragicomedy (1617)
Glover & Waller, Vol. VI
> One Dumb Show, summarizing an important part of the plot.

The Elizabethan Dumb Show

WILLIAM GAGER

Meleager: Tragoedia Nova (1582)
(Oxford, 1592)

One Dumb Show. Short pantomimic scene before the second act, without importance for the action of the play. Only characters from the play itself appear in the pantomime.

GEORGE GASCOIGNE and FRANCIS KINWELMERSH

Jocasta (1566)
Early English Classical Tragedies, ed. J. W. Cunliffe (Oxford, 1912)

Five Dumb Shows before the acts of the tragedy. The atmosphere or the meaning of the following act is foreshadowed in the pantomimes. Only symbolical or allegorical figures appear.

ROBERT GREENE

The Honourable History of Friar Bacon and Friar Bungay (1589)
The Plays and Poems, ed. J. Ch. Collins (Oxford, 1905), Vol. II

Through a magic glass the Prince sees events which take place at a great distance. Only the audience is supposed to hear the speeches. For the Prince, however, it is a dumb show.

The Scottish History of James the Fourth, Slain at Flodden (1590)
Collins, Vol. II

Three Dumb Shows, introduced by Oberon within the 'frame' of the story. The vanity of the world is illustrated by the fall of princes. The characters are different from those in the play.

A Looking Glass for London and England (1590)
Collins, Vol. I

Brief pantomimic scene during the Usurer's soliloquy: '*The euill Angell tempteth him, offering the knife and rope.*' Several pantomimic stage directions.

Appendix I

Nero: Tragoedia Nova (1603)
(London, 1603)
> One Dumb Show. Before the first act Nemesis and the Furies bring in a pantomime in which part of the plot is revealed. The characters are the same as those in the play.

THOMAS HEYWOOD

The Brazen Age (1611)
The Dramatic Works of Thomas Heywood, ed. R. H. Shepherd (London, 1874), Vol. III
> Four Dumb Shows before the acts, introduced and explained by Homer. Important parts of the plot are summarized in this way. The characters are the same as those in the play.

The Fair Maid of the West (1610)
Shepherd, Vol. II
> One Dumb Show, containing a brief and not very important part of the plot.

The Four Prentices of London (1600, 1592?)
Shepherd, Vol. II
> Four Dumb Shows, explained by a Presenter, showing the fate of the four brothers after their shipwreck. The plot is thus telescoped.

The Golden Age (1610)
Shepherd, Vol. III
> Five Dumb Shows, mostly between the acts. They are introduced and explained by Homer and summarize important parts of the plot.

If You Know Not Me, You Know Nobody, Part 1 (1604)
Malone Soc. (1935)
> Three Dumb Shows presenting parts of the plot. One of them reveals a dream of Princess Elizabeth which has symbolic significance. Two angels appear in it.

A Maidenhead Well Lost (1633)
Shepherd, Vol. IV
> Three Dumb Shows, summarizing important parts of the plot. Only characters from the play appear in them.

The Silver Age (1611)
Shepherd, Vol. III
> Five Dumb Shows before the acts, introduced and explained
> by Homer. They summarize important parts of the plot and
> often serve to introduce a new episode and new characters.

THOMAS HUGHES

The Misfortunes of Arthur (1588)
Ed. J. W. Cunliffe, op. cit.
> Five Dumb Shows before the acts, foreshadowing the atmos-
> phere and significance of each act. Allegorical and symbol-
> ical figures appear, some of them indirectly representing the
> main characters of the tragedy.

THOMAS KYD

The Spanish Tragedy (1587)
The Works of Thomas Kyd, ed. F. S. Boas (Oxford, 1901)
> Two Dumb Shows. One of them is a historical pageant, pre-
> sented by Hieronimo to entertain the Court; the second is
> introduced by Revenge and foreshadows the final catastrophe.

The First Part of Jeronimo (1604)
Ed. F. S. Boas, op. cit. (but almost certainly not by Kyd)
> One Dumb Show, showing Hieronimo's installation as
> Marshall before the beginning of the actual play.

THOMAS LEGGE

Richardus Tertius (1580)
Ed. Barron Field, for the Shakespeare Society (London, 1844)
> Pantomimic stage directions in English, especially during
> the last battle. Ceremonious processions at the end of each
> section. No proper dumb shows.

JOHN LYLY

Endimion, the Man in the Moon (1588)
The Complete Works, ed. R. W. Bond (Oxford, 1902), Vol. III
> One Dumb Show (first in Blount's edition of 1632).
> Endimion's dream is shown as a pantomime. Symbolic
> figures appear. The dream is narrated in detail by Endimion
> later in the play.

Appendix I

GERVASE MARKHAM and WILLIAM SAMPSON

The True Tragedy of Herod and Antipater (1622)
(London, 1622)
> Four Dumb Shows. Two of them foreshadow Antipater's crimes in symbolic form. Historical or legendary figures appear. The other two summarize parts of the plot. The third pantomime is explained by Josephus, who acts as Chorus in this tragedy.

CHRISTOPHER MARLOWE

The Tragical History of Doctor Faustus (1592)
Ed. W. W. Greg (Oxford, 1950)
> One Dumb Show (only in the edition of 1616). A magic apparition, conjured up by Faustus (Alexander and Darius), without importance for the action of the play.

JOHN MARSTON

Antonio and Mellida (1599)
The Plays of John Marston, ed. H. H. Wood (Edinburgh, 1934–39), Vol. I
> One Dumb Show. Dumb action on the main stage commented on from the gallery. Only characters from the play appear in it.

Antonio's Revenge (1600)
Wood, Vol. I
> Three Dumb Shows before some of the acts. Parts of the action are summarized.

The Insatiate Countess: a Tragedy (1610)
Wood, Vol. III
> One Dumb Show. Short scene before the third act, not very important for the plot of the play.

The Malcontent (1604)
Wood, Vol. I
> One Dumb Show. Short scene before the second act leading up to dialogue.

Parasitaster, or *The Fawn* (1605)
Wood, Vol. II
> One Dumb Show. A short scene (part of the plot) before the last act.

What You Will (1601)
Wood, Vol. II
> One Dumb Show. Brief pantomimic scene with comic effect.

The Wonder of Women, or *The Tragedy of Sophonisba* (1605)
Wood, Vol. II
> Two Dumb Shows. The first two acts open with a pantomime leading up to dialogue.

PHILIP MASSINGER

The Fatal Dowry (1619)
Ed. A. Symons (London, 1889), Vol. II (*Mermaid Series*)
> Festive Processions (Wedding, Funeral). No dumb shows proper.

The Roman Actor (1626)
Symons, Vol. II
> Ingenious use of the play within a play and pantomimic elements. No dumb shows proper.

THOMAS MIDDLETON

The Changeling (1622)
The Works of Thomas Middleton, ed. A. Dyce (London, 1840), Vol. IV
> One Dumb Show before the fourth act. An important part of the plot is summarized in this way.

A Chaste Maid in Cheapside (1611)
Dyce, Vol. IV.
> One Dumb Show. A mock-funeral is presented as pantomime. Dialogue follows immediately.

A Game at Chess (1624)
Ed. R. C. Bald (Cambridge, 1929)
> One Dumb Show. Brief scene, not very important for the plot.

Appendix I

Hengist, King of Kent, or *The Mayor of Queenborough: a Comedy* (1618)
Ed. R. C. Bald (New York, 1938)
Three Dumb Shows, introduced and explained by Raynulph, the Monk, summarizing important parts of the plot. Apart from the characters of the play itself Fortune appears in the first dumb show.

Women Beware Women (1621)
Dyce, Vol. IV
Pantomimic elements and an elaborate masque at the end, but no dumb shows in the strict sense of the term.

Your Five Gallants (1605)
Dyce, Vol II
One Dumb Show. The main characters are introduced by a Presenter at the beginning of the play. Masque at the end.

ANTHONY MUNDAY

The Downfall of Robert, Earl of Huntingdon (1598)
TFT (1913)
One Dumb Show, fairly extensive, in which the main characters and the action are introduced. The pantomime is explained by Skelton, functioning as Chorus, and is performed twice in succession in order that it be more easily understood.

The Death of Robert, Earl of Huntingdon (1598)
TFT (1913)
Three Dumb Shows, revealing three visions of King John and explained by Skelton. Apart from characters of the play allegorical figures appear, like Austria, Ambition, Insurrection.

THOMAS NORTON and THOMAS SACKVILLE

The Tragedy of Gorboduc (1562)
Ed. J. W. Cunliffe, op. cit.
Five Dumb Shows before the acts of the tragedy, in which the general significance of the play is foreshadowed. Only symbolic or allegorical figures appear.

GEORGE PEELE

The Arraignment of Paris (1581)
Malone Soc. (1910)
> Three Dumb Shows. Brief mythological or allegorical *tableaux*, explained by the three Goddesses who introduce them.

The Battle of Alcazar (1589)
Malone Soc. (1907)
> Three Dumb Shows before some of the acts, introduced and explained by a Presenter. Parts of the plot are presented in pantomimic form. Some fragmentary stage directions make it seem probable that originally there were more dumb shows.

JOHN PICKERING

The History of Horestes (1567)
TFT (1910)
> No proper dumb shows, but some particularly interesting examples of pantomimic stage directions, some of them similar to later dumb shows.

SAMUEL ROWLEY (?)

The Noble Soldier: a Tragedy (1626)
TFT (1913)
> One Dumb Show. Brief pantomime at the beginning in which the two parties are introduced. Pantomimic stage directions.

WILLIAM ROWLEY

The Birth of Merlin (1608)
The Shakespeare Apocrypha, ed. T. Brooke (Oxford, 1908)
> Three Dumb Shows. Allegorical and symbolical apparitions, conjured up and explained by some magicians, often with a prophetic meaning. Not only characters from the play appear in them.

Appendix I

WILLIAM SHAKESPEARE

The Tragical History of Hamlet, Prince of Denmark (1601)
Facsimile Edition of the Folio, prepared by Helge Kökeritz
(Fourth Printing, New Haven, 1963)
(Other editions of Shakespeare's plays are quoted in the footnotes to the relevant chapters)
> One Dumb Show before the play within the play. The action of the following play is exactly foreshadowed in the pantomime.

The Life of King Henry the Eighth (1613)
Folio Facsimile
> One Dumb Show in which Katharine's vision of her heavenly coronation is revealed. Ceremonious processions.

The Tragedy of Macbeth (1606)
Folio Facsimile
> One Dumb Show ('Show of Kings') conjured up by the witches and described by Macbeth as he sees it. No pantomimic scene, but a kind of pageant, foreshadowing future events.

A Midsummer Night's Dream (1595)
Folio Facsimile
> One Dumb Show (only to be conjectured from the text) before the play of the craftsmen, in which the plot of the play is foreshadowed.

Pericles, Prince of Tyre (1608)
Quarto Facsimile, ed. W. W. Greg (London, 1940)
> Three Dumb Shows, introduced and explained by Gower. Important parts of the plot are summarized in this way. Only characters from the play appear.

The Tempest (1611)
Folio Facsimile
> One Dumb Show. A banquet, conjured up by Prospero. Only 'strange shapes', no characters from the play appear in it.

The Two Noble Kinsmen (1613)
The Shakespeare Apocrypha
> No dumb shows proper, but elaborate processions which in performance possibly assumed the character of dumb shows.

RICHARD TARLETON

Seven Deadly Sins, Part II (1585)
Plot in W. W. Greg, *Dramatic Documents from the Elizabethan Playhouses* (Oxford, 1931), *Reproductions and Transcripts*, Plate II.
> Two or possibly three Dumb Shows, introduced and explained by Lydgate. Important parts of the plot are summarized. The third dumb show can only be guessed at, as the full text of the play is lost, but it seems probable that King Henry's dream at the beginning of the play was also presented as a pantomime.

CYRIL TOURNEUR

The Revenger's Tragedy (1606)
The Works of Cyril Tourneur, ed. A. Nicoll (London, 1929)
> One Dumb Show. The installation of the new Duke, Lussurioso, is presented in dumb show, followed by a banquet and a masque.

JOHN WEBSTER

The Tragedy of the Duchess of Malfi (1614)
Ed. F. L. Lucas (London, 1958)
> One Dumb Show. An important part of the plot is presented in pantomimic form and commented on by two pilgrims.

The White Devil (1612)
Ed. F. L. Lucas (London, 1958)
> Two Dumb Shows, produced by a magician, in which the two murders instigated by Brachiano are revealed to him.

JOHN WEBSTER and WILLIAM ROWLEY

The Thracian Wonder: a Comical History (1599)
(London, 1661)
> One Dumb Show, explained by a Chorus, in which an important part of the plot is summarized.

Appendix I

GEORGE WHETSTONE

The Right Excellent and Famous History of Promos and Cassandra (1578)
TFT (1910)
  No dumb shows proper, but various pantomimic scenes. The preparations for a pageant and the pageant itself are shown.

ROBERT WILMOT

The Tragedy of Tancred and Gismund (1591)
Malone Soc. (1914)
  Four Dumb Shows ('Introductions') before the acts, leading up to dialogue. Parts of the action are presented as pantomimes, but these are not necessary for an understanding of the plot.

ROBERT WILSON

The Cobbler's Prophecy (1590)
TFT (1911)
  One Dumb Show at the beginning of the play. A procession of Gods across the stage. Not all of them reappear in the play. Several pantomimic stage directions.

The Three Lords and Three Ladies of London (1588)
TFT (1912)
  Several ceremonious processions and pantomimic battle scenes. Some of them must have been very much like dumb shows in performance.

ANONYMOUS PLAYS

Appius and Virginia (by R. B.) (1564)
Malone Soc. (1911)
  Pantomimic stage direction which is very much like some of the later dumb shows.

The Bloody Banquet (by T. D.) (1639)
TFT (1914)
  Two Dumb Shows, introduced and explained by a Chorus. Important parts of the plot at the beginning and in the middle are summarized by pantomimes.

185

Captain Thomas Stukeley (1596)
TFT (1911)
>   One Dumb Show, explained by a Chorus, in which a lengthy part of the plot is briefly summarized. Dialogue situations are presented in pantomime.

John of Bordeaux, or *The Second Part of Friar Bacon* (1592)
Malone Soc. (1936)
>   Several 'Shows' by which Friar Bacon proves his magic art. No pantomimes in the stricter sense.

A Knack to Know an Honest Man (1594)
Malone Soc. (1910)
>   A festive procession, called 'pompious show' in the stage direction, but not specified exactly. It is observed and briefly commented on by Sempronio, a character from the play.

The Launching of the Mary (by W. M.) (1633)
Malone Soc. (1933)
>   Two extensive stage directions which might have assumed the character of dumb shows in performance. They are immediately followed by dialogue.

The Lamentable Tragedy of Locrine (by W. S.) (1591)
Malone Soc. (1908)
>   Five Dumb Shows before the acts, introduced and explained by Ate. Symbolic and emblematic figures, including animals, appear to foreshadow the content and the moral of the following act.

Look About You (1599)
Malone Soc. (1913)
>   Pantomimic stage directions and ceremonious processions. No dumb shows in the stricter sense of the term.

The Stately Tragedy of Claudius Tiberius Nero (1607)
Malone Soc. (1914)
>   Ceremonious processions and entries. No proper dumb shows.

Appendix I

The Rare Triumphs of Love and Fortune (1582)
Malone Soc. (1930)

Five 'Shows' introduced by Mercury, illustrating the power of Love and Fortune by means of historical and mythological figures. There is no actual plot in these shows, as far as can be judged from the stage directions. Pantomimic stage directions throughout the play.

The Two Noble Ladies: a Tragi-comical History (1622)
Malone Soc. (1930)

One Dumb Show, summarizing part of the plot. No Chorus. Only characters from the play itself appear in it.

The Valiant Welshman (by R. A.) (1612)
TFT (1913)

One Dumb Show, introduced and explained by a Bard. An important part of the plot is summarized. Pantomimic elements throughout the play.

A Warning for Fair Women (1599)
TFT (1912)

Three Dumb Shows, introduced and explained by Tragedy. Characters from the play and allegorical figures (Lust, Chastity) appear side by side. Important parts of the action are summarized or foreshadowed in this way.

The Weakest Goeth to the Wall (1600)
Malone Soc. (1912)

One Dumb Show at the beginning, relating briefly some event which is supposed to have taken place many years before the beginning of the play. The pantomime is explained by a Prologue.

Further Texts of Dumb Shows

1 *Allegorical and Symbolic Dumb Shows*

GEORGE GASCOIGNE AND FRANCIS KINWELMERSH, 'JOCASTA'
[See Chapter 3 for a discussion of this play.]

The order of the thirde dumbe shewe.
Before the beginning of this .iij. Act did sound a very dolefull noise of cornettes, during the which there opened and appeared in the stage a great Gulfe. Immediatly came in .vi. gentlemen in their dublets & hose, bringing vpon their shulders baskets full of earth and threwe them into the Gulfe to fill it vp, but it would not so close vp nor be filled. Then came the ladyes and dames that stoode by, throwing in their cheynes & Iewels, so to cause it stoppe vp and close it selfe: but when it would not so be filled, came in a knighte with his sword drawen, armed at all poyntes, who walking twise or thrise about it, & perusing it, seing that it would nether be filled with earth nor with their Iewells and ornaments, after solempne reuerence done to the gods, and curteous leaue taken of the Ladyes and standers by, sodeinly lepte into the Gulfe, the which did close vp immediatly: betokning vnto vs the loue that euery worthy person oweth vnto his natiue country, by the historye of Curtius, who for the lyke cause aduentured the like in Rome. This done, blinde Tyresias the deuine prophete led in by hys daughter, and conducted by Meneceus the son of Creon, entreth by the gates Electrae, and sayth as followeth.

The order of the fourth dumbe shewe.
Before the beginning of this fourth Acte, the Trumpets, drummes and fifes sounded, and a greate peale of ordinaunce was shot of: in the which ther entered vpon the stage .vj. knights armed at al points: wherof three came in by the Gates Electrae, and the other three by the Gates Homoloides: either parte being accompanied with .vij. other armed men: and after they had marched twice or thrice about the Stage, the one partie menacing the other by their furious lookes and gestures, the .vj. knights caused their other attendants to stand

by, and drawing their Swords, fell to cruell and couragious combate,
continuing therein, till two on the one side were slayne. The third
perceiuing, that he only remayned to withstand the force of .iij.
enimies, did politiquely runne aside: wherewith immediatly one of
the .iij. followed after him, and when he had drawen his enimie thus
from his companie, hee turned againe and slewe him. Then the
seconde also ranne after him whom he slewe in like manner, and
consequently the thirde, and then triumphantly marched aboute the
Stage wyth hys sword in his hand. Hereby was noted the incomparable
force of concorde betwene brethren, who as long as they holde togither
may not easily by any meanes be ouercome, and being once disseuered
by any meanes, are easily ouerthrowen. The history of the brethren
Horatij & Curiatij, who agreed to like combate and came to like ende.
After that the dead carkasses were caried from the Stage by the
armed men on both parties, and that the victor was triumphantly
accompanied out, also came in a messanger armed from the campe,
seeking the Queene, and to hir spake as foloweth.

The order of the laste dumbe shewe.
First the Stillpipes sounded a very mournful melody, in which time
came vpon the Stage a woman clothed in a white garment, on hir
head a piller, double faced, the formost face fair & smiling, the other
behinde blacke & louring, muffled with a white laune about hir eyes,
hir lap ful of Jewelles, sitting in a charyot, hir legges naked, hir fete
set vpon a great round bal, & beyng drawen in by .iiij. noble
personages, she led in a string on hir right hand .ij. kings crowned,
and in hir lefte hand .ij. poore slaues very meanly attyred. After she
was drawen about the stage, she stayed a little, changing the kings
vnto the left hande & and the slaues vnto the right hand, taking the
crownes from the kings heads she crowned therwith the .ij. slaues, &
casting the vyle clothes of the slaues vpon the kings, she despoyled the
kings of their robes, and therwith apparelled the slaues. This done,
she was drawen eftsones about the stage in this order, and then
departed, leauing vnto vs a plaine Type or figure of vnstable fortune,
who dothe oftentimes raise to heigthe of dignitie the vile and
vnnoble, and in like manner throweth downe from the place of
promotion, euen those whom before she hir selfe had thither aduaunced:
after hir departure came in Duke Creon with foure gentlemen
wayting vpon him and lamented the death of Meneceus his sonne in
this maner.

189

The Elizabethan Dumb Show

The Argument and manner of the second dumbe shewe.
Whiles the Musicke sounded there came out of Mordred's house a man stately attyred representing a King, who walking once about the Stage. Then out of the house appointed for Arthur, there came three Nymphes apparailed accordingly, the first holding a Cornucopia in her hand, the second a golden braunch of Oliue, the third a sheaffe of Corne. These orderly one after another offered these presents to the King who scornefully refused. After the which there came a man bareheaded, with blacke long shagged haire downe to his shoulders, apparailed with an Irish Iacket and shirt, hauing an Irish dagger by his side and a dart in his hand. Who first with a threatning countenance looking about, and then spying the King, did furiously chase and driue him into Mordred's house. The King represented Mordred. The three Nymphes with their proffers the treatice of peace, for the which Arthur sent Gawin with an Herault vnto Mordred who reiected it: The Irish man signified Reuenge and Furie which Mordred conceiued after his foile on the Shoares, whereunto Mordred headlong yeeldeth himselfe.

The Argument and manner of the fourth dumbe shewe.
Dvring the Musicke appointed after the third act, there came a Lady Courtly attyred with a counterfaite Childe in her armes, who walked softly on the Stage. From an other place there came a King Crowned, who likewise walked on an other part of the Stage. From a third place there came foure Souldiers all armed, who spying this Lady and King, vpon a sodaine pursued the Lady from whom they violently tooke her Childe and flung it against the walles; She in mournefull sort wringing her hands passed her way. Then in like manner they sette on the King, tearing his Crowne from his head, and casting it in peeces vnder feete draue him by force away; And so passed themselues ouer the Stage. By this was meant the fruit of Warre, which spareth neither man woman nor childe, with the ende of Mordreds vsurped Crowne.

The Argument and manner of the fift and last dumbe shewe.
Sounding the Musicke, foure gentlemen all in blacke halfe armed, halfe vnarmed with blacke skarffes ouerthwart their shoulders should

190

come vppon the stage. The first bearing alofte in the one hand on the trunchion of a speare an Helmet, an arming sworde, a Gauntlet, &c. representing the Trophea: in the other hand a Target depicted with a mans hart sore wounded & the blood gushing out, crowned with a Crowne imperiall and a Lawrell garland, thus written in the toppe. En totum quod superest, *signifying the King of Norway which spent himselfe and all his power for Arthur, and of whom there was left nothing but his heart to inioy the conquest that insued. The seconde bearing in the one hand a siluer vessell full of golde, pearles, and other iewels representing the Spolia: in the other hande a Target with an Olephant and Dragon thereon fiercely combating, the Dragon vnder the Olephant and sucking by his extreme heate the blood from him is crushed in peeces with the fall of the Olephant, so as both die at last, this written aboue,* Victor, an Victus? *representing the King of Denmarke, who fell through Mordreds wound, hauing first with his souldiers destroyed the most of Mordreds armie. The third bearing in the one hand a Pyramis with a Lawrell wreath about it representing victorie. In the other hand a Target with this deuise: a man sleeping, a snake drawing neere to sting him, a Leazard preuenting the Snake by fight, the Leazard being deadlie wounded awaketh the man, who seeing the Leazard dying, pursues the Snake, and kils it, this written aboue,* Tibi morimur. *Signifying Gawin King of Albanye slaine in Arthurs defence by Mordred, whom Arthur afterwardes slewe. The fourth bearing in the one hande a broken piller, at the toppe thereof the Crowne and Scepter of the vanquisht King, both broken asunder, representing the conquest ouer vsurpation: in the other hand a Target with two Cockes painted thereon, the one lying dead, the other with his winges broken, his eyes pecked out, and the bloode euerye where gushing foorth to the grounde, he standing vppon the dead Cocke and crowing ouer him, with this embleme in the toppe,* Qua vici, perdidi, *signifying Cador deadly wounded by Gilla whom he slewe. After these followed a King languishing in complet Harnesse blacke, brused & battered vnto him, besprinkled with blood. On his head a Lawrell garland, leaning on the shoulders of two Heraults in mourning gownes & hoods, th' on in Mars his coate of arms, the other in Arthurs, presenting Arthur victoriously but yet deadly wounded, there followed a page with a Target whereon was portraited a Pellican pecking her blood out of her brest to feede her young ones, through which wound she dieth, this writen in the toppe,* Qua foui, perii, *signifying Arthurs too much indulgencie of Mordred, the cause of his death. All this represented the dismayed and vnfortunate victorie of Arthur, which is the matter of the Act insuing.*

GERVASE MARKHAM AND WILLIAM SAMPSON, 'HEROD AND ANTIPATER' (1622, C 3)

ANTIPATER: [In a monologue he reveals his determination to win the Crown for himself.]

My breast swels to a Mountaine; and I breed
A Monster, past description; to whose birth,
Come Furies, and bee Mid-wiues. Harke! O harke!

Dumbe Shew.
Musique: and, Enter Egystus and Clitemnestra dancing a Curranto, which is broken off by the sound of Trumpets: then, enter Agamemnon, and diuers Noblemen in Triumph: Egystus whispers with Clitemnestra, and deliuers her a sleeuelesse shirt; then slips aside: Clitemnestra imbraces Agamemnon, he dismisses his Traine; shee offers him the shirt, he offers to put it on, and being intangled, Egystus and she kils him; then departs, leauing at Antipaters feete two Scrowles of paper.

ANTIPATER: So shall it be; shall it? no shalls; tis done, dispatcht: Who can resolue, can doe;

[The dumb show here is a kind of hellish apparition, instructing Antipater who successfully acts on this 'advice'. The same happens again later in the play. Antipater cannot make up his mind and asks for instruction (F 3)]:

ANTIPATER: . . . O Hell awake, awake;
And once for all instruct me.

Dumbe Shew.
Musique: and, Enter Miscipsa, Iugurth, Adherball, Hiempsall, Miscipsa makes them ioyne hands, and giues each a Crowne, and departs: then in mounting the tribunall Hiempsall and Adherball sit close to keepe out Iugurth, he deuides them by force, Hiempsall offers to draw, and Iugurth stabs him; Adherball flies and comes in againe with the Roman Senators, they seeme to reconcile them: and being

departed, Iugurth stabs Adherball, and leaues at Antipaters feete a Scrowle.

> O resolute Iugurth; what afford'st thou me?
> *Non mordent mortui*; Dead men doe not bite.

2 'Mixed' Dumb Shows

'A WARNING FOR FAIR WOMEN' (1599)
[See Chapter 6 for a discussion of this play.]

TRAGEDY: . . . now appeares
> Unrest, and deepe affliction of the soule,
> Delight proues danger, confidence dispaire,
> As by this folowing shew shall more appeare.

Enter Iustice and Mercy: when hauing taken their seates Iustice falls into a slumber, then enters wronged Chastitie, and in dumbe action vttring her griefe to Mercie, is put away, whereon she wakens Iustice, who listning her attentiuely, starts vp, commanding his Officers to attend her. Then go they with her, and fetch forth master Sanders body, mistris Sanders, Drurie, and Roger, led after it, and being shewne it, they al seeme very sorrowful, and so are led away. But Chastitie shewes that the chiefe offender is not as yet taken, whereon Iustice dispatcheth his seruant Diligence to make further enquirie after the murderer, and so they depart the stage with Chastitie.

[The dumb show is then explained by Tragedy.]

THOMAS DEKKER, 'THE WHORE OF BABYLON' (1606)
[A Prologue introduces the play and the dumb show before the first Act.]

A Dumb shew
He drawes a Curtaine, discouering Truth in sad abiliments; vncrownd: her haire disheueld, and sleeping on a Rock: Time (her father) attired likewise in black, and al his properties (as Sithe, Howreglasse and Wings) of the same Cullor, vsing all meanes to waken Truth, but not being able to doe it, he sits by her and mourns. Then enter Friers, Bishops, Cardinals before the Hearse of a Queen, after it Councellors, Pentioners and Ladies, al these last hauing

scarfes before their eyes, the other singing in Latin. Trueth suddenly awakens, and beholding this sight, shews (with her father) arguments of Ioy, and Exeunt, returning presently: Time being shifted into light Cullors, his properties likewise altred into siluer, and Truth Crowned, (being cloathed in a robe spotted with Starres) meete the Hearse, and pulling the veiles from the Councellers eyes, they woundring a while, and seeming astonished at her brightnes, at length embrace Truth and Time, and depart with them: leauing the rest going on.

This being done, Enter Titania (the Farie Queene) attended with those Councellors, and other persons fitting her estate: Time and Truth meete her, presenting a Booke to her, which (kissing it) shee receiues, and shewing it to those about her, they drawe out their swordes, (embracing Truth,) vowing to defend her and that booke: Truth then and Time are sent in, and returne presently, driuing before them those Cardinals, Friers &c. (that came in before) with Images, Croziar staues &c. They gon, certaine graue learned men, that had beene banished, are brought in, and presented to Titania, who shewes to them the booke, which they receiue with great signes of gladnesse, and Exeunt Omnes.

[This is, of course, very much like some of the pageants devised for Queen Elizabeth, who is here presented as Titania. For the Bible presented to the Queen cf. the pageant quoted in Chapter 1 and Heywood's *If You Know Not Me, You Know Nobody*, Part I.]

3 Great Ceremonies as Dumb Shows

'THE FIRST PART OF JERONIMO' (1604)
(I, 1)

Sound a signate, and passe ouer the stage. Enter at one dore the King of Spaine, Duke of Castile, Duke Medina, Lorenzo, and Rogero: at another doore, Andrea, Horatio, and Ieronimo. Ieronimo kneeles downe, and the King creates him Marshall of Spaine: Lorenzo putes on his spurres, and Andrea his sword. The King goes along with Ieronimo to his house. After a long signate is sounded, enter all the nobles, with couerd dishes, to the banquet. Exeunt Omnes. That done, enter all agen as before.

KING: Frolick, Ieronimo; thou art now confirmd
Marshall of Spaine, by all the dewe
And customary rights vnto thy office.

Appendix II

[Francis Guicchardine opens the play and introduces the dumb show before the first Act.]

And first by what vngodly meanes and Art,
Hee did attaine the Triple-Diadem,
This vision offerd to your eyes declares.

Hee with a siluer rod mooueth the ayre three times.
Enter.

At one doore betwixt two other Cardinals, Roderigo in his purple habit close in conference with them, one of which hee guideth to a Tent, where a Table is furnished with diuers bagges of money, which that Cardinall beareth away: and to another Tent the other Cardinall, where hee deliuereth him a great quantity of rich Plate, imbraces, with ioyning of hands.

Exeunt Card. Manet Roderigo.

To whome from an other place a Moncke with a magical booke and rod, in priuate whispering with Roderick, whome the Monke draweth to a chaire en midst of the Stage which hee circleth, and before it an other Circle, into which (after semblance of reading with exorcismes) appeare exhalations of lightning and sulphurous smoke in midst whereof a diuill in most vgly shape: from which Roderigo turneth his face, hee beeing coniured downe after more thunder and fire, ascends another diuill like a Sargeant with a mace vnder his girdle: Roderigo disliketh. Hee discendeth: after more thunder and fearefull fire, ascend in robes pontificall with a triple Crowne on his head, and Crosse keyes in his hand: a diuill him ensuing in blacke robes like a pronotary, a cornerd Cappe on his head, a box of Lancets at his girdle, a little peece of fine parchment in his hand, who beeing brought vnto Alexander, hee willingly receiueth him: to whome hee deliuereth the wryting, which seeming to reade, presently the Pronotary strippeth vp Alexanders sleeue and letteth his arme bloud in a saucer, and hauing taken a peece from the Pronotary, subscribeth to the parchment; deliuereth it: the remainder of the bloud, the other diuill seemeth to suppe vp; and from him disroabed is put the rich Cap the Tunicle, and the triple Crowne set vpon Alexanders head, the Crosse-keyes deliuered into his hands; and withall a magicall booke: this donne with thunder and lightning the diuills discend: Alexander aduanceth himselfe, and departeth.

GUICCHARDINE: Thus first with golden bribes he did
     corrupt
     The purple conclaue: then by diuelish art
     Sathan transfigur'd like a Pronotarie
     To him makes offer of the triple Crowne
     For certaine yeares agreed betwixt them two.
     The life of action shall expresse the rest.

[The play is about the life of Pope Alexander VI.]

ROBERT DABORNE, 'A CHRISTIAN TURNED TURK' (1610)
(After l. 1251)
The dumbe shew, with Chorus of Ward turning Turke.

. . .

CHORUS: And with a blushlesse front he dares to doe,
     What we are dumbe to thinke, much more to shew:
     Yet what may fall beyond vncertaine guesse
     Your better favours binde vs to expresse.

*Enter two bearing halfe-moones, one with a Mahomets head
following. After them the Muffty, or chiefe Priest: two meaner
Priests bearing his traine. The Muffty seated, a confused noyse of
musicke, with a showt. Enter two Turkes, one bearing a Turban
with a halfe-moone in it, the other a robe, a sword: a third with a
Globe in one hand, an Arrow in the other: two Knights follow. After
them Ward on an Asse, in his Christian habite, bare-headed. The
two Knights, with low reuerence, ascend, whisper the Muffty in the
eare, draw their swords, and pull him off the Asse. He layd on his
belly, the Tables (by two inferiour Priests) offered him, he lifts his
hand vp, subscribes, is brought to his seate by the Muffty, who puts
on his Turban and Roab, girds his sword: then sweares him on the
Mahomets head, vngirds his sword, offers him a cuppe of wine by the
hands of a Christian: Hee spurnes at him, and throwes away the
Cuppe, is mounted on the Asse, who is richly clad, and with a showt
Exeunt.*

[Apparently the incident was considered unsuitable for presentation in dialogue. Another dumb show in this play is introduced
by the Chorus with the words 'what befell This shew presents,
which words deny to tell.']

Appendix II

4 Dumb Shows Summarizing Parts of the Plot

RICHARD TARLETON, 'SEVEN DEADLY SINS', PART II (1585)
(III)

[The text of the play itself is not known. Only the 'Stage Plot'
has survived, containing two or three dumb shows. Even the
names of the actors are mentioned.]

A senitt. Dumb show.
Enter King Gorboduk with 2 Counsailers. R. Barbadg. mr Brian.
Th. Goodale. The Queene with ferrex and Porrex and som
attendaunts follow. saunder w sly Harry J Duke. Kitt. Ro Pallant.
J Holland. After Gorboduk hath Consulted with his Lords he brings
his 2 sonns to to seuerall seates. They enuing on on other ferrex offers
to take Porex his Corowne, he draws his weopon The King Queen
and Lords step between them They Thrust Them away and
menasing ech other exit. The Queene and L(ords) Depart Heuilie.
Lidgate speaks.
[He probably explained the meaning of the dumb show.]

THOMAS HEYWOOD, 'THE FOUR PRENTICES OF LONDON'
(1592-1600)

[The four brothers have suffered shipwreck. The Presenter
gives an account of their various adventures and introduces the
dumb shows.]

We will make bold to explaine it in dumbe Show:
For from their fortunes all our Scene must grow.

Enter with a Drum on one side certaine Spaniards, on the other side
certaine Citizens of Bullen: the Spaniards insult vpon them, and
make them do them homage: to the Citizens enter Godfrey, as newly
landed & halfe naked, conferres with the Citizens, & by his
instigation they set vpon the Spaniards, & beate them away, they
come to honour him, and he discloseth himselfe vnto them; which
done, they Crowne him, and accept him for their Prince: and so
Exeunt.

197

JOHN DAY, 'THE TRAVAILS OF THE THREE ENGLISH BROTHERS'
(1607)
(Bullen, pp. 403–4)

FAME: But would your apprehensions helpe poore art,
Into three parts deuiding this our stage,
They all at once shall take their leaues of you.
Thinke this *England*, this *Spaine*, this *Persia*:
Yours fauours then, to your obseruant eyes
Weele shewe their fortunes present quallities.

Enter three seuerall waies the three Brothers; Robert with the state of Persia as before; Sir Anthonie with the King of Spaine and others, where hee receiues the Order of Saint Iago, and other Officers; Sir Thomas in England, with his Father and others. Fame giues to each a prospective glasse, they seme to see one another and offer to embrace, at which Fame parts them, and so: Exeunt.

MANET FAME: To those that neede farther description
Wee helpe their vnderstandings with a tongue:
[Fame explains the incidents.]

THOMAS DEKKER, 'MATCH ME IN LONDON' (1611)
(V, 3)
Dumbshew.

Hoboyes: Enter two Fryers setting out an Altar, Enter Iago, Alphonso, Gazetto, Malvento, two Churchmen, Tormiella next and the King, Ladies attending, Cordolente steales in, and stands in some by place, the King stayes or sits in a chayre, Tormiella is brought to him, as she is comming the King meets her; as the ring is putting on, Cordolente steps in rudely, breakes them off, Tormiella flyes to his bosome, the King offers to stab him, is held: she kneeles, sues, weepes, Cordolente is thrust out, Gazetto laughs at all, they are preparing to it againe, it Thunders and Lightens: all affrightedly – Exeunt.
[There is no Chorus or Presenter. The incident is explained in the following scene.]

Appendix II

(*Hoboys.*)
A Dumb Shew.

Enter at one Dore the Souldan with souldiers, from the other a Herald meets him, delivers him a paper. The Souldan sends in a souldier, who brings Lysander. Hee kneels, the Souldan embraces him, and shews him the paper, hee kisses it, beckons to the Herald, houlds out the paper with his left hand and lays his right hand on his sword. With courtesy they part. The Souldan and Herald goe of severally. Lysander stays.

LYSANDER: How princes when they stand in need of men
          can faune vpon their subiects! the proud Souldan
          that lately banisht me the camp, in haste
          now sends for mee, embraces, honours mee
          with wishing I had led his army vp
          to Babilon at first, for then hee thinckes
          he had not tane the foyle. . . .

RICHARD BROME, 'THE QUEEN AND CONCUBINE' (1635)
(II, 1)
(*Loud Musick.*)

Enter four Lords, two Bishops, King, Prince: they sit; Eulalia in black, Crowned; a golden Wand in her hand, led between two Friers; she kneels to the King, he rejects her with his hand. Enter at the other door, a Doctor of Physick, a Midwife, two Souldiers; the King points them to the Bishops, they each deliver Papers, Kiss the Bishops Books and are dismissd. The Papers given to the King, He with his Finger menaces Eulalia, and sends her the Papers: she looks meekly. The Bishops take her Crown and Wand, give her a Wreath of Cypress, and a white Wand. All the Lords peruse the Papers. They shew various countenances: some seem to applaud the King, some pity Eulalia. Musick ceases. King speaks.
[The Queen, wrongly accused, is banished.]

Select Bibliography

H. Baker, *Induction to Tragedy*. Louisiana State U.P., 1939.

G. E. Bentley, *The Jacobean and Caroline Stage*. Oxford, 1941–56.

S. L. Bethell, *Shakespeare and the Popular Dramatic Tradition*. London, 1944.

F. S. Boas, *An Introduction to Tudor Drama*. Oxford, 1933.

F. T. Bowers, *Elizabethan Revenge Tragedy 1587–1642*. 2nd ed. Gloucester, Mass., 1959.

M. C. Bradbrook, *Themes and Conventions of Elizabethan Tragedy*. 2nd ed. Cambridge, 1957.

R. Brotanek, *Die englischen Maskenspiele*. Wien-Leipzig, 1902.

E. K. Chambers, *The Mediaeval Stage*. Oxford, 1903.

E. K. Chambers, *The Elizabethan Stage*. Oxford, 1923.

W. Clemen, *English Tragedy Before Shakespeare: The Development of Dramatic Speech*. London, 1961.

J. W. Cunliffe, 'Italian Prototypes of the Masque and Dumb Show', *PMLA*, XXII (1907), 140–56.

J. W. Cunliffe, *The Influence of Seneca on Elizabethan Tragedy*. New York, 1925.

M. Doran, *Endeavors of Art: A Study of Form in Elizabethan Drama*. Madison, 1954.

U. Ellis-Fermor, *The Jacobean Drama: An Interpretation*. London, 1936.

F. A. Foster, 'Dumb Show in Elizabethan Drama before 1620', *Englische Studien*, 44 (1912–13), 8–17.

R. Freeman, *English Emblem Books*. London, 1948.

L. G. Gibbs, *A History of the Development of the Dumb Show as a Dramatic Convention*. Univ. of South Carolina Dissertation, 1959.

M. T. Herrick, *Tragicomedy: Its Origin and Development in Italy, France, and England*. Urbana, 1955.

C. W. Hodges, *The Globe Restored: a Study of the Elizabethan Theatre*. London, 1953.

G. K. Hunter, *John Lyly: the Humanist as Courtier*. London, 1962.

Select Bibliography

G. R. Kernodle, *From Art to Theatre: Form and Convention in the Renaissance.* 3rd ed. Chicago, 1947.

W. J. Lawrence, *The Elizabethan Playhouse and other Studies.* Stratford-upon-Avon, 1912–13.

W. J. Lawrence, *The Physical Conditions of the Elizabethan Public Playhouse.* Cambridge, 1927.

C. Leech, *The John Fletcher Plays.* London, 1962.

F. L. Lucas, *Seneca and Elizabethan Tragedy.* Cambridge, 1922.

J. Nichols, *The Progresses, and Public Processions, of Queen Elizabeth.* London, 1788–1821.

A. Nicoll, *Stuart Masques and the Renaissance Stage.* London, 1937.

R. Ornstein, *The Moral Vision of Jacobean Tragedy.* Madison, 1960.

T. M. Parrott and R. H. Ball, *A Short View of Elizabethan Drama.* New York, 1943.

B. R. Pearn, 'Dumb-show in Elizabethan Drama', *RES*, XI (1935), 385–405.

I. Ribner, *Jacobean Tragedy: The Quest for Moral Order.* London, 1962.

A. Righter, *Shakespeare and the Idea of the Play.* London, 1962.

A. P. Rossiter, *English Drama from Early Times to the Elizabethans.* London, 1950.

L. L. Schücking, *Shakespeare und der Tragödienstil seiner Zeit.* Bern, 1947.

E. Th. Sehrt, *Der dramatische Auftakt in der Elisabethanischen Tragödie: Interpretationen zum englischen Drama der Shakespearezeit.* Göttingen, 1960.

B. Sunesen, 'Marlowe and the Dumb Show', *ESts*, XXXV (1954), 241–53.

A. S. Venezky, *Pageantry on the Shakespearean Stage.* New York, 1951.

E. M. Waith, *The Pattern of Tragicomedy in Beaumont and Fletcher.* New Haven, 1952.

E. Welsford, *The Court Masque: a Study in the Relationships between Poetry & the Revels.* Cambridge, 1927.

G. Wickham, *Early English Stages* 1300–1660. Vol. I (1300–1576). London, 1959. Vol. II (1576–1660), Part I. London, 1963.

R. Withington, *English Pageantry: an Historical Outline.* Cambridge-Oxford-London, 1918–20.

Index

The more important references are indicated by figures in bold type. The names of editors have not always been included.

Index